The latter half of the fifteenth century, the period between John Lydgate and Richard Skelton, is one of the most neglected in English literary history. Yet this period in England is important both for the volume of writing it produced and for profound changes in the relations between author, publisher, and audience brought about by the widespread use of printing and the growth of a bourgeois reading public. Changes in the vernacular were so drastic that poets were compelled continually to reassess their language and literary conventions. *Illuminator, Makar, Vates: Visions of Poetry in the Fifteenth Century* defines a major shift in attitude toward poetry and the role of the poet during that period.

Lois A. Ebin demonstrates that, instead of being inept imitators of Chaucer and his company, the poets of this time departed from their supposed models. The poetry between Lydgate and Skelton reveals a shift from the salvation-oriented to the secular; from God's word to the poet's language as a manifestation of order; from a quest for truth to one for wisdom and political order; from the poet as an "enluminer" to the poet as a "makar," a master craftsman, a public servant, and model of virtue—to the "vate," or seer and laureate, who did not scorn worldly fame. These changes in vision have had important implications for poets ever since, forcing them to search for a significant shared context for their art. In considering the critical vocabulary developed in the fifteenth century and the myths and thematic digressions introduced in the poetry then, Ebin documents the development of a poetics in English earlier than commonly supposed. Her book provides new criteria for dealing with the literature of the late Middle Ages and for determining the importance of its changing vision of poetry.

Lois A. Ebin, who has taught at Barnard College, Columbia University, and New York University, is the editor of *Vernacular Poetics in the Middle Ages* (1984) and author of *John Lydgate* (1985).

University of Nebraska Press: Lincoln and London

LOIS A. EBIN

Illuminator

Makar

Vates

Visions of Poetry in the Fifteenth Century

Library of Congress
Cataloging
in Publication Data
Ebin, Lois.
Illuminator, makar,
vates: visions of
poetry in the
fifteenth century/
Lois A. Ebin.
p. cm.
Bibliography: p.
Includes index.
ISBN 0-8032-1812-5
paper/alkaline
1. English poetry –
Middle English,
1100-1500 –
History and
criticism.
2. Scottish poetry –
To 1700 – History
and criticism.
3. Poetics.
I. Title
PR521.E25 1988
821'.2'09–dc19
87-22683 CIP

TO LAUREN, JULIE, AND TOM

ontents

reface

The period between Lydgate (fl. 1410–40) and Skelton (fl. 1483–1528), roughly one hundred years, is among the most neglected in English literary history. One finds few extended studies of this literature, and, in fact, very little criticism of any sort. Yet this period in England is important both for the volume of writing it produced—Lydgate alone wrote more than 145,000 lines—and for the profound changes in the literary process that occurred. The fifteenth century witnessed a broadening of the domain of literature and an increasing awareness of the importance of writing in the vernacular. With the expansion in the production and copying of texts, the widespread use of printing, and the birth of an influential new reading public, the relations among author, text, and audience changed radically.[1] At the same time, the vernacular underwent such dramatic alteration that the English at the beginning of the century was archaic by the end. These changes and the rapid absorption of continental models by translation into English compelled the poets continually to reassess the literary language and the medium in which they worked.

The importance of this reassessment for an understanding of late medieval and early Renaissance literature and for English literature in general has not been recognized. Underlying the voluminous body of fifteenth-century literature in England is a major shift in attitude toward poetry and the role of the poet. Within the matrix of the verse itself, the poets of that period articulate ideals and assumptions about poetry, in part their own invention, in part drawn from continental sources, which depart significantly from their immediate models. In the fifteenth-century poets' self-conscious consideration of their craft and in the responses of poem to poem in this period in defining their own art, one finds a precursor to a formal poetics in English.

The traditional approach to the period, which we have inherited from late eighteenth- and early nineteenth-century writers, as an anticlimax to the age of Chaucer has in part obscured the serious revaluation of the poetic process that is evident within many fifteenth-century poems. Conditioned by C. S. Lewis and others to view the fifteenth century as a "dark age," a transition from civilization to "barbarism," we have until recently overlooked the significance of its literature.[2] Although since the 1960s scholars have turned again to this period in an attempt to reestablish its importance, their studies raise a further problem—that of determining a viable critical basis for dealing with fifteenth-century literature.[3] In many cases, the methods used to approach earlier texts are not effective for fifteenth-century works, which are occasional, topical, and, by Chaucerian standards, discursive and unwieldy. By reconsidering in detail one area of fifteenth-century literature, the work of the major English and Scots poets, in light of the assumptions about the literary process that they articulate in their poems, this book will attempt to define new criteria for dealing with much of the literature of the late Middle Ages and for determining the importance of its changing vision of poetry.

In general, the critics who have approached fifteenth-century literature in an effort to restore its reputation have relied upon one of three methods. Some scholars, including Walter Schirmer and Alain Renoir, have suggested that although the literature between Lydgate and Skelton is not as immediately appealing as fourteenth-century literature, it is nevertheless crucial to an understanding of the Renaissance, because many of the themes and forms characteristic of later literature first appeared in English in this period.[4] A second group of critics, including H. S. Bennett, Eleanor Hammond, and, more recently, Rossell H. Robbins, Derek Pearsall, A. S. G. Edwards, Richard Green, and N. F. Blake, attempts to justify fifteenth-century literature on its own historical grounds.[5] Rejecting the notion that these works are important because they anticipate the Renaissance, these critics insist that the literature of the fifteenth century must be read in the context of the political, social, and historical events of its own age and in terms of the changing linguistic environment and patterns of patronage in the period. In a series of studies that appeared between 1922 and 1947, Bennett and Hammond survey the discordant conditions in England during the fifteenth century—the continual warfare at home and abroad, the weakness of the administration, the disintegration of medieval social ideals, the "stereotyping society" of the aristocracy, the rise of a new bourgeois reading public—arguing that these circumstances produced a climate hostile to the development of great literature.[6] Rather than using the historical and social conditions of the time as an excuse for the allegedly poor quality of fifteenth-century poetry, Robbins, Pearsall, Green, and Olson, among others, attempt to make this poetry accessible to the modern reader by reconstructing the context of its composition and dissemination and clarifying its social and political significance. Dismissing Bennett's and Hammond's explanation of the quality of fifteenth-century literature as too simple, they encourage us to re-orient ourselves historically and attempt to approach this literature as readers of the age did.[7] Finally, a few scholars have applied tenets of modern criticism to fifteenth-century texts. Typical is A. C. Spearing's use of Harold Bloom's "anxiety of influence" in his careful analysis of several major fifteenth-century texts to explain the fifteenth-century poets' "misreading" of Chaucer.[8]

Although the approaches of these scholars have been very helpful in dealing with fifteenth-century literature, particularly the methods of the historical critics which have provided an informed social, political, economic, linguistic, and aesthetic context for the poems, even the best of these studies leave important questions about the nature of fifteenth-century poetic practices unanswered. Many of the poems are neither primarily reflections of the moral, social, and political concerns of the time, nor are their conspicuous formal and stylistic features explicable in these terms. In this book I turn from earlier approaches to fifteenth-century literature to the evidence within the poems themselves about the distinct poetic practices and ideals of good poetry that underlie the poets' attempts to develop a new literary medium in the vernacular. Although no formal poetics have survived in English from before the end of the sixteenth century, the fifteenth-century poets produced a striking number of poems that address the role of the poet and the process of poetry as central themes. These poems, which either have been ignored or treated exclusively from other points of view, provide a survey of the poetics of the period that is more comprehensive and relevant to the practices of the fifteenth-century poets than the earlier treatises of the rhetoricians to which we usually turn for an understanding of the medieval poet's craft.

Although the fifteenth-century poets reveal their familiarity with some of the rhetorical texts, both transmitted directly by writers like Geoffrey of Vinsauf and John of Garland and indirectly in the poems of Dante, Jean de Meun, Chaucer, and other poets, they draw most heavily on the examination of the poetic process within their own and earlier poems, including the self-conscious consideration of poetry and the poet's role in Dante's *Commedia,* the French love visions, Chaucer's *Hous of Fame, Troilus,* and *Canterbury Tales.* John Gower's *Confessio Amantis,* and on treatises like John of Salisbury's *Policraticus* and Boccaccio's *De Genealogia deorum.* Minnis has pointed out that behind these thirteenth- and fourteenth-century poems is a theory of *auctors,* developed in the prologues of several generations of schoolmen, which was adapted in the fourteenth century from scriptural to secular writers. The result was a more liberal attitude to classical poetry and a shift in the way secular poets envisioned themselves and their work.[9]

I suggest that the fifteenth-century poets viewed Dante, Chaucer, and certain of the French poets as *auctors* and models for their own eventual assumption of that role. In their self-conscious examination of their craft within the body of their works, the fifteenth-century poets respond to each other and to earlier poets in an ongoing dialogue about the purpose and effect of poetry. This book focuses on this explicit thematic redefinition of the poetic process in the poems of the period in an attempt to define the attitudes and assumptions about poetry that underlie fifteenth-century literature. As part of this process, I will consider the fifteenth-century poets' effort to develop a critical vocabulary to define the qualities of good poetry by coining words where none existed and assigning new meanings to terms that were used in English before for different purposes. As we have not heretofore recognized, by means of this vocabulary these writers articulate with considerable sensitivity the artistic preoccupations that dominate the poetry of the period. The vision of poetry that emerges is refined and reinforced by the recurring metaphors and myths of the poetic process these poets introduce in their poems. Finally, I assess the manifestations of the fifteenth-century poetic ideals in the dominant styles and forms of the period.

This investigation of the fifteenth-century poets' conceptions of poetry provides a different view of the period from historical interpretations. The fifteenth-century poets, in many cases, depart from the models and concerns of their so-called masters. Their poetry represents a significant redefinition of the relation of poets to their medium and a reassessment of the importance of poetry as a vehicle of truth and a means of ennobling humanity and reaffirming political order and harmony in the realm. These concerns find form in the fifteenth-century poets' attempts to develop a literary language and a high poetic style in the vernacular, the medium that they consider most worthy of their purposes as poets, and in many of the characteristic poetic practices of the period—the fondness for amplification, aureate diction, intricate verbal design, and attenuated forms. The issues the fifteenth-century poets grapple with in their poems also have implications for our understanding of Renaissance literature. The self-conscious thematic treatment of the value and effect of poetry evident in the body of fifteenth-century literature suggests the formulation of a poetics in English earlier than so far recognized, based on a secularized view of the poet's role. With some notable exceptions, including Spenser and Milton, the vision of the poet as a potential instrument of divine truth and a spiritual guide is put to rest by the fifteenth-century poets. Their attention shifts from the quest for salvation, embodied in the journeys of Dante's poet, Chaucer's pilgrim, and William Langland's Will, to the activity of individuals in the world in its ethical and political contexts. Rather than encouraging human beings to transcend the mutable reality of earthly experience, poetry in this period becomes a legitimate vehicle of immortality as an artifact that endures beyond the temporal events it records. This change in direction and turning away from long-standing assumptions, rather than any specific theoretical innovation, prepares for the birth of many of the attitudes about poetry we still hold.

Two poets, John Lydgate and John Skelton, provide the boundaries for this investigation of fifteenth-century poetics. Lydgate, the most prolific writer of the period, at the beginning of the century embodies the thematic and artistic concerns that dominate the age. To an even greater extent than Chaucer's poetry, his works introduce the poetic ideals and practices that recur during the fifteenth century. The conception of poetry and the role of the poet that Lydgate popularizes at the outset of the century are confirmed and qualified in the writing of each of the major English and Scots poets—James I of Scotland, Robert Henryson, William Dunbar, Gavin Douglas, and Stephen Hawes. Throughout the century, these poets reiterate, refine, and extend the vision of the poet as an "enluminer" whose writing enlightens and leads humanity to wisdom, harmony, and political order, and the corresponding high styles and amplificatory modes linked with these views. Skelton, writing between 1483 and 1528, manifests the dissolution of the poetic ideals that dominate the period. His work questions and challenges the basic assumptions of fifteenth-century poetry, particularly the relation of the poet as an illuminator of the poetic medium, the ability of poetry to lead one to wisdom, and the effectiveness of poetry in its current forms to insure the well-being of the state. In his efforts to deal with these problems, Skelton, though linked to his predecessors, abandons the various solutions of the fifteenth-century poets.

* * *

The research for this book was supported by generous grants from the National Endowment for the Humanities, the American Council of Learned Societies, and Barnard College. Students and colleagues at Barnard College and Columbia University, particularly Ruth Kivette and Howard Schless, have provided helpful suggestions and criticisms of various drafts of the manuscript. I am also grateful for the valuable assistance of many scholars in the field, including the late E. Talbot Donaldson, George Economou, Vernon J. Harward, Roderick J. Lyall, Judith Neaman, Robert O. Payne, Derek Pearsall, Walter Scheps, and Eugene Vance.

ne

"The Firste Fyndere of Our Fair Language"

As assessment of fifteenth-century attitudes toward poetry properly
begins with a reconsideration of the poets' relation to Chaucer, for, to
a great extent, our assumptions about Chaucer's influence in the
period have colored our understanding of this poetry. For the fifteenth-century poets, Chaucer is the "laureate," their "maister
deere," their father "reuerent," the "noble rethor poete" of Britain,
the "flour of eloquence," the universal father of "science," the
mirror, lamp, and lodestar of poets.[1] His importance as a model for
their writing is considerable. Following their "maister," fifteenth-
century poets extended the *Canterbury Tales,* supplying missing
links, additional stories, and even new pilgrims. They provided se-
quels to the *Troilus,* wrote an ending for the *Hous of Fame,* and
responded directly to many of Chaucer's short lyrics and complaints.
Their poetry includes full-scale imitations of the *Book of the Duchess,*
the *Parliament of Fowls,* the *Hous of Fame,* the *Troilus,* the opening
of the *General Prologue,* the *Knight's Tale,* the *Nun's Priest's Tale,*
the *Wife of Bath's Tale,* the *Tale of Sir Thopas,* and several of the

lyrics. Finally, their writing repeatedly borrows Chaucerian lines, forms, and meters.

But although Lydgate, Thomas Hoccleve, James I, Henryson, Dunbar, Douglas, Hawes, and Skelton admired Chaucer and imitated him closely in many passages, their aims and purposes differed substantially from his. Paradoxically, in turning from Chaucer to these poets, one is impressed by the striking divergence of their work from his, a departure that cannot be accounted for simply by faulty imitation. Beyond the diversity of fifteenth-century poems lie shared assumptions about poetry that distinguish the poets of this period from their so-called master. By examining the evidence provided by the fifteenth-century tributes to Chaucer, the relative popularity of his works between 1400 and 1500, the early manuscript traditions, and the development of the Chaucer apocrypha, one gains new insight into these poets' attitudes toward Chaucer's work. Such an investigation reveals that Chaucer is significant to the fifteenth-century poets for reasons that are different from the ones we have recognized and that their views of poetry and their conceptions of their roles as poets often reflect concerns that are not prominent in his work.[2]

Underlying Chaucer's conception of poetry is an essential uneasiness about the truthfulness of poetry and the limitations of mortals with their mutable language and imperfect "entente" as artists. These concerns, which each of the major fifteenth-century poets responds to, find form in Chaucer's repeated questioning of the relation between the poets' moral and artistic vision, between the truths a poet knows by experience, authority, and vision and the illusions created by language.[3] While Chaucer emphasizes the superficial and transitory nature of earthly experience, he is also aware of its undeniable attractiveness, and, of the way in which the poets' created images become part of the mutable reality they seek to transcend. His position as poet, which critics suggest has its counterpart in the shift from the synthesizing vision of the thirteenth-century philosophers to the increasing skepticism of the fourteenth-century nominalists,[4] is reflected in the formal and stylistic solutions of his poems, particularly in his strategies of indirection, thematic and structural contrast, and irony, and in his mistrust of high style, rhetorical amplification, and the "ars poetical" that were to become the staples of the fifteenth-century poets.

In the writing of many of the fifteenth-century poets, the problems that Chaucer considers so anxiously no longer are apparent. Rather, their work reveals a confidence in the power of poetry to ennoble humanity and to lead readers to truth. Underlying much of their writing is a vision of the poet as an "enluminer" and enlightener whose heightened language adorns the poet's matter and renders it significant and enduring. The poet's activity, which they link with the activity of the legendary Amphion and later David, has the power to inspire people and bring political order and harmony to the state. Behind the formal and stylistic practices of these poets, particularly their characteristic strategies of amplification and their conspicuous efforts to develop a high style in English, are conceptions of the value and effect of poetry, in part their own development, in part derived from Dante, Boccaccio, and other continental sources, which are not evident in Chaucer's work.

A good starting point for considering the departure of these poets from the Chaucerian model and for reassessing the terms of Chaucer's influence in the late Middle Ages is provided by the elaborate tributes that the fifteenth-century poets have written in praise of Chaucer. To a great extent, we have misinterpreted these passages. Put off by the artificial language of their praise, we have concluded that the fifteenth-century poets admired Chaucer for the wrong reasons—for his rhetorical skill and ornate language.[5] In fact, as Kean has demonstrated, the fifteenth-century poets' terms of praise had a much broader significance than has been recognized and referred not simply, as we have assumed, to stylistic elaboration but to an effective relation between style and content.[6] This larger range of meanings, for example, is illustrated by Thomas Feylde's eulogy of Chaucer, Gower, and Lydgate where the terms "rethoryk," "rethorycien," and "eloquence" suggest not only poetic skill, but also excellence of content:

Cancer [sic] floure of rethoryke eloquence
Compyled bokes pleasaunt and meruayllous
After hym noble Gower experte in scyence
Wrote moralytes herde and delycyous
But Lydgate's workes are fruytefull and sentencyous
Who of his bokes hathe redde the fyne
He wyll hym call a famus rethorycyne.[7]

Even more important than the connotations of the terms in the tributes to Chaucer are certain emphases in these passages that have gone undetected in our preoccupation with the fifteenth-century conception of Chaucer as a "rethorician." In the first place, the fifteenth-century poets stress that Chaucer is of a stature different from that of all other English poets. He is the "father of poets," the "floure of rethoryk" and "elloquence," the "mirror of excellence," the "laurer," the "sun" among dimmer stars, the "lodesterre."[8] Throughout the century, these images cluster and recur to draw attention to Chaucer's preeminent position among poets. Lydgate, for example, praises Chaucer as the "floure of poets / throughout al breteyne / which sothly hadde / most of excellence / In rethorike and in eloquence" and later as the "laurer" and sun which outshines all other stars.[9] Hoccleve, too, combines these images in his famous eulogy: "O, maister deere, and fadir reuerent! / Mi maister Chaucer, flour of eloquence, / Mirour of fructuous entendement, / O, vniuersel fadir in science."[10]

Second, the fifteenth-century poets emphasize that, in his writing, Chaucer did something distinctly new that has changed the course of English poetry. His achievement, in their view, is above all the transformation of his native tongue into a language suitable for poetry. Lydgate first articulates this notion at length in the *Life of Our Lady* in a passage later printed by Caxton as "a commendacion of Chauceris":

> The noble rethor Poete of breteine
> . . . .
> That made firste to distille and reyne
> The golde dewe droppis of speche and eloquence
> In-to oure tounge thourʒ his excellence
> And founde the flourys first of rethoryk
> Oure rude speche oonly to enlumyne
> That in oure tunge was neuer noon him like. . . .[11]

Again in the prologue to the *Siege of Thebes* (1420), he praises Chaucer as the "pris / honoure / and glorye // Of wel seying / first in our language . . ."[12] and in the *Pilgrimage of the Life of Man* (1426) as the "ffyrste in any age / That amendede our language."[13] Finally, before Lydgate sums up Chaucer's achievement in the *Fall of Princes,* he pauses to remind us of Chaucer's role in developing English as a literary language:

> My maistir Chaucer dede his besynesse,
> And in his daies hath so weel hym born,

Out off our tunge tauoiden al reudnesse,
And to refourme it with colours of suetnesse;
Wherefore lat us yiue him laude & glory. . . .[14]

Lydgate's assessment of Chaucer as the reformer of the English
tongue is confirmed by writers who follow him throughout the century. Hoccleve, in the *Regiment of Princes,* for example, addresses
Chaucer as "the firste fyndere of our fair language."[15] John Shirley, in
his prologue to Chaucer's translation of Boethius, reports that the
work was "laboured" by Chaucer who "first enlymned þis lande with
retoryen and eloquent language of oure rude englisshe modere
tonge."[16] Echoing these writers, William Caxton, at the end of the
century, refers to Chaucer as "the worshipful fader & first foundeur &
embellisher of ornate eloquence in our englissh."[17] John Rastell,
Dunbar, and Skelton, at the beginning of the sixteenth century, repeat
this praise of Chaucer. Rastell commends Chaucer for his elegant
writing; Dunbar refers to him as the light of all our English; and
Skelton addresses him as "Noble Chaucer, whos pullisshyed eloquence / Our englysshe rude so fresshely hath set out."[18]

Chaucer's effort to amend his language, the fifteenth- and early
sixteenth-century writers emphasize, resulted in the inclusion of English among the great literatures of the other nations. Although before
Chaucer English had but "litel reputation," after he wrote, it attained
a stature equal to the best of continental languages.[19] Lydgate explicitly introduces this view in the *Troy Book* as he concludes his
praise of Chaucer by linking him with Petrarch as one of the two poets
who excelled in their native tongues.[20] Likewise, in the *Fall of
Princes,* he places Chaucer in the tradition of the great national
writers, "Daunt in Itaille, Virgile in Rome toun, / Petrak in Florence. . . ."[21] Finally, at the end of the century, George Ashby extends this idea to include Gower and Lydgate, "Primier poetes of this
nacion" who changed the course of English literature and made it
worthy of renown.[22]

Thus, for the fifteenth-century poets, Chaucer's significance lay in
the tremendous prestige he gave to English literature. His writing, and
especially his innovative use of language, opened up possibilities for
working in English, which, in these poets' view, did not exist before
he transformed their native language into a medium suitable for
poetry. In acknowledging Chaucer as their master, these poets refer

not to the specific lines and phrases they borrow, but to their awareness of working within a tradition newly vitalized and extended by a
poet greater in stature than any English writer before him.

The fifteenth-century poets' view of their debt to Chaucer is
underscored by an important shift in the emphasis of the tributes as the
century progresses. In the early stanzas in praise of Chaucer that first
begin to appear in number shortly after 1400, the year of his death,
each of the leading poets steps forward to lament his loss, assess
Chaucer's position as an English poet, and define his own relation to
his master.[23] About 1440, however, after Lydgate has achieved considerable prominence, the tone and emphasis of the tributes begin to
change. Some of the intensity of the early eulogies subsides, while the
relation of Chaucer to the English poets who follow him is brought
into focus even more sharply. In many of the tributes, his name is
linked with Lydgate's and Gower's, and his individual poetic achievement becomes less important than the role he now shares with these
poets as innovators and amenders of the English language. In an
anonymous poem entitled "A Reproof to Lydgate," the poet makes
the importance of this relation between Chaucer and Lydgate clear.
Since Chaucer is dead, Lydgate, his rightful successor, must now
"occupy his place" and inspire the pen of this poet.[24] Again, in an
account of Lydgate (c. 1450), the anonymous author refers to the
Monk of Bury as the imitator of Chaucer in that he continued to enrich
the English language, and, like Chaucer, "was a great Ornament of ye
English Toung."[25] By the first quarter of the sixteenth century, another shift in emphasis occurs. The achievement of Chaucer, though,
considerable, is no longer as relevant to poets working in English as it
had been in the fifteenth century. Henry Bradshaw, for example,
writing in 1513, refers to a variety of English models, each with his
distinct achievement: "Fyrst to maister Chaucer and Ludgate senten-
cious. / Also to preignaunt Barkley nowe beyng religious / To inuen-
tiue Skelton and poet laureate."[26] Likewise, although Skelton praises
Chaucer in "Phyllyp Sparowe," his narrator indicates scornfully that
some writers now find his English obsolete and in need of correction:

> And now men would have amended
> His Englyssh, whereat they barke
> And mar all they warke;
> Chaucer, that famus clerke,

His termes were not darke,
But plesaunt, easy and playne:
Ne worde he wrote in vayne.[27]

Thus, as the fifteenth century progressed, Chaucer's position as the "firste fyndere" of our literary English, the amender of our language, became even more important than the influence of his specific works. The evidence of the tributes suggests that poets sought to follow his example not simply by copying his poems, but by attempting to extend the limits of their literary language and poetic forms. The effect is seen in the tremendous volume of writing these poets produced, in the scale of the works they undertook, in their manipulation of traditional forms, and in their conspicuous effort to develop a high poetic style in English.

The relative popularity of Chaucer's works in the fifteenth century provides a second indication of the attitudes of these poets toward his poetry and of their changing concerns as poets. On the basis of the number of manuscripts that have survived, we have assumed that the fifteenth-century reading public admired Chaucer principally as a narrative poet and a moral and didactic writer. Among the early works, those most frequently copied in the fifteenth century include the *Astrolabe* (in twenty-five manuscripts and fragments), the *Troilus* (with thirty-two manuscripts and fragments and three early prints), the *Legend of Good Women* (in twelve manuscripts and one early print), the "Complaint of Chaucer to his Purse," the complaints to "Pity," "Mars," "Venus," and *Anelida and Arcita* (each at least in eight manuscripts).[28] With reference to the *Canterbury Tales,* certain of the tales, principally the romance and exemplary tales, exist in more manuscript groups than the other tales.[29] In addition, some tales appear to have circulated both separately and with other tales in anthology manuscripts. In these collections, by far the most popular tales were first the religious and moral tales—the *Clerk's Tale,* the *Prioress' Tale, Melibee,* the *Parson's Tale,* the *Second Nun's Tale,* and the *Man of Law's Tale*—and, to a lesser extent, the romances—the *Wife of Bath's Tale,* the *Knight's Tale,* the *Franklin's Tale*—a factor that has reinforced our impression of Chaucer's popularity in the fifteenth century as a narrative and didactic writer.[30]

But when one turns from the manuscript evidence to the testimony of the poetry of the period, a different picture emerges. An investigation of the poetic imitations and allusions to Chaucer reveals that the fifteenth-century poets' interest in their "maister" centered on a few important poems, in many cases, not the ones most popular among the reading public. In contrast both to Chaucer's image of himself as a fledgling poet and an outsider from love and to the modern view of him as a complex and ironic writer, these poets consider him principally as a court poet and poet of love, the author of the *Troilus,* the visions, complaints, and selected lyrics. From the perspective of their poetry, the work with the most profound impact was the *Troilus,* which was alluded to in fifteenth-century writing more than three times as often as any other Chaucerian piece,[31] and which directly influenced several fifteenth-century poems.[32] As Patterson demonstrates, the poem served both as an impressive model of earthly love and as a work of stylistic and rhetorical significance.[33] Although the early visions, the *Anelida and Arcita,* and the complaints remain popular, particularly for their experimentation in structure and verse forms, the *Hous of Fame* appears to have been more important to the fifteenth-century poets than the number of manuscripts indicates. Several poets, including Lydgate and Hawes, allude to Chaucer's unfinished vision and the *Hous of Fame* is linked closely to Lydgate's experimentation in the *Temple of Glas,* Gavin Douglas's *Palice of Honour* and prologue to the *Aeneid,* Book I, and Skelton's "Garlande of Laurell."[34] Critics also have underestimated the importance of the *Legend of Good Women* to the fifteenth-century poets. Portions of this poem, especially the prologue and the Dido legend, copied in anthology manuscripts, had a recurrent impact on the miscellaneous court poems of the period, including *The Flower and the Leaf, The Court of Love, The Letter of Dido to Aeneas,* and *The Louer's Mass.*[35]

Among the *Canterbury Tales,* the most important works were the *Knight's Tale,* which influenced *The Kingis Quair, The Complaint of the Black Knight, The Cuckoo and the Nightingale, The Siege of Thebes, The Floure of Curtesye, The Court of Love,*[36] and the *Wife of Bath*'s prologue, which lay behind the thematic and stylistic emphasis of Dunbar's "The Tretis of the Tua Mariit Wemen and the Wedo," Lydgate's "The Pain and Sorrow of Evil Marriage," and Hoccleve's "Dialogue Cum Amico."[37] The *Nun's Priest's Tale,* the *Monk's Tale,* the *Prioress' Tale,* and *Sir Thopas* were imitated directly though not as frequently as the *Knight's Tale* and the *Wife of Bath*'s prologue.[38] Finally, the fifteenth-century poets repeatedly borrowed from four other *Canterbury Tales*—the *Clerk's Tale,* the *Merchant's Tale,* the *Squire's Tale,* and the *Franklin's Tale*—as well as several significant passages in other parts of the poem, including the opening lines of the *General Prologue* and the rhetorical outbursts against Fortune in the *Man of Law's Tale.*[39]

The poetic imitations and allusions to Chaucer in the fifteenth century indicate that in their poems Chaucer's immediate successors turned principally to his love poetry, especially the *Troilus* and the *Knight's Tale,* the dream visions, complaints, and selected lyrics as sources for their own experimentation. Their borrowings reflect the literary and social concerns that were increasingly important in the fifteenth century—the use of literature as an instrument of social display and play, a repository of stances and statements to be embellished and adopted for specific patrons and occasions; the poem as a continuing refinement of social interaction on the one hand and as a celebration or statement of topical or political relevance on the other, and the increasing concern during this period with absorbing into English the greatness of continental models.[40] Stylistically and formally, the fifteenth-century poets find in Chaucer an example of this achievement and they turn with particular interest to the separate passages in which he experiments with a high style in English—the complaints in the *Anelida and Arcita,* the "ABC," the set speeches in the *Knight's Tale,* the *Troilus* palinode—which they refine and modify throughout the century.

The vision of Chaucer as preeminently a court poet and a poet of love is confirmed by the development of the Chaucer apocrypha, the body of more than forty-five spurious works attributed to the dead poet.[41] As these poems reveal, to a considerable extent fifteenth-century writers and editors remade Chaucer in their own image, adding works to the canon which reflected their own conception of good poetry. As Bonner points out, several conditions combined to encourage the proliferation of works attributed to Chaucer in the fifteenth century—Chaucer's own ambiguous catalogues of his writing in the *Legend of Good Women,* the introduction to the *Man of Law's Tale,* and the *Retraction;* the testimony of his contemporaries Gower and Lydgate; the methods of manuscript transmission in the fifteenth century, particularly the practice of assembling collections of works by various authors that were copied by several scribes and then bound together for distribution; and the efforts of early editors to make their Chaucer volumes saleable by including newly discovered Chaucerian texts.[42] Yet at least as important was a factor that Bonner ignores—the changing poetic preoccupations of the time. As the fifteenth century progressed, the works that became attached to the Chaucer canon defined a poet who epitomized the new poetic ideals and tastes of the period.

The differences between the works added to the Chaucer canon during the fifteenth century and those added in the sixteenth century provide a good example of this process. In the fifteenth century, the majority of works erroneously attributed to Chaucer are love poems, lyrics of complaint, and short moral ballads, similar in style and theme to the larger body of literature of the contemporary court poets. The earliest of these poems include several conventional love lyrics, for example, the "Balade to His Mistress, Fairest of Fair," "To Alisoun," and "To My Sovereign Lady."[43] Between 1450 and 1500, a number of longer "love aunters" and miscellaneous courtly and moral poems are added to the canon in manuscript collections such as MS Trinity Cambridge 599 and Fairfax 16. Particularly striking in these manuscripts is the ascription to Chaucer of certain popular fifteenth-century narrative types, for example, the love allegories that differ from his original works in style and technique, but are clearly related to the endeavors of the popular English Chaucerians of the period. Among other poems, this group includes *The Court of Love, The Court of Venus, The Craft of Lovers, The Isle of Ladies,* and *The Assembly of Ladies.*[44] Also, in these manuscripts, several decorative pieces are assigned to Chaucer that have more in common with the occasional court verse of the fifteenth century than with the authentic works of the canon, for example, the "Epistle to His Mistress, Signed Chaucer," "Virelai," "The Describing of a Fair Lady," and "A Praise of Women."[45]

Moreover, as the scribes and poets of the second half of the fifteenth century linked Chaucer, Gower, and Lydgate, they obliterated by their additions to the canon some of the essential differences among these poets. This process is especially apparent in the case of Chaucer and Lydgate. In the fifteenth-century manuscripts and editions, more than fifteen of Lydgate's works are attributed to Chaucer. The Trinity MS R. 3. 19, for example, assigns Lydgate's "Ten Commandments of Love" to Chaucer, whereas Seldon B 24 concludes Lydgate's *Complaint of the Black Knight* with the colophon

"Here endith the maying and disport of Chaucer."[46] Likewise, Richard Pynson, William Thynne, and John Stow respectively attribute to Chaucer "Utter thy Language," "In Commendation of Our Lady," and "Doubleness." The effect of these and other similar additions was to produce a Chaucer much more akin to Lydgate than he actually was, a poet who turned to the genres and styles that were popular in the fifteenth century—the complaint, the courtly commendation, the witty and amplified love conceit, the moral ballad.

In the sixteenth century, in contrast, while editors continued to add love poems to the Chaucer canon, for the first time they also began to include works that reflected the religious controversy and tumult of their own time. Unlike the fifteenth-century apocryphal poems, the religious works were not found in manuscripts with Chaucer's genuine poems nor were they similar in content and style to the authentic works of the canon. In 1542, for example, Thynne included in his edition of Chaucer the *Ploughman's Tale,* a rather fierce attack on the Catholic church, which, as Lounsbury points out, "Nothing but the bitterness of religious controversy . . . could have imputed to Chaucer."[47] Likewise, about 1538, *Jack Upland,* a bitter complaint in prose against "antichrist and his disciples," was printed and attributed to Chaucer.[48] This work was referred to by Thomas Speght in 1598 and added to his edition of 1602.[49] In addition, between 1532 and 1602, Thynne, Stow, and Speght introduced an increasing number of satiric poems that undermined the form and content of fifteenth-century love poetry, for example, "The Describing of a Fair Lady," "O Mossie Quince," and "A Praise of Women." These poems mock the conventions of the courtly poetry popular in the fifteenth century and suggest a reappraisal of some of the dominant fifteenth-century styles and themes.[50]

The attitudes of the fifteenth-century poets toward Chaucer are complicated by problems of secondhand and simultaneous influence. In many cases, although these poets knew Chaucer's original work, they were also familiar with the adaptations by his early imitators—particularly Lydgate, who provides his own version of more than ten of Chaucer's poems, reworking the *Book of the Duchess* in *The Complaint of the Black Knight,* the *Hous of Fame,* in the *Temple of Glas,* the *Troilus* in his expanded *Troy Book,* the *Monk's Tale* in the *Fall of Princes,* the opening of the *Canterbury Tales* and the *Knight's Tale* in his *Siege of Thebes,* and many of Chaucer's best-known lyrics in his own short poems. In these adaptations of Chaucer, which were extremely popular in the fifteenth century, the characteristics of his writing were exaggerated and, in turn, imitated by later poets, forming the basis for many of the stylistic and metrical practices of the period.

A striking example of this process is found in Lydgate's treatment of Chaucer's vocabulary, syntax, and rhetorical figures. Typically, in imitating Chaucer, Lydgate adapts devices that Chaucer uses only rarely and introduces them with such frequency and prominence that they become a staple of the fifteenth-century poets who follow him. This dissemination of selected Chaucerian techniques is immediately evident in Lydgate's popularization of Chaucer's poetic vocabulary. In Lydgate's writing, many words that occur only a limited number of times in Chaucer's usage are developed as significant terms. The word "licour," for example, found in its various forms only four times in Chaucer's poetry, appears more than thirty times in Lydgate's work, both with its Chaucerian meaning of "liquid" and in several new figurative senses—as a metaphor for the dew that Titan's fiery heat dries up (*Complaint of the Black Knight,* 26–30), as the "rain" of Ceres' horn of plenty (*Troy Book,* I, 1300), and finally, as a term to describe poetic power or inspiration, a meaning that is entirely absent in Chaucer's writing.[51] Lydgate's uses of the term "licour," particularly as a metaphor for the poetic process, recur throughout the century. Caxton, for example, introduces the term in this sense in *The Book of Curtesye,* referring to the "lusty lyquour / of that fulsom fontayne" to praise the writing of the dead Chaucer.[52] As the studies of Reismuller, Nichols, and Hammond reveal, many other examples of this adoptive process occur in Lydgate's writing.[53]

As Courmont points out, Lydgate also introduces syntactical devices that Chaucer practices only occasionally to vary his lines.[54] One of the most common of the techniques Lydgate adapts is Chaucerian inversion, transposing the auxiliary and verb and the verb and object pronoun with such frequency that this practice becomes a characteristic mark of his style, in turn copied by the poets who follow him. In addition, Lydgate transforms many of the larger syntactical patterns characteristic of Chaucer. The most familiar example is perhaps the opening of the *Siege of Thebes* in which Lydgate attempts to imitate the first sentence of the prologue to the *Canterbury Tales*. Lydgate, however, extends Chaucer's nineteen-verse sentence to sixty-five verses, and, whereas Chaucer leads us swiftly through his series of clauses with the repetition of "whan," "whan," "thanne," Lydgate distorts this pattern by doubling the number of "whan" clauses so that we do not reach the main point of the sentence until more than sixty lines have passed.

As Pearsall demonstrates, Lydgate's exaggeration of Chaucerian devices is not simply an instance of faulty imitation; his changes are intended to be an improvement, a more "deluxe" version of his master's work.[55] In adapting two lines from the *Friar's Tale,* for example, Lydgate makes a number of characteristic alterations in Chaucer's rhetorical scheme that suggest this motive. Chaucer writes, "His eyen twynkled in his head aryght, / As doon the sterres in the frosty nyght" (I [A] 267–68). Lydgate transforms the lines to read, "Whos brennyng eyes sparklyng of ther licht / As doon sterris the frosti wyntres nicht" (*Fall of Princes,* VI, 27–28). Typically, he amplifies the lines by adding more details ("wyntres," "of ther licht"), a greater number of images ("brennyng" as well as "spar-klyng"), and the contrast between "brennyng" and "frosti."[56] Simi-lar tendencies are apparent in Lydgate's description of Criseyde in the *Troy Book.* In writing about Criseyde's hair, for example, Chaucer simply says: "And ofte tyme this was hire manere, / To gon ytressed with hire heres clere / Doun by hire color at hire bak behynde, / Which with a thred of golde she wolde bynde" (*Troilus and Criseyde,* V, 809 ff). Lydgate embellishes this description with the addition of adjec-tives, celestial similes, comparisons, and repetition for emphasis:

> Hir sonnysche her, liche Phebus in his spere,
> Bounde in a tresse, briȝhter þanne golde were,
> Doun at hir bak, lowe doun be-hynde,
> Whiche with a þrede of golde sche wolde bynde
> Ful ofte syþe of a-custummaunce.
> (*Troy Book,* II, 4741–45)

Later poets like Dunbar, Hawes, and Douglas in turn copied and elaborated Lydgate's figures. Douglas, for example, in *The Palice of Honour* describes Venus with some of these devices:

> . . . like Phebus in hiest of his Spheir
> Hir bewtie schane, castand sa greit ane glance.
> All fairheid it opprest baith far and neir.

> Scho was peirles of schap and portrature.
> In hir had nature finischit hir cure.
> As for gude hauingis thair was nane bot scho,
> And hir array was sa fine and sa pure
> That quhairof was hir Rob I am not sure
> For nocht bot Perle and stanis micht I se;
> Of quhome the brichtnes of hir hie bewtie
> For to behald my sicht micht not Indure. . . .[57]

Likewise, Dunbar adopts and extends many of these stylistic features. In the "Thrissil and the Rois," he describes the sunrise with typically Lydgatian embellishments—celestial similes, repetitions, inversions, qualifying clauses, and paired adjectives:

> The purpour sone with tendir bemys reid
> The orient bricht as angell did appeir
> Throw goldin skyis putting up his heid,
> Quhois gilt tressis schone so wondir cleir
> That all the world tuke confort fer and neir,
> To luke upone his fresche and blisfull face,
> Doing all sable fro the hevynnis chace.[58]

As these examples suggest, Chaucer's influence in the fifteenth century was filtered through the work of Lydgate and other early imitators who, in their writing, modified many of his techniques and adopted poetic dictions and styles that departed considerably from his.

Even when the late fifteenth-century and early sixteenth-century poets used Chaucer in an unadulterated form, they often imitated his poems simultaneously with other poets', producing works that differed from any of their sources. Several instances of this simultaneous borrowing are found in Dunbar's poems, for example, in his famous "Tretis of the Tua Mariit Wemen and the Wedo." Although the poem is generally linked with Chaucer's *Wife of Bath*'s prologue which it resembles, it also draws freely upon Lydgate's "The Pain and Sorrow of Evil Marriage."[59] Dunbar takes hints for the three women's characters and their colorful speeches from the Wife's experiences with her five husbands, but many of the specific features of the satire are suggested by the Lydgate poem—the first Wife's desire to imitate the mating habits of birds, her image of herself at pilgrimages and gatherings, the description of the widow's duplicity and several of her devices.[60] Even more important is the relation between Lydgate's poem and the theme of bestiality in the "Tua Mariit Wemen." From Lydgate's description of the husband in wedlock and the wives which "been bestes very unstable," Dunbar appears to have developed the idea for the recurrent animal imagery of his poem, a central device of his satire and the means by which he establishes a contrast between the beautiful courtly appearance of the women and the ugliness beneath, an emphasis that finally distinguishes his poem from both of his sources. In a somewhat different form, we find the simultaneous influence of Chaucer and Lydgate in Stephen Hawes's *Pastime of Pleasure*. In this poem, the structure of the work itself represents an effort to join the love narrative modeled on *Troilus and Criseyde* with the large-scale allegorical form of Lydgate's *Pilgrimage of the Life of Man* and the Lydgatian *Courte of Sapyence*. Though often cumbersome, Hawes's ambitious form is another indication of the ways in which the fifteenth-century poets used Chaucer in the context of his early imitators.

The stylistic, structural, and thematic borrowings of the fifteenth-century poets draw attention to certain important peculiarities that underlie many of the adaptations of Chaucer in the period. Although these poems differ considerably from each other in purpose and technique, many of the Chaucerian imitations in the fifteenth and early sixteenth centuries exhibit similar tendencies. Rather than attempting to imitate Chaucer by reproducing his effects, as we have assumed, the so-called English and Scottish Chaucerians often appear to be experimenting with Chaucer's innovations in an effort to extend them to their furthest limits. In a sense, they attempt to improve on the work of their master by going beyond his poetic solutions. Although Pearsall has noted a few stylistic examples of this phenomenon in Lydgate's poetry, the same tendency is evident on a much more significant scale in the fifteenth-century poets' treatment of entire poems.[61]

Two good examples of this development are Lydgate's *Troy Book* and James I of Scotland's *The Kingis Quair*. The *Troy Book* provides a large-scale example of the stylistic embellishment and elevation by which Lydgate transforms individual passages from Chaucer. Although many of the changes from his source, Guido della Colonna's *Historia destructionis Troiae,* particularly his restructuring of the narrative and his numerous additions about war, serve to accentuate the central theme of his version—the dangers of war—curiously, this thematic emphasis does not appear to have been Lydgate's main concern in reworking the Troy story. Rather, the bulk of his additions, nearly one third of the entire poem, reveals his effort to create a more spectacular version of the Troy story than any of those writers before him including Chaucer's famous poem. Although many critics have judged these passages to be extraneous,[62] rhetorically they serve to amplify and elevate the action, to make Lydgate's account the most grandiose of all the versions, and to expand the story Chaucer popularizes in English to its most elevated limits.

The effect Lydgate achieves is particularly striking in Book IV, the longest section of the narrative. In this book, he uses numerous devices to extend his material. Most obviously, he punctuates the narrative with a series of eloquent set speeches, more than twenty major ones in this book alone, and a number of highly rhetorical laments that build in intensity to his climactic lament for the fallen Troy (IV, 6930–7108). In addition, he introduces elaborate seasonal prefaces, other descriptive passages, and eloquent sections of comment and invective. Finally, he repeatedly works to elevate the language of his descriptions, to transform the rather colorless account of Guido into highly charged rhetorical passages as in the following report of Achilles' death. Guido simply states:

> Achilles and Antilochus were dead in the temple of Apollo, wickedly killed by Paris. Paris ordered the bodies of Achilles and Antilochus to be cast out to the crows and dogs, but by the prayers and advice of Helen they were merely cast forth from the temple of Apollo into the square, so that they could be seen clearly by all of the Trojans.[63]

Lydgate extends and elaborates Chaucer's rhetorical techniques in the famous "palinode" to the *Troilus*—his exclamations, repetitions, word pairing and amplification—to create an account that is much loftier in its effect:

> And afterward þe body was out drawe
> Of Achille fro þe holy boundis,
> And cruelly þrowen vn-to houndis,
> To be deuourid in þe brode strete,
> þe canel rennyng with his wawes wete—

With-oute pite or any maner routhe.
Loo! here þe ende of falshed & vntrouþe,
Loo! here þe fyn of swiche trecherie,
Of fals deceit compassid by envie!
Loo! here þe knot and conclusioun,
How God quyt ay slauȝter by tresoun!
Loo! here þe guerdon & þe final mede
Of hem þat so deliten in falsehede.
(IV, 3204–16)

In the *Kingis Quair* James experiments generally with the familiar Chaucerian dream vision to enlarge the possibilities of this form.[64] Whereas Chaucer had significantly changed the dream vision, particularly by the insertion of a book section between the narrator's introduction and the dream itself in his early versions, James carries Chaucer's innovations even further. Following his master's lead, he adds a second section between the introduction and the dream that makes the thematic possibilities inherent in the Chaucerian form explicit. In contrast to the French sources that were his models, Chaucer's expansion of the dream vision had rendered the form structurally suitable for an examination of the relation between the three realms of experience accessible to man (life, books, and dreams) and the truths one perceives by the characteristic mode of each realm (experience, authority, and vision) defining these perspectives in the three separate sections of the vision. James's similar expansion of the Chaucerian vision, his addition of a third section before and after the dream in which the poet-narrator steps forward to examine his narrative as literature, adds a perspective only hinted at in Chaucer's frames to the *Book of the Duchess* and the *Hous of Fame*— the role of literature as the mediator among the past, present, and future, and books, experience, and vision. Drawing attention to his role as poet and the process of writing in this section, James encourages us to consider the means by which one's experiences acquire significance when translated into the ordered medium of poetry. Though he begins with Chaucer's form and techniques, in the *Quair*, James thus enlarges the form he borrows to develop some of the thematic and structural relationships that Chaucer introduces in his vision.

The reworking of Chaucer in the fifteenth century reflects attitudes and assumptions about poetry that depart from Chaucer's. Although the distortion of the Chaucerian model, to some extent, was inherent in its process of transmission, the reshaping of Chaucer's writing in the fifteenth century also represents a conscious deviation from his techniques and concerns. In imitating Chaucer's efforts to extend the limits of his literary language and poetic forms, these poets go beyond his poetic solutions in directions that reveal different standards of poetic excellence. Their efforts suggest a confidence in the power of poetry and in their roles as poets which contrasts sharply with Chaucer's anxiety about the ambiguity of his medium and the limits of mortals as artists. The fifteenth-century poets' views echo the increasing number of defenses of poetry that appear on the continent in the late Middle Ages, yet their attitudes are not simply a reiteration of these works. Their ideals of good poetry reflect an appreciation of Chaucer's accomplishments as an English poet, "the firste fyndere of our fair language," and a vision of the possibilities of his newly established literary vernacular. In this context, the poetic ideals that they share with their continental counterparts acquire a new emphasis and significance, and, as they are embodied in the particular critical terms, metaphors, and myths of the fifteenth-century poets, they anticipate many of the preoccupations of the Renaissance poets in England. It is in the work of John Lydgate at the outset of the fifteenth century that we first find articulated the distinct concerns that dominate the period.

The "Noble Rethor Poete"

Lydgate's poetry (c. 1410–40) introduces a major shift in attitude in English literature toward the process of writing and the role of the poet. In the numerous digressions about poetry that appear in his work—for the most part his original additions to his sources—Lydgate defines ideals of poetry that are significantly different from Chaucer's and also central enough to an understanding of fifteenth-century writing to warrant more careful attention than they have received. In contrast to his immediate English predecessors, who are anxious about the limits of the poet's craft and the ability of language to embody truth, Lydgate defends the inherent truthfulness of poetry and the poet's intention. He envisions the poet essentially as an illuminator who uses the power of language to shed light on the poet's matter and make it more significant and effective. Like the sun with its intense light, the poet transforms common matter into works that are fairer than the ordinary and more enduring. This process of illumination has the power to dispel the darkness of the human mind and draw it to virtue. Finally, Lydgate links the activities of the poet with the well-being of the state, suggesting the ability of the poet to turn humanity from chaos and disorder to harmony and order. These views of poetry, though virtually ignored by critics, provide a key to an understanding of Lydgate's purpose as a poet and to the poetic ideals and practices that dominate the fifteenth century.

The shift in attitude toward poetry represented by Lydgate's work is reflected in striking form in the vocabulary he develops to describe the characteristics of good poetry. In his digressions, Lydgate creates a new critical language, coining words where none existed and, to a greater extent than we have recognized, assigning new meanings to terms that had been found in English before his time but that were not applied to poetry. The most important of his critical ideals are embodied in eight terms—"enlumyne," "adourne," "enbelissche," "aureate," "goldyn," "sugrid," "rethorik," and "elloquence"—terms that are linked by strong metaphoric associations. These words, which Lydgate popularizes or develops with new meanings, are adopted by every major writer of the fifteenth century and become the standard critical language of the period.

Central to Lydgate's vocabulary is the highly charged word "enlumyne," which draws together associations from the art of manuscript illumination and from the religious tradition of spiritual illumination. In Lydgate's usage, "enlumyne" suggests both the process of "lighting up" or "throwing light upon" (illuminare) words or matter and "enlightening" or "giving spiritual insight or intelligence." In the first sense, the word is found in English (in the forms "enlumyne" and "enlomyne") as far back as the thirteenth century to refer to the process of embellishing the initial capitals and borders of manuscripts by decorative works in brilliant colors and with gold or, more rarely, silver leaf.[1] As Diringer points out, illumination was distinguished from the related art of illustration by the use of gold or silver to literally "light up" or "illuminate" the page of the manuscript.[2] When skillfully applied, the metallic leaf produced a startling transformation of the text, giving it sudden brilliance and depth. The process, which spread at the outset of the Middle Ages and declined with the development of printing, in its ideal form served to increase the splendor of the word and to draw attention to its significance. As Robb argues, "Illumination, the 'causing of words to be resplendent,' can be a creative process only when the written word is held in such high regard . . . that its form is appropriately made more illustrious."[3] Within the context of many manuscripts, moreover, the process of illumination was carefully calculated to stress and make visible and memorable essential portions of the text, thereby bringing added attention to their meaning. The art thus provided a good image of the poetic process in its taking in ("enluminer") of invisible light from outside to light up or illuminate the significance of the word.

In a second context, derived from the experience of spiritual illumination, "enlumyne" refers to the process of "enlightening" the mind or heart or dispelling ignorance or sin by divine inspiration. At the outset of the Middle Ages, Augustine introduces this meaning repeatedly in his discussions of divine illumination. Developing Plato's concept of the Good as the "cause of all things right and beautiful," the origin of light in the visible world and truth and reason in the intelligible, Augustine suggests that the effect of God, the "intelligible light" on the mind is analogous to the sun's activity in the natural world.[4] As the sun's light makes corporeal things visible to the eye, so divine light makes eternal truths visible to the human intellect. Unaided, the human mind cannot apprehend the changelessness and necessity of eternal truths that transcend it and are superior to it "for no creature, howsoever rational and intellectual, is lighted of itself, but is lighted by participation of eternal Truth."[5] Thus, in Augustine's view, divine illumination is necessary to dispel ignorance and to allow the mind to see beyond the mutable realm of human experience. "God hath created man's mind rational and intellectual, whereby he may take in His light . . . and He so enlighteneth it of Himself, that not only those things which are displayed by the truth, but even truth itself may be perceived by the mind's eye."[6]

The Augustinian concept of divine illumination is developed, among other thinkers, by Bonaventura, Matthew of Aquasparta, Robert Grosseteste, and Alexander of Hales in the thirteenth century. In the *Itinerarium mentis in Deum,* for example, Bonaventura maintains that the mind can apprehend eternal truth and achieve certitude only through divine light. This light, "which illuminates all men coming into this world" penetrates the darkness of the mind and leads one to an awareness of supertemporal truths.[7] Linking the divine light with Christ's words, Bonaventura describes this process of illumination explicitly as the enlightenment of our intellect: "Christ is the interior teacher and no truth is known except through Him, not by His speaking as we speak, but by His enlightening us interiorly. . . . He is ultimately present to every soul and by His most clear ideas He shines

upon the dark ideas of our minds."[8] Although the Platonic-Augustin-
ian tradition of divine illumination ultimately is rejected by Thomas
Aquinas and John Duns Scotus, who maintain that the active intellect
by its natural power and without any special illumination from God is
capable of apprehending universal truths, the earlier associations of
"illuminare" often are retained by the poets who introduce the word
with the Augustinian connotations of spiritual illumination.[9] Hoccleve, for example, suggests this meaning when he prays to God "þat
of the holy goost he menlumyne."[10] Similarly, Chaucer introduces
the word in the sense of "to illuminate" or "enlighten," "to give
spiritual insight" in the *Parson's Tale* to reveal God's power to
transform the sinful: "God wole the rather enlumyne and lighte the
herte of synful man."[11]

In exploiting the term "enlumyne" to define the poetic process,
Lydgate brings together associations both from the artistic and from
the spiritual traditions, introducing a link between the poet's rhetorical enhancement of language and the illumination of meaning that
enlightens the reader. Although the word "enlumyne" is used in
English on a few scattered occasions before Lydgate to refer to poetry,
it lacks this important range of meanings that is central to Lydgate's
conception of good poetry. In his single application of the term to
poetry in the Clerk's famous praise of Petrarch (IV [E] 33), Chaucer,
for example, introduces the word with more limited meaning "to
render illustrious or splendid," citing Petrarch, "whose rethorike
sweete / Enlumyned al Ytaille of poetrie."[12] Like Chaucer in the
Clerk's prologue, in a few cases Lydgate introduces "enlumyne" to
signify the poet's power to make something illustrious, brilliant, or
famous by means of art. The striking praise of Dante in Book IX of the
Fall of Princes, for example, echoes this sense: "Thou hast enlumyned Itaile & Lumbardie / With laureat dites in thi flouryng
daies."[13] But even when Lydgate borrows from Chaucer, he extends
the significance of the term, drawing attention to the implications of
the poet's activities as illuminator by means of an elaborate analogy
between the sun and the poet. In the example just cited, he addresses
Dante as the "cleerest sonne, daysterre and souereyn liht / Of our cite,
which callid is Florence" (*Fall of Princes,* IX, 2522–23), suggesting
the relation between the sun's radiance and the radiance of Dante's
verse. On several other occasions in the *Fall of Princes,* Lydgate is
even more explicit. Praising Cicero in Book VI, he extends the

analogy to link the sun's beams of light as they illuminate the world with the poet's beams of rhetoric and eloquence that transform his matter:

> Lik a sunne he dide hem [the Romans] enlumyne
> Bi hih prowesse of knihtli excellence;
> And thoruh the world his bemys dede shyne
> Of his rethorik & his elloquence . . .
> (*Fall of Princes,* VI, 3081–84)

In addition to expanding Chaucer's usage, Lydgate exploits the term "enlumyne" to describe the poet's process of working on his matter in several ways that are not anticipated by earlier examples. Most commonly, he introduces the word with the sense "to color" or "to embellish" to refer to the poet's style or the way in which he evokes the colors or flowers or rhetoric to illuminate his matter. In the envoy to the *Troy Book,* for example, Lydgate submits his work for correction and apologizes that it is "enlumined with no floures / Of Rethorik" but only with white and black.[14] Second, in an even more significant sense for fifteenth-century writing, Lydgate adapts the term "enlumyne" to define the poet's process of enriching or extending his medium. Used in this way, "enlumyne" points specifically to the poet's effort to raise the level of his language, to make his English suitable for poetic endeavors. This sense, for example, is apparent in the *Serpent of Division* when Lydgate praises Chaucer as the "first that euer elumined our language with flowers of rethorik."[15] Again, in the *Life of Our Lady,* Lydgate exploits the term with this meaning to draw attention to Chaucer's achievement as the poet who found "floures, first of Rethoryke / Our Rude speche, only to enlumyne," that is, as the poet who first made English elegant and poetic.[16]

Lydgate also introduces "enlumyne" with a cluster of meanings derived from the application of the word in descriptions of intellectual and spiritual illumination. In his famous eulogy of Chaucer in the prologue to the *Siege of Thebes,* for example, he uses the term in this sense to emphasize the poet's role in clarifying or shedding light on the significance of his content, praising Chaucer for "keping in sybstaunce // The sentence hool / with-oute variance, // Voyding the Chaf / sothly for to seyn, // Enlumynyng / þe trewe piked greyn // Be crafty writing."[17] Similarly, Lydgate develops Chaucer's earlier meaning of "enlumyne" as "to inspire" by refining his broad connotation of spiritual inspiration to make the term refer directly to the poet's activity. In the *Life of St. Edmund*, for example, Lydgate prays to God to "Send doun of grace thi licour aureate / Which enlumynyth these rhetoricians," linking the poet's power to affect the audience with God's might. In an even more striking example in the *Life of Our Lady*, Lydgate suggests that God's grace enters the actual pen with which the poet writes, giving him power to illuminate his work. He prays to Mary: "the licour of thy grace shede / Into my penne, tenlumyne this dite" (I, 57–58). Like the divine illumination that inspires it, the poet's "enlumyng" sheds light on the significance of his matter and enlightens reader's minds. As Lydgate explains: "God sette writyng & lettres in sentence, / Ageyn the dulnesse of our infirmyte, / This world tenlumyne be craft of elloquence" (*Fall of Princes*, IV, 29–31). The two traditions of "enlumynge" in the sense of lighting up or increasing the splendor of words, Lydgate indicates, serves the purpose of illuminating their content and enlightening the reader.

Linked to "enlumyne" are two other terms, "adourne" and "enbelissche," which, like "enlumyne," in Middle English draw together associations both from secular and religious contexts.[18] "Enbelissche," in the fourteenth and fifteenth centuries, has the primary meanings of "to decorate" from the Old French "embeliss." Frequently, the word also was used in the narrower sense of "to endow with beauty or increase the beauty of attractiveness of nature, a created thing, or a person," and, after Lydgate, with the specialized meaning of "to make words or poetry more beautiful or attractive."[19] At the same time, however, the word also had the secondary meaning of "to add or increase spiritual beauty of excellence." In the *Legend of Good Women*, Chaucer, for example, refers to Lucretia's "teres ful of honeste" that "embelished hire wifly chastite" (1737) and in the translation of Boethius's *Consolation* to the possibility of being "distyngwed and embelysed by the spryngynge floures of the first somer sesoun" (2, prosa 5, 66–67). Similarly, although "adourne" in Middle English generally meant to "decorate or embellish something" or "to beautify, ornament, or make more distinguished," the word, by a confusion with the Middle English word "adouren" (to worship) acquired the meaning "to honor" or "adore" as in the following line from John Hardyng's *Chronicle* (1464), "And Mars, the god of armes, they dyd adorne."[20]

In Lydgate's usage, "adourne" and "enbelissche" serve to clarify one aspect of the meaning of "enlumyne"—the ability of the poet to extend language, to make it more striking, effective, and enduring, and hence to give it the power to increase the beauty or excellence of its content. It is this quality that Lydgate suggests when he praises Chaucer in the *Troy Book* as the poet "gan oure tonge first to magnifie / And adourne it with his elloquence" (III, 4243). In his role as "adourner" or "enbelisscher" of our language, Lydgate indicates that the poet is like the more skillful artist, Nature, who when she pleases uses her art to form creatures of lasting splendor and beauty:

> . . . se how I, Nature,
> When [þat] me list, enbelissche can my wirke:
> · · · · · · · · · · · · · · · · · ·
> Riȝt as me list adourne & make fair,
> So peint & florische, it schal nat apeire;
> And my colours so craftily dispose.
> Of þe lillie and þe fresche rose,
> And so ennew þat þei schal nat fade,
> But ay ben on. . . . (*Troy Book*, II, 5024–34)

Like Nature, the poet is so skillful in his art that it improves his object, an emphasis that underscores the difference in meaning between Lydgate's use of "adourned" and "enbelissched" and the modern connotations of decorated.

Closely related to the terms "enlumyne," "adourne," and "enbelissche," which describe the poet's process of working on his matter, is a second group of words that Lydgate coins to define the effects of the poet's activities. The most important of these terms, "aureate," "goldyn," and "sugrid," refer to the qualities of the diction and style the poet produces. Each of these terms points particularly to an ideal, an aspect of good writing, which for Lydgate is the antithesis of the "rude style" of bad writers.

"Aureate," a term Lydgate introduces for the first time in English, suggests the special nature of the poet's medium, the heightened poetic quality that sets it off from ordinary speech and writing. As Norton-Smith points out, Lydgate's coinage probably was based on the late Latin *aureatus* that is recorded once in literary usage as a *difficilio lectio* and has the meaning "gold-adorned," but unlike Lydgate's term, does not refer to language.[21] Although Lydgate's coinage has the obvious connotation of "goldyn" suggested by the Latin root and, in this sense, reinforces the suggestion of "enlumyne," he develops three more significant meanings by means of the striking metaphoric associations with which he repeatedly surrounds this word—"eloquent," "fragrant" (that is, poetical not only in a visual sense), and "inspired." The most familiar of these meanings, "eloquent," is suggested by the recurrent metaphor "aureate colors." In Lydgate's special sense, this phrase refers to the golden or eloquent style the poet creates, the result of his "enlumyng." This meaning, for example, is apparent in Book VIII of the *Fall of Princes* when Boccaccio praises his master Petrarch for providing a model of good poetic style. Significantly, Lydgate changes his source to define Boccaccio's indebtedness in terms of the metaphor "aureate colors." In his version, Boccaccio praises Petrarch as the "Cheef exaumplaire to my gret auauntage, / To refourme the rudness of my stile / With aureat colours of your fressh langage" (*Fall of Princes,* VIII, 79–80). As Lydgate makes clear in several other examples of this phrase, "aureate colour" does not refer simply to a superficial process of painting or decorating, but to a suitable relation between the poet's style and subject matter, that is, to an appropriate use of eloquent and golden language.[22]

A second important meaning of "aureate" is suggested by the metaphor "baume aureate." When used alone, the term "baume aureate" refers to fragrance and introduces a potent analogy between the intoxicating and perfumed secretion of a flower and the poet's rhetorical or poetical output that overwhelms the reader not only by its appearance but by its pleasing effect. Characteristically, Lydgate uses the metaphor "baume aureate" to describe what the poet produces, the particular kind of writing that makes one recognizable as a poet. In the "Mumming for Mercers," for example, he makes this meaning clear, referring to "Tulius," "Macrobye," "Ovyde," "Virgilius," "Petrark," and "Bocas," and adding that "Thoroughte þat bawme aureate / þey called weren poetes laureate."[23]

Finally, Lydgate develops the striking metaphor "aureate licour" to draw attention to the inspired nature of the poet's writing.[24] As Lydgate suggests, this quintessential liquid or "aureate licour" is transmitted directly from God and the muses to the poet and enables him to write in a manner worthy of his subject. At the beginning of the "Ballade at the Reverence of Our Lady," for example, Lydgate seeks encouragement for his poetic journey and prays: "O wynd of grace, now blowe in to my saile. / O auriat licour off Clyo, for to wryte / Mi penne enspire, of that I would endyte."[25] At the outset of the *Fall of Princes,* he apologizes for his lack of poetic skill and points out that the muses who sing on Parnassus "with ther sugred aureat licour / Thei be nat willi for to doon fauour" (I, 461–62). In several of the religious poems, Lydgate uses this metaphor even more explicitly to refer to the poetic power, the substance of poetic inspiration, which comes directly from God and enables the poet to deal adequately with sacred matter. At the outset of the "Invocation to Aynte Anne," for example, he fervently prays to God to inspire him to write in a manner that will do justice to this lady:

> þou first moeuer, þat causest every thing
> To haue his keping thoroughte þe prouydence,
> And rightfully art callid lord and kynge,
> Having þe lordship of eche Intelligence,
> Destille adoune þy gracious Influence
> In-to my brest þat dulle is for rudenesse,
> Of holy Anne some goodly word expresse.
>
> . . . .
> Shed from abouen þy licuor aureate. . . .[26]

Thus the term "aureate" means more than "golden" in a narrow sense. In Lydgate's usage, it points to an aspect of good writing, an ideal of poetic style that distinguishes the "baume" of the poet from ordinary speech or writing, and, at the same time, suggests the source of this inspiration.

Like "aureate," Lydgate introduces the term "goldyn" as a term of praise to refer to the poet's or orator's heightened style. When used alone, the word is more specific than "aureate" and points principally to the eloquence of the poet's language, its richness, luster, visual splendor, and stylistic perfection. It is these qualities, for example, that Lydgate has in mind when he praises Dares Phygius in the *Fall of Princes* for his "goldene style" (IX, 3402). Likewise, in "As a Mydsomer Rose," he refers to Chrysostom's "goldene mouth" to draw attention to his excellence as a poet.[27] In addition to introducing "goldyn" alone, on many occasions Lydgate combines the word with the recurrent metaphors of "rain" or "dew," life-giving forces that bestow new luster and vitality to the objects they fall upon. In its most striking and frequently used sense, this metaphor refers to the distillation of poetic excellence, the golden liquid of the poet's speech or rhetoric that, like the rain or dew in its action, gives the poet's medium new potency and effectiveness. This meaning of the phrase, which is not suggested by the metaphors for "aureate," is quite common in Lydgate's praise of Chaucer, for example, in the *Life of Our Lady* where he commends Chaucer as the one who "made firste, to distille and rayne / The golde dewe, dropes of speche and eloquence / Into our tunge, thurgh his excellence" (II, 1632–34).

Complementary in significance to "goldyn" and "aureate," Lydgate introduces the term "sugrid," which refers specifically to the sound of the words the poet produces, to the sweetness or melodiousness of language rather than to its visual splendor or luster. Occasionally, Lydgate employs the term literally to refer to the mouth or the tongue of the skilled poet, the source of pleasing language, for example, in the prologue to the *Siege of Thebes* where he admires the "sugrid mouth of Chaucer," or, again in "As a Mydsomer Rose," where he defines Cicero's power as an orator in terms of his "sugryd tonge."[28] But Lydgate's most common and most original use of the word "sugrid" is as a descriptive term for the pleasing sound of speech, music, or poetry. In Book IV of the *Troy Book,* for example, he draws attention to this meaning when he praises Antenor's elegant and effective speech: "His tale gan with sugred wordis swete. / Makyng þe bawme outward for to flete / Of rethorik and of elloquence" (IV, 5201–3). In the *Fall of Princes,* he refers to the "sugrid langage & vertuous daliaunce" of rhetoricians (VI, 3467). At other times, Lydgate uses the term "sugrid" to describe the harmonious and enticing sound of music, as in the phrase the "sugrid melodie" of Charbydes (*Troy Book,* V, 2864) or "þe soote sugred harpe" of Mercury (*Siege of Thebes,* 273). But most important for our purposes is his application of the adjective "sugrid" to the sound of poetry. In the *Fall of Princes,* Book IX, for example, he refers to the "sugryd dytees of Omer" (IX, 3402) that are unlike his own rude writing. In an even more striking example in the prologue to the *Troy Book,* Lydgate links good poetry with the "hony swete / Sugrest tongis of rethoricyens" and the sounds of "musicyens" as he prays for inspiration to Calliope, the mother of the poet-musician Orpheus and the muse who best represents the "sugrid" sounds of all three arts (Prol., 53–62).

Finally, Lydgate gives added weight and a new significance to two very important words, "rethorik" and "elloquence," which in his critical passages represent the epitome of good poetry. Although earlier writers use these terms, it is Lydgate who gives them their particular meanings and importance as pivotal critical terms in the fifteenth century, the embodiment of the ideals of good poetry. The extent to which Lydgate popularizes and changes the connotations of "rethorik" and "elloquence" is underscored by a brief comparison with Chaucer. On the one hand, Chaucer uses these terms only rarely; each appears only six times in his writing, and, when he uses these words, he either does not apply them directly to poetry, or with a few notable exceptions, he introduces them with an ironic or a perjorative meaning.[29] Lydgate, in contrast, uses each term more than thirty times, very frequently together, and always as terms of commendation.[30] Eloquence in Lydgate's writing is a positive attribute of style and refers to the way writers or orators use their medium elegantly, effectively, and appropriately. As Lydgate emphasizes, the eloquence of an author improves the subject. Referring to Guido, who wrote the version of the Troy story he translates, Lydgate remarks that "he enlymyneth by crafte & cadence; / This noble story with many fresche colour / Of rethorik, and many riche flour / Of eloquence to make it sownde bet" (Prol., 362–65). But in praising writers or orators for their eloquence, in many cases Lydgate has a very specific sense of the word in mind that we have not recognized. In his usage, the word is linked with prudence, wisdom, and discretion and thus means much more than "fair langage." In the *Troy Book,* for example, Lydgate remarks that Elphenor is pleased to listen to Ulysses "To here hym talke, for his elloquence / For his wysdam & his hiʒe prudence" (V, 2143–44). Again in Book IV of the *Troy Book,* he places the eloquence of Ulysses in the context of these virtues, "Wyse Vlixes, ful of elloquence; / Gan his tale prudently deuyse" (IV, 1698–99). And he refers to Aeneas as one who "hadde of fame of passyng ellouqence, / Wys of counseil and of gret sapience" (II, 4915–16). As Lydgate emphasizes in his chapter on rhetoric and oratory, Nature has given eloquence only to human beings. When it is "conveied bi prudence," it is a "thyng couenable in especiall" (*Fall of Princes,* VI, 3383–84). It teaches one to live in harmony and to be stable in virtue (*Fall of Princes,* VI, 3403–9).

Similarly, "rethorik" is a favorable term in Lydgate's writing, a distinct mark of praise. Its weight and significance are perhaps best revealed by the phrase that Lydgate repeatedly introduces to distinguish his master Chaucer, "the noble rethor poete." In the *Troy Book*, Lydgate, for example, sums up Chaucer's achievement by characterizing him as "þe noble Rethor that alle dide excelle" (III, 553). Again, in the *Life of Our Lady*, Lydgate refers to Chaucer as "the noble Rethor, poete of Brytayne" (II, 1629). For Lydgate, "noble Rethor" represents the highest form of praise, a distinct shift from Chaucer's more ambiguous use of the term.

Most frequently, Lydgate introduces the word "rethorik" in the familiar sense of the colors or flowers of rhetoric to refer to the successful style of the good poet or orator. At the outset of the *Troy Book*, for example, he praises Guido "For he enlvmyneth by crafte & cadence / This noble story with many fressche colour of rethorik" (Prol., 362–64). In the *Life of Our Lady*, he celebrates Chaucer as the poet who "fonde the floures, first of Rethoryk / Our Rude speche, only to enlumyne" (II, 1635–36). This meaning, also found in Chaucer's *Franklin's Tale* and *Squire's Tale*, is common, but Lydgate, unlike Chaucer, repeatedly clarifies the significance of these metaphors to make their positive sense clear. Following Boccaccio, he carefully distinguishes between natural rhetoric learned in youth and "crafft of rethorik" that comes to one only by great diligence:

> Bochas eek tellith, touchyng rethorik,
> Ther been too maneres: oon is of nature,
> Lernyd in youthe, which doth oon speke[e] lik
> As he heereth & lerneth bi scripture;-
> Crafft of rethorik youe to no creature
> Sauff to man, which bi gret dilligence
> Be studie kometh to crafft of elloquence.
> (*Fall of Princes*, VI, 3409–16)

Rhetoric, in the sense in which he uses the term as a characteristic of good poetry or speech, requires long study and a great deal of skill.

Lydgate makes it clear, moreover, that "crafft of rethorik" involves more than skillfully ornamented style or elegant language, the meaning suggested by Chaucer's references in the *Clerk's Tale* and *Squire's Tale*. "Rethorik" in Lydgate's work more often has the broader meeting of good writing, good speech, or noble style. This emphasis is apparent in the following lines from the *Siege of Thebes* when Lydgate bids the reader refer to Boccaccio for an example of noble style: "Lok on the book / that Iohn Bochas made // Whilom of wommen / with rethorikes glade, // and directe / be ful souereyn style" (3201–3). Lydgate stresses the links between his term "rethorik" and "souereign style" in his praise of Virgil in Book IV of the *Fall of Princes*. Briefly reviewing the Latin poet's writing, he singles out the *Aeneid* as the work "which that dide excell / In rethorik be souereynte of stile" (72–73).

But more important, "rethorik" in the sense in which Lydgate defines it—good writing, "souereign style"—serves to illuminate the essential truth of a story. As he explains in the prologue to the *Troy Book*, poets "Han trewly set thoruȝ diligent labour, / And enlumyned with many corious flour / Of rethorik, to make vs comprehende / The trouthe of al, as it was kende" (Prol., 217–20). Used in this way, the term suggests connotations very different from the ones we find in Chaucer's work. We learn to suspect the motives of the rhetoricians in the *Canterbury Tales*—the Reeve, the Man of Law, the Summoner, the Pardoner, the Merchant, the Franklin, the Nun's Priest, and even the "goode wife of biside Bathe"—but in Lydgate's work the "rethor" is "noble" and his art is the epitome of good poetry.

Although the vocabulary Lydgate develops either is not commonly found earlier in English or is introduced with a different meaning, after Lydgate, these terms become the standard critical language of the fifteenth century. One need only compare the praise of Chaucer before and after Lydgate's time to gain some idea of the impact of his terms. In the passages before Lydgate, one finds very little trace of the vocabulary we have been considering. Gower, for example, in the first recension of the *Confessio Amantis* (1390), has Venus praise Chaucer simply as "mi disciple and mi poete: / For in the floures of his youthe / In sondri wise, as he wel couthe, / Of Ditees and of songes glade, / The whiche he for mi sake made, / The lond fulfild is overal."[31] Thomas Usk, in the *Testament of Love* (1387), commends Chaucer's writing principally for its appropriateness and gentility: "his noble sayings can I not amende: In goodnes of gentyl manlyche speche / Without any maner of nycite of stories ymagynacioun in wytte and in good reason of sentence he passeth al other makers."[32] After Lydgate, however, the new critical terms are used conspicuously in the work of every major writer of the period. Hoccleve, for example, in the *Regiment of Princes,* praises Chaucer as "the flour of eloquence" who "with bookes of his ornat endytyng, /

That is to al þis land enlumynyng."[33] Shirley, at the end of his edition
of Chaucer's translation of Boethius, refers to the poet as "famous
Chaucyer which first enlumyned þis lande with retoryen and eloquent
langage of oure rude englisshe modere tonge."[34] A few years later, an
anonymous poet again repeats Lydgate's language as he assesses the
dead Chaucer's achievement:

> Maister geffrey Chauucers þat now lith graue
> þe noble Rethor poete . of grete bretayne
> þat worthi . was the laurer to have
> Of poyetry . And þe palme atain
> þat furst made to still & to rain
> þe gold dew Dropes . of speche in eloquence
> In to english tonge / þorow his excellens.[35]

Even more significant than the extreme popularity of Lydgate's
terms are the implications of his vocabulary. His critical language
places a conspicuous emphasis on craft, not only by the number of
words he coins to describe the poet's process of working on his
matter, but by the importance he attaches to the ideal of the "noble
rethor poete," the craftsman skilled in the language of poetry, who
treats his subject eloquently and appropriately. "Rethor," for Lydgate, is a mark of distinction or skill, attained by only the best of
poets, who combine the orator's mastery of language with a worthy
vision and purpose. Several of Lydgate's terms draw attention to the
ideal of poets as the improvers and extenders of their medium, self-
conscious in their effort to "enlumyne," "adourne," and "enbelissche" their matter and make it more brilliant, significant, and
enduring. The recurrent analogies with the sun and Nature emphasize
the importance of this role. Like the sun, which illuminates the natural
world with its light, the poet transforms the matter of a poem by
rhetoric and eloquence, illuminating its underlying meaning. Finally,
Lydgate's critical vocabulary reveals a confidence in the power of
poetry to dispel mortals' darkness, inspire them, and move them to
virtue. Unlike Chaucer, who repeatedly questions the relation between appearance and reality, experience and authority in his writing
and the limitations the poet's craft imposes on his effort to create a
truthful vision, Lydgate neither doubts the inherent truthfulness of
good poetry, nor does he question the master poet's intentions.[36] In
his work, the problems that Chaucer considers so anxiously no longer

are apparent. Rather, Lydgate's digressions point to an unfailing assurance that the poet is noble and his writing is a source of truth.

Lydgate's conception of poetry as ennobling manifests itself in his conspicuous interest in high style and in his preoccupation with amplification, two aspects of his poetic practice that critics have misunderstood. As we have seen, several of Lydgate's terms draw attention to his interest in creating a heightened poetic style, in making his language more "goldyn," "sugrid," and "eloquent." His serious effort to develop such a style in English contrasts sharply with the concerns of his predecessors. As Burrow points out, high style is not characteristic of the late fourteenth-century writers, who prefer to approach their material more indirectly and ironically.[37] Chaucer and many of his contemporaries, in fact, deliberately make the reader nervous about the unequivocal use of high style, keeping one on guard by means of ironic undercutting and comic innuendo. Lydgate's unrestrained interest in high style thus represents a major shift in attitude.

To some extent, the changed vision of high style in Lydgate's writing is linked historically and socially to certain developments that occurred at the outset of the fifteenth century. Of primary importance was the new status that English attained as a literary language after Chaucer. In turning to their own vernacular, the fifteenth-century poets, unlike their predecessors, had the possibility of working within a medium that was once again firmly established as a literary language, equal to the best of continental tongues. Their efforts were encouraged by a new class of patrons like Humphrey of Gloucester who supported the production of ambitious works in the vernacular on the scale and scope of continental models.[38] Finally, these poets were influenced by the demands of an expanding literate audience, the increased awareness on the part of patron and audience of an enlarged function of poetry, and the incipient separation of the roles of poetry and prose. As Pearsall observes, "Poetry is deprived of its middle ground by prose, thus sharpening the distinction between the low vernacular style and the artificially inflated high style."[39]

These changes contribute to an atmosphere that is conducive to the development of high style, yet they do not sufficiently explain Lydgate's particular attitude toward this style. It is important to recognize that Lydgate's concern with high style is not simply an interest in style for its own sake but is a direct outgrowth of his conception of poetry, the counterpart of his vision of poetry as ennobling, a source of wisdom and truth. As Lydgate repeatedly stresses, he seeks to find a medium worthy of the poet's role as an "enluminer" or extender of his matter. At the outset of the *Troy Book,* for example, Lydgate prays to Mars and the muses of poetry "to do socour my stile to direct" so that he can write in a manner that will do justice to his subject. He then provides a long digression on the importance of poetry, emphasizing its power to reveal truth, to withstand time, and to lead men to virtue (Prol., 216–25). Lydgate then reviews the writing of all the poets who narrated the story of Troy before him and concludes that Guido was the best for he told the story in the style most worthy of its subject (Prol., 372–74).

Lydgate's concern with finding a style appropriate to his purpose as poet is even more apparent in the digressions in his religious verse. These poems are filled with his repeated pleas to God to guide his style, to raise it to the level of the sacred matter he narrates. Typical is his protest at the end of the first book of the *Life of Our Lady,* that his "mater is so Inly spirituall, / That [he] dar nat, so high a style pace" (871–72). Without Mary's grace, he cannot find words lofty enough for his charge. In some of the religious lyrics, Lydgate articulates his concern with creating a new poetic medium in English suited to the ennobling role he envisions for his matter. In these lyrics, he at once defines an idea of high style and a stunning example of its fulfillment. A good example of this process is found in his famous "Ballade at the Reverence of Our Lady Qwene of Mercy."[40] In this poem, Lydgate announces his intention to "redresse" or reform his style to develop a new poetic medium capable of expressing his unsurpassed praise of Mary, "I wil now pleynly my stile redress, / Of on to speke at Nede that will not faile" (8–9). Echoing the Troilus narrator's concluding admonition, he rejects the style of "olde poets," the poets of love:

A thowsand storiis kowde I mo reherse
    Off olde poetis, touchynge this matere,
How that Cupide the hertis gan to perse
    Off his seruantis, settyng tham affere;
Lo, here is the fin of the errour and the werre!
Lo, here of loue the guerdoun and greuaunce
That euyr with woo his seruauntis doth avaunce!
(1–7)

The body of the poem provides the response to Lydgate's plea, a celebration of the Virgin in a style distinct from that of the "olde poets" of stanza 1. Repeatedly, Lydgate extends the Latin rhetorical traditions in which he works to create a medium that is more dazzling than any before him. His technique is to amass striking images, allusions, and epithets, to overwhelm the reader by his unusual coinages from the Latin, his elaborate aureation, his exploitation of internal rhymes, alliteration, and meter, and thus move the reader to awe and admiration. While he combines many of the traditional images of Mary in his tribute—the star of stars, the jewel, the enclosed garden, the "fructifying" olive, the healing balm, the flower of flowers—he presents these images in such rapid succession and with such an elaboration of stylistic and linguistic devices that the overall effect is quite different from the passage of Alain de Lille's *Anticlaudianus,* his immediate source.[41] The first stanza with its elaborate imagery, alliteration, repetition, and intricate pattern of sounds is typical of his treatment:

> O sterne of sternys with thi stremys clere,
> > Sterne of the see, [on]-to shipmen lyght and gyde,
> O lusty lemand, moost pleasaunt to appere,
> Whos bright bemys the clowdis may not hide.
> O way of lyfe to hem þat goo or ryde,
> > Haven aftyr tempest surrest as to ryve,
> > On me haue mercy for thi Ioyes fyve. (22–28)

The effect of Lydgate's treatment of style in the "Ballade at the Reverence of Our Lady" is even more pronounced when one compares his poem with Chaucer's "ABC," the most famous earlier example of this kind of celebration in English. The difference between the two lyrics is not simply one of increased aureation but involves a changed conception of the role of style itself. Chaucer opens with a stately and dignified address to the Virgin and the poem reaches a few moments of high style in Lydgate's sense, for example, in stanza 14:

> O verrey light of eyen that ben blynde,
> O verrey lust of labour and distresse,
> O tresoreere of bountee to mankynde,
> Thee whom God ches to mooder for humblesse!
> (105–8)

But this is not Chaucer's main concern in the lyric. Rather, he subordinates style to his theme of Mary as our refuge, our comfort. Lydgate, in contrast, focuses all of his efforts on his medium, his attempt to create a new mode of religious praise in English. To a great extent, his theme is his poetic effort and the style he develops forms an essential part of the poem's meaning, conveying a sense of Mary's importance and invoking our admiration for her glory.

Lydgate's assumptions about the function of poetry also underlie his preoccupation with amplification. His concern with amplifying not only specific lines and phrases but also extended passages and frequently entire structures is not primarily a stylistic impulse, a decadent development of the rhetorical practices of the fourteenth-century poets, as critics have assumed, it is a moral instrument that is linked directly to his vision of poetry as a source of truth. In his preface to the *Fall of Princes*, Lydgate articulates this connection most clearly. As he begins his longest work, he suggests that amplification is the means by which the poet makes the essential meaning of the story apparent. To underscore his point, he expands and modifies Laurent de Premierfait's preface to his translation of Boccaccio's *De Casibus*, the source of Lydgate's own translation, adding passages that draw attention to the importance of amplification. For example, Laurent merely says that he will amplify only those stories that the authors have told so briefly that they provide little more than the names.[42] Lydgate gives the passage an entirely different emphasis by changing Laurent's reason for amplifying, indicating that he will extend a story whenever its theme is virtuous.[43] And Lydgate concludes this section of the prologue by adding two stanzas for which there is no basis in Laurent in order to clarify and defend the process of amplification. In these stanzas, he equates amplification with plainness and clarity, arguing that a story that is told too briefly prevents readers from comprehending its truth:

> For a story which is nat pleynli told,
> But constreynyd vndir woordes fewe
> For lak off trouthe, wher thei be newe or old,
> Men bi report kan nat the mater shewe;
> These ookis grete be nat doun ihewe
> First at a stroke[e], but bi long processe,
> Nor longe stories a woord may not expresse.
> (92–98)

This view of amplification, it is important to note, represents a significant deviation from the statements of the rhetoricians. According to Geoffrey of Vinsauf, for example, the poet has two courses: "either you will proceed discursively, or you may skip along hastily; either you will note a thing briefly, or draw it out in an extended treatment."[44] In contrast to Lydgate, he suggests the poet chooses the broad path primarily to give variety and pleasure:

> You may give pleasure with this device; without it your meat may be abundant enough, but with it your mere dishes become excellent courses. A parade of courses coming more numerously, and tarrying at the banquet table that proceeds more deliberately, is a mark of distinction. Long and richly we feed the ears with varied material.[45]

Everard l'Allemand and John of Garland also treat amplification as one of the two important modes of variation that is pleasing to the reader. Everard explains, a long delay pleases us more than brevity.[46] Similarly, John of Garland treats amplification as a device for "dressing up naked matter," distinguishing five efficient structural methods, digression, vivid description, periphrasis, prosopopoeia, and apostrophe, and five stylistic modes, reduplication, exclamation, hypophora, indecision, and synonomy.[47] By emphasizing clarity and truthfulness rather than variety and pleasure, Lydgate thus changes the definition of amplification to one that is more in line with his own assumptions about poetry.

Lydgate, however, articulates the relation between the ideals his critical terms define and his purpose as a poet most explicitly in his chapter "On Poets and Writing" in the *Fall of Princes,* IV, a section that he adds entirely to his source. In this chapter, Lydgate stresses the importance of writing and its relation to the larger design of human knowledge. He begins in the same vein as Chaucer in the *Parliament* and the *Legend of Good Women* by defining the powers of poetry to preserve past wisdom (IV, 1–7). But then Lydgate moves beyond the ideas found in these words to suggest that poetry not only preserves knowledge, but it has a restorative power. As he indicates, writing is the "frut of the tre of lyff" that can renew hearts and restore the five wits. The natural food of lively and healthy minds, it enables one to triumph over sloth and live a virtuous life. But most important, as Lydgate indicates by means of his central metaphor of light, poetry has the power to dispel the darkness of the mind and "enlumyn" the world around one. God ordained writing to compensate for human ignorance and to make the world intelligible to one's infirm wit: "God sette writyng & lettres in sentence, / Ageyn the dulnesse of our infirmyte, / This world tenlumyne be crafft of elloquence" (IV, 29–31). This process of illuminating the design of the world, Lydgate indicates, is the supreme test of the poet.

Although Lydgate borrows some of the ideas from the rhetorical treatises of the twelfth and thirteenth centuries, John of Salisbury, Dante, and Boccaccio, he adds considerably to the hints he takes from these sources. The most extended example of his reshaping of earlier discussions is provided by the relation of his work to Boccaccio's *De Genealogia deorum,* Books XIV and XV, a text on which he relies heavily in his digressions about poetry. Like Boccaccio, Lydgate fervently defends the powers of poetry, its sublime effects, its ability to lead mortals to virtue, and its source of inspiration in God. In developing these ideas, he echoes and expands many of the points Boccaccio makes in his famous definition of poetry in Book XIV, chapter VII, of the *Genealogia:*

> This poetry, which ignorant triflers cast aside, is a sort of fervid and exquisite invention, with fervid expression, in speech or writing, of that which the mind has invented. It proceeds from the bosom of God, and few, I find, are the souls in whom this gift is born; indeed so wonderful a gift it is that true poets have always been the rarest of men. This fervor of poetry is sublime in its effects; it impels the soul to a longing for utterance.[48]

Like Boccaccio, Lydgate emphasizes that the poet must be well trained in his craft. Boccaccio explains, "For, however deeply the poetic impulse stirs the mind to which it is granted, it very rarely accomplishes anything commendable if the instruments by which its concepts are to be wrought out are wanting—I mean, for example, the precepts of grammar and rhetoric."[49] As we have seen, this is a recurrent theme in Lydgate's digressions. Finally, the two agree that the poet must often remain apart from others in the leisure and solitude of contemplation.[50]

Although his discussions reiterate these views, Lydgate's conception of poetry and the ideals to which his critical terms point ultimately differ from Boccaccio's. Of greatest significance is Lydgate's considerable emphasis on craft. Whereas Boccaccio includes as a major concern in his definition of poetry a discussion of the poet's powers of invention, Lydgate ignores this aspect of the poetic process and concentrates instead on the role of the poet in presenting and improving the matter that is given. Boccaccio, for example, in his definition of poetry stresses invention in the opening lines and adds a passage to the end that describes the power of the poet to create new worlds, a passage that could just as well have appeared later in Sir Philip Sidney's *Apology:*

> Further, if in any case the invention so requires, it can arm kings, marshal them for war, launch whole fleets from their docks, nay, counterfeit sky, land, sea, adorn young maidens with flowery garlands, portray human characters in its various phases. . . .[51]

Lydgate mentions the function of invention only briefly and centers instead on the poet's power to "adourne," "enbelissche," and "enlumyne," to perfect and extend the limits of the medium. Without exception, as we have seen, his critical terms point to this function of the poet. Boccaccio dwells on the role of poetry as a veil that covers "truth in a fair and fitting garment of fiction."[52] Lydgate, in many of his works, envisions poetry as a process of "enlumynyng," of rendering his work glorious, illustrious, and brilliant, but also of shedding light on difficult matter to clarify and illuminate its significance.[53]

Finally, Lydgate establishes an important relationship among his role as a poet, the "goldyn" language he creates, and the well-being of the state, a concern only briefly touched upon in Boccaccio's *De Genealogia* and not evident at all in Chaucer's work. As an illuminator or enlightener, the poet uses heightened language to underscore significant truths and to lead readers to order and harmony. His "fair" words have the power to "ympe" or engrave the "sothefast pyth" in our minds, "To seen eche thing trewly as it was, / More bry3t and clere þan in any glas" (*Troy Book,* Prol., 169–70) and inspire us to virtue. In his association of the poet's "enlumynyng" and the aureate, golden style it produces with wisdom, virtue, and political order, Lydgate appears to be returning to Dante as his primary model, and, in a manner that is not anticipated by either Chaucer or Boccaccio, introducing a similar conception of poetry in English. At the center of

Lydgate's poetics is the configuration of ideals, though in a much diluted form, which Dante evolves in his major treatises and poems.

In Dante's poetics, several important themes from rhetorical, philosophic, religious, and literary traditions converge. Though his orientation is that of the Ciceronian tradition as modified by Augustine, with its conception of poetry as an aspect of rhetoric and a blend of instruction, persuasion, and delight oriented to the commonwealth, Dante defines this relationship at once in broader and in more specific terms. Of primary importance is his emphasis on the truthfulness of poetry, which distinguishes his vision both from the ambivalence of Chaucer about the effects of poetry and from the strong emphasis of the twelfth- and thirteenth-century scholastic thinkers on the deceptive nature of poetry. In their final version in the *Comedy,* Dante's views also differ from the late medieval theories of poetry as a veil that conceals hidden meanings, a corollary of the falsity of poetry tradition. For Dante, as for Lydgate, poetry is an art of illuminating, a joining of wisdom and eloquence to engender goodness. The poet's language is an integral part of this process in its ability to move humanity and incite the will to virtue, and its effectiveness is both a manifestation of a divine gift and of a perfection of human craft. The effort of both poets to develop a vernacular literary language is linked to the moral and intellectual rectitude that underlies their visions, and, in its ideal form, is the linguistic image of the order they seek to inspire. Indeed, both visions manifest themselves in specific political terms. Following Brunetto Latini, Dante links his conception of poetry with its association of eloquence, wisdom, and virtue to a particular set of political conditions, those of the thirteenth-century Italian city-state. As Colish suggests, "For Dante, the pursuit of wisdom and virtue demand [sic] that he take an attitude toward the Europe of his own day" and his writing exhibits an increasing tendency to define the activity of the poet in the context of these ethical and political concerns.[54] But Dante's vision culminates in the expansion of the mission of poetry to include the realm of theology; Lydgate, except in a few rare instances, does not take this final step. His views, much less cohesive than the richly developed poetics of Dante, in the end are didactic and moral rather than philosophical or epistemological.

The configuration of the ideals of eloquence, wisdom, virtue, and political order in Lydgate's writing are particularly apparent in the long poems, where Lydgate clarifies that his definition of good poetry extends beyond the definition offered in Book IV of the *Fall of Princes*. Poetry not only "enlumyns" the world and leads people to virtue in a general sense, but in many cases, it has a specific political application. As Lydgate remarks in his chapter "On Rhetoric and Oratory" in the *Fall of Princes,* the poet's or orator's words have unique powers to bring concord out of discord, order out of disorder, civilization out of chaos:

> Of rhetoriciens whilom that wer old
> The sugrid langage & vertuous daliaunce
> Be goode exaumples & prouerbes that thei tolde,
> Woordes pesible enbelisshed with plesaunce,
> Appesid of tirauntes the rigerous vengaunce,
> Sette aside ther furious sentence
> Bi vertu onli of prudent elloquence.
> (VI, 3466–72)

The poet's heightened language reinforces the political value of peace, an ideal that Lydgate emphasizes throughout his poetry and that has a particular relevance in England in the 1420s between the conclusion of the Hundred Years War and the death of Henry V. Echoing the words of the Treaty of Troyes, the peace agreement between England and France, in his *Siege of Thebes,* Lydgate prays that "the venym / and the violence / / Of strif, of werre / of contek, and debat. . . . / Shal be proscript and voyded out of place" and that "Pees and quyet / concord and vnyte" reform the realm.[55] The word, he argues, is a more effective instrument than the sword (4690–4703). Similarly, Lydgate underscores the role of the poet in reinforcing the office of the prince, both by providing models of the good ruler and subject and in moving humanity to embrace these ideals.

Lydgate makes the relation of the poet, the golden language of poetry, and the well-being of the state even more explicit by his unusual exploitation of the myth of Amphion, the legendary founder of Thebes, Significantly, he introduces this figure at least four times in his work when no mention of Amphion is prompted by his sources.[56] In each case, Lydgate develops Amphion as a symbol of the relation between the poet and the state fully realized—the poet, orator, and statesman, who through his golden language, brings harmony and order to the realm. By his treatment of the myth, he defines a central tenet of his poetics that becomes increasingly important in the work of the fifteenth-century writers who follow him.

The most extensive treatment of the Amphion legend is found in the *Siege of Thebes*.[57] At the outset of this poem, Lydgate departs from his "auctour" and introduces a lengthy account of Amphion's founding of Thebes. Though he draws on other accounts of Amphion, especially Boccaccio's *De Genealogia,* Book V, chapter 30, he makes several changes that point up his own treatment of the myth. Like Boccaccio, Lydgate says in the *Siege of Thebes* that Amphion built the walls of Thebes only with "the swetnesse / and melodious soun / / And armonye / of his swete song" (202–3) and without craft "of eny mannys hond."[58] As the two poets explain, Amphion had a unique power, which he received from Mercury at birth, that he should be "Most excellent / be craft of Rethorik."[59] Adding to Boccaccio's account, Lydgate, however, links his "song" with his "crafty speech" and "his wordes swete" that were so "pleasaunt," "favorable," and "mete" that they caused all to do his bidding in concord: "In her Eerys / that shortly was ther noon / / Disobeysaunt / with the kyng to goon, / / Where so euere / that hym list assigne" (231–33). Thus the city was built through the "syngyng of this king" (241).

Lydgate concludes by drawing the following moral from the story: the "ssote surged harpe" of Mercury is more fortunate than the sword of Mars "whetted kene and sharpe." A prince can gain more by fair language than by war:

> I take record / of Kyng Amphyoun,
> Thay bylte Thebes be his elloquence
> Mor than of Pride / or of violence,
> Noble and riche / that lik was nowher non,
> And thus the walles / mad of lym and stoon
> Were reised first / be syngyng of this king,
> Lich as Poetes / feyn in her wrytyng.
> (*Siege of Thebes,* 286–92)

Again this conclusion is not prompted by his source. Boccaccio merely relates the brief legend of Amphion without considering the broader implications of his actions or the political significance of the story.[60]

By means of these changes, Lydgate uses the myth of Amphion to introduce a major theme of the *Siege of Thebes*—the opposition of the word and the sword. In his version, the entire poem represents an example of this theme. Reworking his sources, Lydgate develops a series of incidents that point out the significance of the example of Amphion with which he opens and the value of effective language rather than force in ordering humanity. On the one hand, he introduces several instances of the unsuccessful triumph of words over the sword. When Polyneices and Tydeus first meet in a storm, for example, their impulse is to fight it out to see who will win the right to stay in the shelter. Adrastus awakens, and like Amphion, with his eloquent words persuades the two men to lay down their swords. The outcome is favorable to both men as Adrastus befriends them, marries them to his daughters, and gives each of them riches and half of a kingdom (1236–1649). A second example occurs when the Greeks are befriended by Lady Hypsipyle (2998–3504). As she goes out to fetch water for the weary men, a serpent poisons the son of King Lycurgus who had been in her care. Lycurgus, however, rather than seek revenge by means of the sword as the queen at first would have him do, is moved by Adrastus's "sweet words" to avoid strife and forgive Hypsipyle.

Juxtaposed with these examples, on the other hand, are a number of incidents, disastrous in their outcome, in which the sword gains precedent over the word. The first example occurs when Tydeus rides to Thebes in an attempt to persuade Eteocles to fulfill his agreement with Polyneices and turn the kingdom over to him for a year (1874–2122). Tydeus speaks eloquently, but Eteocles refuses to listen. The result is the beginning of the devastating war of Thebes in which both kingdoms are destroyed. Again, during the wars, the prophet Amphiorax tries to persuade the Greeks to give up their siege (2794–2988). But his words are ignored and their effort ends in disaster. Finally, in an episode that directly parallels the incident in which Tydeus acts as a messenger to Eteocles, Jocasta enters the Greek camp with the hope of persuading her son Polyneices to cease fighting and become reconciled with Eteocles (3726–3821). Her words also fail, the siege continues, and both sides are devastated. As Lydgate points out, this is the inevitable result when war wins over words, when the sword of Mars is favored more than the harp of Mercury:

> . . . in the werre is non excepcioun
> Of hegh estat / nor lowh condicioun,

But as fortune / and fate, both yffere,
List to dispose / with her double chere,
And Bellona / the goddes in hir char
Aforn provydeth; / wherefor ech man be war
Vnavysed / a werre to bygynne.
For no man woot who shal lese or wynne.
And hard it is when eyther party leseth.
(4645–53)

One finds an even more interesting development of the myth of
Amphion in Book VI of the *Fall of Princes*. Here, Lydgate goes
beyond the suggestions of the *Siege of Thebes* and the opposition of
the word and the sword to consider the relation between poetry and
Fortuna, the force that threatens not only king and state, but all human
civilization and order. Reorganizing the structure of Book VI, he sets
up the story of Amphion as a frame for the events of this crucial
section of the *Fall*. At the outset of this book, Lydgate diverges from
his source and inserts a reference to Amphion into the lively debate
between Fortuna and Boccaccio. As Boccaccio warns Fortuna, the
power of poetry is considerable whether it be the eloquent language of
Tullius or his own plain style. To prove his point, he cites the example
of Amphion, who, by means of his "fair langage" and his "song,"
first civilized men (*Fall of Princes*, VI, 335–41). He then provides a
brief history of civilization, stressing the role of eloquent language in
reforming humanity and creating order:

Peeplis of Grece, of Roome & off Cartage,
Next in Itaille, with many a regeoun,
Wer inducid by swetnesse of langage
To haue togidre their conuersacioun,
To beelde castellis & many roial toun.
What caused this?—to telle in breef the foorme.
But eloquence rud peeplis to reffoorme.
(VI, 379–85)

Before humans were influenced by poetry and "fair speche," Lydgate
states, they were rude and bestial. But through the power of eloquent
language they have come together "In goldene cheynys of pes and
vnite" (VI, 391).

At the end of Book VI, Lydgate inserts a long chapter "Ageyn /

Ianglers and / diffamers of Rethorique" in which, following Laurent, he provides a brief description of the skills of the rhetorician and stresses the unique advantage humans have as a result of their powers of speech (*Fall of Princes*, VI, 3277–3490). Significantly, Lydgate again departs from his source to draw attention to the singular powers of the rhetorician to bring concord and comfort, to reconcile warring men and restore the disconsolate. As an example of his point, he cites the experience of Amphion who built the walls of Thebes by means of his song:

> Bexaumple as Amphioun, with song & elloquence
> Bilte the wallis of Thebes the cite,
> He hadde of rethorik so gret subtilite.
>
> In his langage there was so gret plesaunce,
> Fyndyng therbi so inli gret proffit.
> That al the contre kam to his obeissaunce,
> To heere hym speke thei hadde so gret delit;
> The peeple enviroun hadde such an appetit
> In his persone, in pes & in bataille:
> Heer men may seen what rethorik doth auaille!
> (*Fall of Princes*, VI, 3491–3500)

In the context of Book VI, Lydgate's treatment of the Amphion legend is even more significant. The reference to Amphion at the outset marks the conclusion of the debate between Boccaccio and Fortuna and forms the main point of Boccaccio's defense. Fortuna, first accusing Boccaccio of trying to change her nature, argues that he must accept her as she is and not complain of her doubleness. Boccaccio responds that even though worldly things are changeable, he will attempt to finish his book in the hope that he will be remembered for it. Even though his language is not as elegant as Tullius's, he argues, his work will be useful for he seeks to lead mortals to virtue, which is removed from Fortuna's domain. As Boccaccio continues, he adds an important dimension to the view of poetry we have been considering by skillfully setting up an opposition between the power of poetry and the power of Fortuna. While "fair langage" and "fressh ditees" first brought humans into harmony, Fortuna, in contrast, introduced strife and discord. If it had not been for the power of "fair langage," mortal kingdoms and cities would have been destroyed:

Afftir the sharpe[nesse] of thi cruel rage
Onli bi mene of speche & fair langage,
Folk be thi fraude fro grace ferr exilid,
Wer be fair speche to vnite reconcilid.
(*Fall of Princes*, VI, 375–78)

Throughout the brief sketch of civilization that follows, Boccaccio repeats this emphasis. Fortuna brings disorder; poetry and eloquence lead mortals back to a civilized and harmonious state. Fortuna makes human beings "incorrigible, / Wilful, froward, causeles at debat"; fair speech reconciles them, for there is no outrage so terrible that "gracious langage" cannot reform it. Boccaccio's arguments in the frame of Book VI thus define a pattern that provides an important perspective for understanding the significance of the stories in the center of the book.

The examples in the body of Book VI describe the downfall of civilization, represented by imperial Rome, through chaos and disorder and the reaffirmation of the power of rhetoric in the person of Cicero. The series begins with the story of Saturnine who caused great trouble in Rome by conspiring with Marius to banish Metellus. Then follows a group of stories of people whom Fortuna helped to make war against Rome—Marius who after lengthy wars was defeated by Sulla; Spartacus, who organized a large group of conspirators and churls to ravage the country; Viriathus, the thief who attacked Rome; Mithridates, whom Fortuna helped make war against Rome for forty years; and finally the bitter feud of Pompey and Caesar that threatened the downfall of the city. The section ends with Caesar's conquest of Egypt, his destruction of Alexandria and the civilization it represents, his death at the hands of Brutus, and renewed warfare and disorder.

In contrast to this long series of examples of the disorder prompted by Fortuna, Lydgate introduces the climactic story of Cicero, the "Laumpe and lanterne of Romeyn oratours," the "prince of elloquence," who restored concord to Rome. Acclaimed for his virtues and thus chosen counsel, Cicero opposed the cruel Catiline and broke up the conspiracy against Rome, saving the city from destruction. By the power of his rhetoric and eloquence, he reconciled rivals and brought order to Rome, "Thoruh his langage this saide Tullius / Reconsilede bi his soote orisouns / To the lordschipe & grace of Iulius, / Princes, kynges of dyuers regiouns, / That suspect stood bi accusaciouns" (*Fall of Princes,* VI, 3130–34). For a brief moment, the power of eloquent language restores the harmony and order Fortuna repeatedly seeks to destroy. But ultimately Cicero is exiled by Antony and slain. Lydgate concludes with a chapter in praise of rhetoric and oratory and the example of Amphion who is linked to Cicero by the power of his speech. Book VI ends with the beginning of a new cycle, the renewal of warfare and disorder under the Triumvirate.

Thus, by his exploitation of the myth of Amphion in the frame of Book VI, Lydgate draws attention to a final theme, the opposition of Fortuna and the poet. Fortuna brings about disorder and chaos, the poet by means of his "fair langage" has the power to restore order and harmony. By extension, this conclusion applies to Boccaccio and hence to his translator Lydgate. Despite Fortuna's arguments at the outset of the book, the two poets will continue their writing, thereby affirming the power of poetry.

Significantly, Lydgate goes even further than Boccaccio. Near the end of his long translation, he describes not only the poet's power but his sacred obligation to write. In the prologue to Book VIII, the next to the last book of the *Fall of Princes,* Lydgate makes several changes in his source to dramatize this point. In contrast to Laurent, he pictures Boccaccio as old and infirm, overcome by weariness with his task, a picture that significantly resembles Lydgate's condition at the end of the *Fall of Princes.* Just as Boccaccio is about to give up and allow himself to be overcome by sloth, Petrarch appears to him. Again changing his source, Lydgate has Boccaccio welcome Petrarch in terms that recall his own view of poetry:

> Wolkome maister, crownid with laureer,
> Which han Itaille lik a sunne cleer
> With poetrie, pleynli to descryue,
>
> . . . .
> Ye haue been lanterne, liht and direccioun
> Ay to supporte myn ocupacioun,
>
> As in writyng books to compile,
> Cheeff exaumplaire to my gret auauantage,
> To refourme the rudnesse of my stile
> With aureat colours of your fressh langage.
> (VIII, 67–81)

In Lydgate's version, Boccaccio concludes by again emphasizing his age and his determination to give up his craft. Petrarch responds by espousing the critical doctrine of the poet's obligation to write:

> . . . he that can and ceseth for to write
> Notable exaumples of our predecessours,
> Of envie men wil hym atwite,
> That he in gardyns leet perishe þe holsum flours
> In sondry caas that myhte do gret socours.
> (VIII, 162–66)

After Petrarch concludes, Boccaccio overcomes the feebleness of his own age and prepares to begin his book. In two stanzas that he adds to his source, Lydgate makes explicit the parallel between himself and Boccaccio and closes the prologue with his renewed determination to write (VIII, 190–203). By these changes, Lydgate thus sums up his view of the poet and the noble function a poet performs. An "enlumyner" who sheds beams of rhetoric and eloquence on the poet's matter, making it brilliant, illustrious, and clear, the poet offsets humanity's "dulness" and brings order and harmony to the world.

In our haste to pass Lydgate off as a poor Chaucerian, we have overlooked the extent to which he deliberately departs from the basic assumptions of his "master." Underlying his writing, his digressions make clear, is a view of poetry that differs substantially from his English predecessors'. This shift is apparent in the critical vocabulary Lydgate develops to describe the poetic process, in his conception of poets as illuminators who lead mortals to truth by means of their heightened language and amplification, in his concern with the relation between poetry and the well-being of the state, and in his belief in the power of poetry to withstand the ravages of Fortune. These ideals coalesce in Lydgate's conception of the "noble rethor poets," who join the orator's skill with language and impact in the public arena with the poet's insight, vision, and noble purpose. Lydgate's view of poetry points to the beginning of a new poetics in English. The poems on poetry produced by his successors, "The Golden Targe," the *Palice of Honour,* the *Pastime of Pleasure,* the "Garlande of Laurell," among others, in their most skillful form are a prelude to the formal poetics that first appeared in English in the sixteenth century.

hree

The "Makaris"

The conception of the poet as an "enluminer" who adorns and embellishes his matter by means of his rhetoric and eloquence underlies many of the early fifteenth-century poems. The influence of this vision of poetry extends from the amplified petitions and complaints of Hoccleve, to the miscellaneous court literature attributed to Chaucer, to the elaborate lyrics of the fifteenth-century collections, and to most of the poetry of the Middle Scots "makaris" ("makar" = maker, composer, craftsman). But it is in the writing of the Scottish poets rather than their English counterparts that one finds the first significant theoretical response to the vision of poetry that Lydgate popularizes at the outset of the fifteenth century. In contrast to Hoccleve and to the early fifteenth-century English court poets who typically do not consider questions about the nature of poetry directly in their poems, the Middle Scots "makaris," James I, Robert Henryson, and William Dunbar, address these issues as central themes. In their writing and in their self-conscious examination of their craft, these poets reassess the value and effect of poetry and their roles as "makaris." Although they differ considerably in their individual artistic solutions, in their poems about poetry they share with Lydgate ideals that are not characteristic of Chaucer and the late fourteenth-century poets. In different ways, the styles to which these poets turn—James's carefully controlled and governed style, Henryson's extreme juxtaposition of styles, and Dunbar's "anamalit" (enameled) style—serve as emblems of their redefinition of the vision of poetry that dominates the early fifteenth century.

"MORALITEE AND ELOQUENCE ORNATE"

The *Kingis Quair,* written c. 1424 by James I shortly after Lydgate's *Temple of Glas,* reaffirms the vision of poetry as ennobling, a source of wisdom and truth. But James reconsiders the means by which poetry "enlumines," to some extent qualifying Lydgate's vision. Although critics have treated the poem almost exclusively as a Boethian consideration of the workings of Fortune and humanity's search for order in a universe only imperfectly understood, the *Quair* is also a significant poem about poetry.[1] At the outset of the poem, James explicitly places his central philosophical themes in the context of his activities as poet, linking the two concerns by means of the same metaphor—the journey. Literally an account of a specific journey the narrator made in his youth, the *Quair* also defines the journey from innocence to experience, from youth to maturity, a journey of the narrator from instability and subjugation to Fortune to wisdom and self-governance. Finally, the *Quair* is the quest of the poet to write the poem, a journey from ineffective and uncontrolled writing to "rype" and purposeful poetry. The relation of these journeys provides an important perspective that is not considered in Boethius's *Consolation,* one that demonstrates the power of poetry to lead an individual into wisdom, self-governance, and strength against Fortune.

As the narrator explains at the outset of the poem, he lacks guidance both as a man and as a poet:

Ryght as the schip that sailith stereles
Vpon the rok[kis], most to harmes hye
For lak of it that suld bene hir supplye;
So standis thou here in this warldis rage
And wantis that suld gyde all thy viage.

I mene this by myself, as in partye.
Though nature gave me suffisance in youth,

The rypenesse of resoun lak[it] I
To gouerne with my will, so lyte I couth,
Quhen stereles to trauaile I begouth,
Amang the wawis of this warld to driue:
And how the case anon I will discriue.

With doutfull hert amang the rokkis blake,
My feble bote full fast to stere and rowe,
Helples, allone the wynter nyght I wake,
To wayte the wynd that furthward suld me throwe.
O empty saile, quhare is the wynd suld blowe
Me to the port, quhar gynneth all my game?
Hekp, Calyope, and wynd, in Marye name!

The rokkis clepe I the prolixitee
Of doubilnesse that doith my wittis pall:
The lak of wynd is the deficultee
In enditing of this lytill trety small:
The bote I clepe the mater hole of all:
My wit, vnto the saile that now I wynd
To seke conning, though I bot lytill fynd.
(101–26)

In James's scheme, Venus or Love provides the first source of stability for the poet-narrator in his search for governance. In contrast to the *Consolation*, where earthly love is one of the false gods of the world, and to Chaucer's *Knight's Tale* and *Troilus*, where Love, however pleasurable, increases one's vulnerability to Fortune, Love in the *Quair* is a positive force that transforms the narrator from a prisoner to a "free thrall," from one buffeted by Fortune to one who seeks to determine his own actions. Extending his metaphor of the "stereles" ship, the narrator suggests that Love offers man a safe harbor and port, a refuge from the "huge weltering wawis fell" (696). Specifically, Venus teaches the narrator discipline and self-control and finally places his personal experience in the larger context of the orderly workings of the universe.

When the narrator has gained self-control and tempered his will to Love's laws, Venus sends him to Minerva who represents a higher form of order than Love—wisdom both in the sense of rational knowledge and in the Christian sense of *sapientia* or knowledge based on divine law.[2] In contrast to Boethius's Philosophy, she is less concerned with Fortune's position in the universe than she is with strengthening the narrator by teaching him how to control his will and rule himself. By associating the narrator's self-governance with God's order, Minerva offers a new guide for his rudderless ship:

> "Tak him before in all thy gouernance,
> That in his hand the stere has of you all,
> And pray vnto his hye purueyance
> Thy lufe to gye. . . ." (904–7)

God's governance is the foundation upon which the narrator's must rest. Offering a new conclusion to the discussion about free will and necessity that appears in the *Consolation* and in the *Troilus,* Minerva indicates that while all are subject to Fortune, one can minimize her effects through wise governance (stanza 149).[3] Warning the poet-narrator of his danger if he fails to join wisdom to his will, she sends him on to Fortune.

The confrontation with Fortune reveals that "wit or resoun" is not sufficient for the narrator; he must also learn by experience. In spite of Minerva's preparation, what the narrator sees as he discovers Fortune hovering over a huge wheel, astonishes and terrifies him:

> And vnderneth the quhele sawe I there
> An vgly pit, depe as ony helle,
> That to behald thereon I quoke for fere.
> But o thing herd I, that quho therein fell
> Com no more vp agane, tidings to telle,
> Of quhich, astonait of that ferefull syght,
> I ne wist quhat to done, so was I fricht.
> (1128–34)

Bluntly mocking the narrator's weakness, Fortune warns him that half of his time or life is gone and he must spend well the "remnant of the day" (1197). As she spins him on her wheel, she bids him learn from the example of its turning, demonstrating by experience what Minerva had taught him—the danger of his position.

When the narrator awakens at the end of the dream, James returns to the related journey as poet. In the stanzas that follow the dream, the narrator suddenly shifts from the past of his adventures to the present moment of his writing, making his role as poet conspicuous. Although he insists that he does not have time to tell the details of his story, he continues for sixteen more stanzas in which he draws attention to his poetic activity by providing an elaborate concluding prayer, a rhetorical series of blessings, and a formal envoy to his book.[4] In these stanzas, the narrator reveals that, unlike Boethius, he does not understand the significance of his dream immediately. Rather the process of writing makes order out of experience and enables him to recognize the truths his vision has revealed.

In the final portion of the poem, the poet-narrator, now in control of his medium, changes his technique by turning away from the specific events of his story and the leisurely narrative manner of his opening sections to focus on the broad significance of his experience. From his present perspective as author, he retraces his steps back to the beginning of the poem, echoing its opening line, "Heigh in the hevynnis figure circulere." But as the narrator rethreads his way through the poem, he introduces an important change in emphasis. Ending with the appropriate metaphor of God the "writer" of our lives, the poet provides the conclusion to both of his journeys:

And thus endith the f[a]tall influence
Causit from hevyn quhare powar is commytt
Of gouirnance, by the magnificence
Of him that hiest in the hevin sitt.
To quham we th[a]nk that all oure [lif] hath writt,
Quho couth it red agone syne mony a yere
"Hich in the hevynnis figure circulere."
(1366–72)

As in Chaucer's *Troilus,* the narrator's self-conscious activity as author becomes an emblem of the philosophic speculation of the *Quair.*[5] His effort to write his poem is the artistic counterpart of the larger search for self-rule in the *Quair.* The ideal of poetry the narrator defines as he refers to his own writing in stanzas 15–18 is one that reflects the governance he seeks on his dream journey—a carefully controlled poetry in which his "wilsum wittis," like the wandering will of his youth, are guided and directed on an effective course. In contrast to the aimless writing of his youth in which he spent "more ink and paper" "to lyte effect," the narrator seeks a poetry that, like Boethius's fair and eloquent Latin, is mature, "rype," and purposeful. During the course of his poetic journey, he changes from a poet who is unable to write because his inspiration fails and his style is prolix and "double" (stanzas 17–18) to one who is firmly in control of his vision and medium. Before his dream, the narrator's verse is marked by false starts, by self-conscious and overly elaborate rhetoric, and by an expansion and frequency of narrative interruption common in Lydgate's visions, but these poetic difficulties are no longer apparent after his dream. The stanzas, though still rhetorical and allusive, are more tightly knit and they are directed swiftly to the conclusion of the poem.

The ideal of a poetry that is effectively guided, the artistic counterpart of the narrator's larger search for a principle of governance, is articulated explicitly in the closing envoy to the "quair." Giving the traditional humility topos a new emphasis, the narrator returns to the central metaphor of the poem in the last four stanzas. As he takes leave of his book, he bids the reader "to reule and to stere" his "quair," to provide poetic control where it is lacking so that the work's frailities may be made firm and its faults may be corrected. Again, in the next stanza, he refers to the lady who inspired the "quair" as the "gyd and stere" of his book, who has the power to mitigate its shortcomings. Finally, in the last two stanzas, the narrator places his completed "quair" in the larger context of the governance of God, the supreme "writer," the ultimate "gyd and stere" for him as man and as poet in the tradition of the great English writers who, like Boethius, were "superlatiue . . . In moralitee and eloquence ornate" (1376–77).

In the *Quair*, James thus views poetry as ennobling, a source of wisdom and truth. As the narrator discovers on his journey, poetry has the power to order experience and to draw attention to its underlying meaning. The journey of the poet to write his poem, though fraught with difficulties, ends with a ripeness of reason and a recognition of the events he has narrated. Corresponding to this vision is James's emphasis on the importance of an explicitly literary style. In defining his ideal of poetry, he, in fact, echoes many of Lydgate's critical terms, praising the poets he admires for their "suete" and "flourit" language and their "rhetoric" and "eloquence ornate."

But, despite this echoing, James's vision of poetry finally qualifies Lydgate's. Although he defines effective poetic style as a combination of "moralitee and eloquence ornate," of language "full of fruyte and rhetorikly pykit," James indicates that the "noble rethor's" style must be guided or directed on an effective course. The poet's journey, like the journey of life, must be governed if the poet's efforts are to be more than "aimless wanderings." The difference between the two poets' conceptions of poetry is summed up by the differences between their central metaphors. For Lydgate, the poet is primarily an "enluminer" who sheds beams of rhetoric and eloquence on his matter, making it "aureate," "goldyn," and "sugrid." His role is to enhance the meaning of his material by his effective use of language and rhetoric and to illuminate the truths that one's "dull wit" would not otherwise comprehend. James, in contrast, defines good poetry in terms of the metaphor of the skillfully guided ship, an emblem of the governance and poetic control the maturing narrator attains. The poet's craft depends upon a combination of inspiration (the "wynd" that blows the sail), "wit" or the ability to write in a style that is "rype," and "connyng" to avoid the rocks (stanza 18) or the obstacles that threaten the carelessly guided poem. While James envisions good poetry as "fair," "fruitful," and "eloquent," he qualifies this ideal by subordinating it to the more important notion of governance in the poet's writing and in his life.

"QUHAT IS IT WORTH TO TELL ANE FENƷEIT TAILL?"

Although, like James, Henryson, writing between c. 1450 and c. 1500, defends the power of poetry to "enlumine" humanity, he reaches this position only after considerable conflict. Whereas his fifteenth-century predecessors begin with the assumption that poetry is truthful, Henryson again raises this question, and, in answering, he considers the problematical relation between the poem and the world and the ambiguous nature of the poet's medium. Two of his three long works, *Orpheus and Eurydice* and *Fables,* address these concerns as central themes.[6] Specifically, the poems consider the way in which poetry, by means of its examples or "fenƷeit fabils" ("fenƷeit" = feigned, invented, imagined), provides prudence and insight in the world. By directing attention away from the transitory and the ephemeral to enduring concerns and by teaching readers to distinguish true wisdom from its false imitation, poetry offers an antidote to human blindness. This defense of poetry is linked to the forms to which Henryson turns and to the extreme juxtaposition of styles characteristic of his major poems.

The *Orpheus and Eurydice* provides the least ambiguous treatment of the view of poetry that dominates Henryson's long poems. The poem describes the potential power of poetry to free one from blinding lust and appetite and to turn one's gaze upward to the realm of "perfyte wisdome." Working within the tradition initiated by Boethius and embellished by Nicholas Trivet, Henryson focuses his story directly on Orpheus's journey to the underworld and his struggle to regain Eurydice. The Boethian version is essentially a moral allegory, an example of the difficulty of men who struggle to free themselves from worldly concerns and "raise [their] minds to sovereign day." Henryson's treatment of the myth, on the other hand, is more directly concerned with the role of Orpheus as poet and with the effect of his music.

For Boethius, the story, which concludes the third book of the *Consolation,* sums up Philosophy's teaching that one must direct one's attention not to the deceptive rewards of Fortune but to the True Good: "Happy is he who can look into the shining spring of good; happy is he who can break the heavy chains of earth." Although Orpheus as poet charms Nature and the inhabitants of the underworld by his "sweet songs," "songs inspired by his powerful grief and the love which doubled his grief," he has no power to console himself. As lover, moreover, he succumbs to blind passion, "a stronger law unto itself," and loses Eurydice, the object of his quest. Warning of the power of passion over the upper part of the soul, Boethius draws the following moral from the fable: "whoever is conquered and turns his eyes to the pit of hell, looking into the inferno, loses all the excellence he has gained."[7]

In some of the medieval commentaries on Boethius's text, the emphasis shifts from Orpheus as an impassioned lover to Orpheus as an embodiment of wisdom and eloquence, as example of the power and limits of art. The origin of this interpretation is provided by Fulgentius's *Mitologiae* where the name Orpheus from *oraia phone* is interpreted as "best voice" and Eurydice from *eur dike* as "profound judgment" and the myth is treated less as a moral allegory than as a consideration of the power of music or eloquence.[8] Later commentators, particularly Trivet (d. 1334), whom Henryson cites, considerably develop these qualities, now locating both wisdom and eloquence together in the figure of Orpheus, who represents "the part of the intellect which is instructed in wisdom and eloquence."[9] In Trivet's commentary, which probably was influenced by Bernardus Silvestris's interpretation of Virgil's *Aeneid*, Orpheus's music assumes an important role both as a civilizing force and a means of redirecting the mind to the True Good. As poet-singer, beloved of the gods, Orpheus has the power to inspire and ennoble humanity and redeem human folly. As Trivet explains, "By his sweet lyre, that is his eloquence, [Orpheus] brought wicked, brutal, and savage men to right reason."[10]

Henryson's version of the Orpheus story increases the emphasis incipient in fourteenth-century commentary on the power of Orpheus's music. Although he follows Trivet, Henryson shifts his focus specifically to Orpheus as poet, cutting the material that is extraneous to this role and expanding the portions of the story that deal with Orpheus as poet-singer. The narrative links the traditional moral allegory of the struggle of the intellect to free itself from worldly concerns with the power of poetry and, in Henryson's version, Orpheus's quest to recover Eurydice also becomes a quest for an effective medium as poet.

In contrast to his sources, Henryson stresses the transformation of Orpheus's song as he undergoes his journey. After the loss of Eurydice, Orpheus's music is discordant and ineffective, "dully" rather than "sweet." Adding a long "Complaint" to earlier narrative, Henryson represents Orpheus as out of tune with Nature. Boethius suggests that Orpheus's song calms Nature—his "sorrowful music . . . made the woodland dance and the rivers stand still. He made the fearful deer lie down bravely with the fierce lions; the rabbit no longer feared the god quieted by his song."[11] Henryson accentuates Nature's ineffective attempt to console Orpheus and his loss of poetic power. In opposition to Orpheus's discordant song, Henryson introduces the harmonious music of the spheres, which prefaces the journey to the underworld in his version and serves as a model of effective music for the poet-singer. In a long digression that he adds to his sources, Henryson represents Orpheus passing through the nine spheres and hearing an impressive music, overwhelming in its power and harmony:

In his passage amang the planetis all,
He herd a hevinly melody and sound,
Passing all instrumentis musicall,
Causit be rollyng of the speiris round;

Quhilk armony, throu all this mappamound,
Quhilk moving ceiss vnyt perpetuall—
Quhilk of this warld, Pluto the saul can call.
(219–25)

From this music, the poet Orpheus learns perfect harmony and proportion and, as Henryson's sudden shift to technical language indicates,
the intricacies of his craft.[12] Significantly, the song that Orpheus
produces after this experience has a new power and effectiveness. It
charms the creatures of the underworld and redeems Eurydice (366
ff.). But although Orpheus, in imitation of divine music, discovers his
medium as poet, as a mortal man he finally fails in his quest when
blinded by lust, he looks backward and loses Eurydice.

The *moralitas* emphasizes both the potential power of poetry to
prevent human blindness and lead one away from the false goods of
the world and the difficulty of achieving this state. The poem, by its
structure, suggests the transitoriness of human happiness. The joy of
Orpheus and Eurydice lasts but a moment, not even an entire stanza in
the design of the poem. As the narrator muses: "off warldly Joy;
allace, quhat sall I say? / Lyke till a flour that plesandly will spring, /
Quhilk fadis sone, and endis with murynyng" (89–91). Repeatedly
reminding us of the quickness of "warldly lust, and all our affectioun" (444), the allegory of the *moralitas* reinforces this view. Although the perfect poetry that the narrator describes can clear human
vision and direct the mind above the mutable realm of appetite and
"affectioun," the human poet's relation to this ideal is tentative and
conditional.[13] Orpheus's journey as poet finally embodies both the
discovery and the loss of poetic power.

In the *Fables,* Henryson develops the view of poetry introduced in
Orpheus and Eurydice. In one sense, the *Fables* is a defense of poetry
that reaffirms the value of fiction in a world that is corrupt and
unstable. Defining more explicitly than Lydgate the way in which
poetry enlightens humanity, Henryson links human moral vision with
that of the blind beast and suggests that poetry by its examples or
"fenʒeit fabils" has the power to clarify human sight and make one
prudent. Although poetry is not always based upon truth, Henryson
emphasizes by his additions to his sources in the "Prologue,"[14] it has
considerable usefulness to humanity. As the earth when worked with
great diligence produces flowers and the grain to sustain men and

women, so the "subtell dyte of poetry" produces a "morall sweit sentence" when well applied (stanza 2). Like a nut with a hard shell but a delectable kernel inside, the "fenʒeit fabill" of poetry surrounds a doctrine that is wise and full of fruit (stanza 3). Finally, as a bow that is always bent becomes ineffective, so a mind that is too serious becomes jaded. By mixing "meriness" with "sad materis," poetry keeps one's mind supple and effective (stanza 4).

In turning to the fable for his defense of poetry, Henryson exploits the inherent implications of this form. In the Middle Ages, the term *fabula* referred both to tales with animal characters and to stories that were fictive, that is, "fenʒeit" or made up.[15] In this double sense, the fable form provides an effective emblem of Henryson's concerns. On the one hand, the fable is the artistic embodiment of a human being's transformation into beast. In Henryson's hands, it defines the consequences of the denial of nobler human qualities—a world of lust, appetite, and selfish desires in which human and animal concerns merge. In contrast to the *Nun's Priest's Tale* in which Chaucer introduces repeated reminders of animal features distinct from man's own, Henryson rarely breaks the illusion of his form but rather gradually grafts the human world onto the animal to indicate how "mony men in operatioun, / Ar like to beistis in conditioun" (48–49).[16] The fable demonstrates that when human beings become preoccupied by "carnall and foull delyte," their true nature is abandoned and they are transformed into beasts (50–56). At the same time, the fable is an image of the "fenʒeit" nature of poetry. Overtly dealing with matter that the poet has made up, the fable for Henryson becomes a symbol of "the subtel dyte of poetry" itself. Like the nut with the hard shell, the fable provides an explicit image of the way in which poetry operates. "Fenʒeit," that is, made-up or imagined, poetry, like the more overt fable form, provides fictions that lead one to "be figure of ane other thing" to more significant truths. In the thirteen fables of his collection, Henryson links these two themes to redefine the way in which poetry can ennoble human beings.

The first five tales in the Bassandyne order introduce a world in which the characters, preoccupied by their desires, do not see clearly.[17] In these tales, the characters' relation to events is uncertain and they have difficulty anticipating the effect of their actions and the choices they make. The central three tales define the implications of this impaired sight and suggest that poetry can help humans see clearly and acquire prudence in the world. The closing frame of five tales reveals the danger of a world without insight in which the characters, now totally bestial, fail to distinguish between good and evil, just and unjust action. The bleakness of this experience underscores the need for each person to seek the wisdom that poetry contains.

The first fable, "The Cock and the Jasp," defines the nature of impaired human sight, indicating the reason for the transformation into beast—a lack of concern with anything beyond immediate physical needs. Considerably changing the strategy of his sources, Henryson presents the body of the tale from the perspective of the Cock, repeatedly reinforcing his limited point of view by means of elaborate rhetoric.[18] As the Cock eloquently explains, the gem (the "Jasp") that he finds is of no use to him; he needs food rather than jewels, grain rather than treasure fit for a king:

> Thow hes na corne, and thairof I had neid;
> Thy cullour dois bot confort to the sicht,
> And that is not aneuch my wame to feid.
>
> . . . .
>
> "Quhar suld thow mak thy habitatioun?
> Quhar suld thow duell, bot in ane royall tour?
> Quhar suld thow sit, bot on ane kingis croun,
> Exalt in worschip and in grit honour?
> Rise, gentill Iasp, of all stanis the flour,
> Out of this fen, and pas quhar thow suld be;
> Thow ganis not for me, nor I for the."
> (99–112)

In the last ten lines of the tale, Henryson suddenly changes direction, shifting to the point of view and style of the poet-narrator, which differ radically from the Cock's. In a plain style that contrasts sharply with the Cock's rhetorical performance, the narrator indicates the "Jasp" has considerable value for the Cock that he has overlooked:

> This ioloe iasp has properteis seuin:
> The first, of cullour it is meruelous,
> Part lyke the fyre, and part lyke to the heuin.
> It makis ane man stark and victorious;
> Preseruis als fra cacis perrillous;

Quha hes this stane sall haue gude hap to speid,
Of fyre nor fallis him neidis not to dreid.
(120–26)

By thus juxtaposing the two conflicting styles and reactions to the precious stone, Henryson begins to make us uneasy about having accepted the Cock's arguments.

The *moralitas* confirms the narrator's position rather than the Cock's, showing that, unlike the grain that the Cock so busily sought, the jacinth or knowledge provides "eternall meit" for the soul.[19] In a crucial last stanza, Henryson applies the problem of the Cock to everyone. The stone is now lost and hidden. We neither seek it nor value it, but like the Cock, are concerned only with material things:

Bot now, allace, this iasp is tynt and hid.
We seik it nocht, nor preis it for to find;
Haif we richis, na better lyfe we bid,
Of science thocht the saull be bair and blind.
Of this mater to speik, I wair bot wind,
Thairfore I ceis and will na forther say.
(155–60)

The narrator concludes with the challenge, "Go seil the Iasp, quha will, for thair it lay" (161). The fables that follow address this challenge in a world of imperfect vision.

The next four tales—"The Two Mice," "The Cock and the Fox," "The Fox and the Wolf," and "The Trial of the Fox"—reveal more specifically than the opening tale the forces that deceive humans. The first two tales provide examples of "blindness" and recovery; the two fox tales that follow present a darker vision of delusion without renewal of sight. In the "Tale of the Two Mice," Henryson again focuses on the limitations of human preoccupation with physical concerns with the example of the country mouse who is blinded by the "wordis hunny sweit" (315) of her sister who offers her sumptuous food and fancy lodging. Although suspicious of her sudden prosperity, the country mouse makes merry at the feast the city mouse prepares only to be brutally awakened to her senses by Gib the cat. The *moralitas* warns of the danger of making the womb a god and of "Grit aboundance and blind prosperitie" (377) that often lead to a bad ending. Rather, the narrator emphasizes by the refrain at the end of each stanza, we must seek the best of earthly joy, "Blyithnes in hart, with small possessioun."

"The Cock and the Fox" points up two further weaknesses that blind humans—flattery and pride.[20] Reworking Chaucer's *Nun's Priest's Tale,* Henryson cuts all but the central episode that focuses on these themes, and, within the episode, he plays up the features of the characters that suggest deception by flattery and pride, introducing the fox as "fenʒeit, craftie, and cawtelows" (402) and making Chantecleir an even easier prey than his predecessor in Chaucer's work.[21] Finally, he adds an episode that is not in his immediate sources in which the three hens react to Chantecleir's capture in order to accentuate the deceitfulness of language and provide a parallel to the Fox's deception of the Cock.[22] Like the "fenʒeit foxe," Pertok speaks with false terms as she rhetorically praises her lost lover: "ʒone was our drowrie, and our dayis darling, / Our nichtingall, and als our orlege bell / Our walkryfe watche" (497–99). But after Sprutok speaks more candidly of Chantecleir's shortcomings, Pertok, like the Fox at the end of the central episode, reveals her true feelings:

> Than Pertok spak, with feinʒeit faith befoir,
> In lust but lufe that set all hir delyte,
> "Sister, ʒe wait, off sic as him ane scoir
> Wald not suffice to slaik our appetyte.
> I hecht ʒow be my hand, sen ʒe ar quyte,
> Within ane oulk, for schame and I dirst speik,
> To get ane berne suld better claw oure breik."
> (523–29)

Tuppok sums up, suggesting that Chantecleir got what he deserved for his vanity and pride.

The *moralitas* portrays the danger of false language, setting up an opposition between the "fenʒeit termis textuall" of the fables (589) and the flattery of the "fenʒeit foxe." As the narrator suggests by his repeated use of the word "fenʒeit," which becomes almost a leitmotif in the tale, we may find "ane sentence richt agreabill, / Under thir fenʒeit termis textuall" of the fable (598–99). But we must beware of the terms of the "fenʒeit foxe" that may seem like sweet sugar but have poison underneath.

> This fenʒeit foxe may weill be figurate
> To flatterais with plesand wordis quhyte,

With fals mening and mynd maist toxicate,
To loif and le that settis thair haill delyte.

. . . .

The wickit mynd and adullatioun,
Of sucker sweit haifand similitude,
Bitter as gall and full of fell poysoun,
To taist it is, quha cleirlie vnderstude.
(600–610)

The problem, like the problem of knowing when to seek the jewel buried in the dung heap and when to be content with one's own simple fare, is how to distinguish one kind of "feȝnyng" from another.

We can note a progression from the simple mouse to the vainglorious Chantecleir, but the central characters in the two tales that follow are even more deluded by their appetites. The Fox in "The Fox and the Wolf" labors to read the stars, but he fails to see the obvious dangers before his own eyes. In a humorous passage, he mistakes "Freir Wolf Waitskaith," in "science wonder sle" for a worthy doctor of divinity and bids him as the "lanterne, and siker way . . . to grace" (677–78) to hear his confession. When the son and heir of the Fox appears in the next tale, he is presented as even more ruled by greed and covetousness than his father, as, to the narrator's horror, he rejoices at his father's death and thinks only of his own gain. The Fox is so bound by his appetite that as the tale progresses, he changes his very appearance to serve his corrupt desires, ironically feigning the loss of sight in one eye. In both tales, the fate of the "blind" characters is worse than in the preceding tales. The Fox is separated from his skin for his efforts while his son and heir ends up on the gallows.

The three central tales of the thirteen in the Bassandyne order—"The Sheep and the Dog," "The Lion and the Mouse," and "The Preaching of the Swallow"—form a kind of "nut" within the "shell" of the work. These tales reveal the implications of the world of the opening tales not only for the deluded characters in these tales but for the innocent as well and turn to the role of poetry as a means of restoring impaired human sight. In "The Sheep and the Dog," the situation of the first five fables suddenly is reversed. The victim in this tale is not a figure blinded by flattery, pride, or covetousness who deserves his or her fate, but the innocent sheep, and the world of the tale is filled not with the orderly catalogue of beasts of the preceding tale, but with a grim catalogue of predators ruled by their appetites, a parody of the Lion's just parliament. The social satire increases sharply as Henryson changes his sources to indicate how widespread the greed, pride, and corruption of the earlier tales are among the very instruments of justice in the state.[23] The innocent Lamb stands no chance against his predators, and, like the Fox of the earlier tale, ends up losing his skin.[24]

The *moralitas* closes with the poignant lament of the sheep based on Psalm 44.23:

> . . . O Lord, quhy sleipis thow sa long?
> Walk, and discerne my cause groundit on richt;
> Se how I am be fraud, maistrie, and slicht
> Peillit full bair, and so is mony one
> Now in this warld richt wonder wo begone.[25]

The world is overturned; the moral order of the previous tales appears to have broken down. We are left with the compelling question of what a mortal is to do. The "Taill of the Scheip and the Doig," thus, reveals the larger implications of the "blindness" of the preceding tales, the danger not only to the characters controlled by their lusts but to the innocent as well who find themselves in a world where clear-cut evaluations are impossible and their vision is inadequate. Like the "fenʒeit" rhetoric of the Fox that is a false version of the "fenʒeit termes" of the fables, and the false "science" of the Wolf that parodies the "science" the jacinth represents, the false trial of this tale is part of a larger series of oppositions in the *Fables* in which the false version mirrors the true one to the dismay of the ordinary person.

"The Lion and the Mouse," which serves as the poetic center of the work, addresses itself to this dilemma.[26] Significantly, Henryson opens the tale with a new prologue, a dream vision in which the poet-narrator confronts Aesop, his master and one of the most important fabulists of antiquity. While Aesop provides one view of poetry, Henryson qualifies it with another. In response to the narrator's request to tell a moral fable (1386–87), Aesop questions the value of poetry, demanding: "quhat is it worth to tell ane fenʒeit taill, / Quhen haly preiching may na thing auaill?" (1389–90). When the world is "roustit" with "canker blak," when man's ear is deaf, when his heart is hard as stone, when he inclines always down to earth, Aesop asks, what effect can poetry have? (1393–96).

Although Aesop implies that poetry is of less value than straight teaching (1389–90), the *Fables* as a whole offers a more hopeful view. The three central tales suggest an answer to Aesop's question.[27] "The Sheep and the Dog" presents a vision of the world in which the majority are blinded by their appetites, a vision that Aesop confirms, but "The Lion and the Mouse" offers a way out. The tale presents an example of fall and recovery, an entrapment in the world and an escape from its nets. The fable opens with a picture of the sleeping Lion, off guard and vulnerable to the dangers of the world, who forms an implicit parallel with the sleeping poet of the prologue to the tale. Enraged by the mice who dance over his sleeping body, the Lion ultimately is persuaded to show pity rather than scorn and pardon his subjects. As the Mouse teaches the Lion, he should not allow himself to be blinded by rage that is unworthy of his nobility, but he should act according to his true nature. While hunting, the Lion then is caught in a net "off hempyn cordis strang" only to be saved by the Mouse he had pitied.

The *moralitas,* with its exhortation to vigilance, applies both to the sleeping Lion, the ruler of humankind, and to the sleeping poet who also is humanity's "gyde and Governour." As the narrator concludes, the ruler "suld be walkrife gyde amd gouernour / Of his pepill, that takis na labour / To reule and steir the land, and iustice keip" (1576–79), reminding both king and people of the relationship that has eroded in the troubled reign of James III.[28] Echoing the descriptions of the "fair forrests" in which the poet and the Lion fell asleep, the narrator warns that the forest is the world with its false pleasures that will ensnare those "Quhilk in thair lustis maist confidence hauis" (1586). Aesop ends with a prayer that Justice will reign in the land and that the lords, the makers of the net, keep their faith unto the king. The tale, thus, provides an effective example of humanity's entrapment and escape from the nets of the world and suggests that the ruler, like the Lion, rather than like Aesop of the prologue, must pity rather than scorn erring mortals.

The final tale of the three, "The Preaching of the Swallow," offers a further response to Aesop's reservations about poetry. Contrary to Aesop's assumptions, the tale suggests that poetry offers a more effective means of enlightening than preaching. Again, Henryson defines a world where people are blind to spiritual operations, where they think only of their own appetites. The tale moves swiftly from the large perspective of God's providence to the limited human view in darkness and delusion. The human soul, the narrator suggests, is like a bat's eye that hides from the light of day and comes out only in darkness. Human eyes are too weak to look at the sun; the soul is too oppressed with fantasies to comprehend God's work. Nevertheless, he suggests, one still may discover God's order through His creation—the firmament moving in harmony, the various creatures He has made to people the earth, and the constant cycle of seasons. The parallel between the creation and the poet's verse is implicit. Both render divine working that is too mysterious for mortals to perceive in its original state in a form that their weak eye can consider.

The tale itself provides a dramatic illustration of the observations of the prologue. Like the fettered man of the prologue, the birds are unable to respond to the working of God's providence and think only of their immediate pleasure. Despite the repeated warnings of the Swallow, they fail to prevent the Churl from growing and harvesting the hemp with which he will make the fatal nets to ensnare them. As the Swallow points out, the birds lack simple prudence, man's version of the "hie prudence" or divine providence with which the fable opens. In a Latin line from the *Distichs* of Cato, which numerically stands at the center of this fable, he sums up the point to the tale and warns the birds to anticipate events that will come and to prepare for the future. "Nam leuius laedit quiquid praeuidimus ante,"[29] which he expands:

"For clerkis sayis it is nocht sufficient
To considder that is befoir thyne ee;
Bot prudence is ane inwart argument,
That garris ane man prouyde befoir and se
Quhat gude, quhat euill is liklie for to be
Off euerilk thingis at the fynall end,
And swa fra perrell ethar him defend."
(1755–61)

Though one's eye may be too weak to discern God's scheme, one may avoid misfortune by being prudent. But the Swallow's preaching is of no avail. The birds ignore his warning and think only of the feast they will have when the hemp is grown. Led astray by their appetites, they mistake the empty chaff that the fowler sprinkles in the snow to lure them for the true seeds and, in contrast to the Lion of the previous tale, they are caught in the fatal nets. The *moralitas* expands the significance of the fable by linking the Churl to the fiend, the chaff to fleshly lust and vain prosperity, and the Swallow to the holy preacher who warns humans to beware of the fiend's nets (stanza 275).

The relationship of the central tales of the *Fables,* numbers 6, 7, and 8, thus clarifies the sentence that underlies the surrounding tales. These three tales provide figures of human blindness and vulnerability to the dangers of the world and the means of recovery. Tales 6 and 8 reveal the causes of humanity's fall—the difficulty of seeing clearly in the world and lack of prudence—and the fable at the exact center, number 7, "The Lion and the Mouse," illustrates humanity's recovery by means of the figure of the Lion who adheres to his noble virtues and wisely heeds the Mouse's warning. In these tales, human blindness is defined explicitly as a lack of prudence, the failure to see the consequences of one's actions or to recognize that they are part of a larger scheme of God's workings. While the Swallow's preaching fails to make the birds see, that is, to act with prudence, the narrator implies that poetry with its "fenȝeit fables" can provide one with a kind of prudence.

The remaining five tales (9–13) present a much darker vision than the opening frame (1–5). These tales reveal the implications of the sentence of the central tales by defining a world entirely without prudence, in which the characters have no recognition of God's workings. Although the opening tales contain contrasts within them between good and evil characters, just and unjust action, these contrasts are excluded from most of the remaining tales. The only perspective is that of the blind beast. The dangers of a world limited to this vision are made increasingly apparent in these tales as the central images of the first half of the poem recur in a literal form.

The atmosphere is defined immediately by the two Fox tales, "The Fox, the Wolf, and the Cadger" and "The Fox, Wolf, and Husbandman." The guile of the Fox in these fables even exceeds his earlier stratagems, and the other characters are represented as entirely preoccupied by their selfish desires. By the end of these tales, we move from figurative to literal blindness, from daylight to a world of total darkness as the Wolf, who imprudently feigns blindness in the first tale, loses his sight and ends up at the bottom of a well. The portrayal of the blind world in the second half of the *Fables* culminates in the "Trial of the Wolf and the Lamb." This tale, which invites comparison with the earlier "sheep" tale, reveals how bleak a world without prudence is. In this fable, Henryson changes his version to make the outlines of the earlier tale recur in even harsher form. Again the Lamb, the figure of the common man, is wrongly accused by his predator. Again, he has no recourse in a world governed by lust, pride, and greed. But while the Sheep in the first half of the *Fables* is permitted a trial, though a sham, and escapes with the loss of his skin, the naive and innocent Lamb, who foolishly expects the Wolf to adhere to the laws he cites, is denied even the pretense of justice. Despite the Lamb's articulate legal pleas, which Henryson adds to his version, the Wolf takes matters into his own hands and murders his innocent victim. The ending is much more gruesome than in the earlier tales as Henryson incorporates in his version a graphic description of the Wolf drinking the poor Lamb's blood and feasting on his flesh.[30]

The final tale, "The Paddock and the Mouse," draws together many of the concerns of the earlier tales. The Mouse in this tale not only is totally blinded by her appetite like the Cock, the Wolf, and the birds of Henryson's preceding fables, but like the Sheep and the Lamb, she naively relies on her own powers of persuasion to deal with her enemies.[31] While the Sheep and the Lamb recognize their predators for what they are, the Mouse in this tale, though instinctively repelled by the Frog's hideous appearance, is beguiled by his false rhetoric and blindly puts her life in his hands. Again, the narrator reminds us of her folly by echoing some of the earlier tales. Like the foolish birds in "The Preaching of the Swallow," the Mouse bids the Frog, "Let be thy preiching" so that she can fill her stomach just as, ironically, he is making a point that she might do well to heed:

"Off sum the face may be flurischand,
Off silkin toung and cheir rycht amorous,
With mynd inconstant, fals, and wariand,
Full off desait and menis cautelous."
(2847–50)

Like the Wolf in "The Fox, the Wolf and the Cadger," the Mouse relies on her enemy's false oath to serve her, again ignoring her better judgment. Her realization of the Frog's true intent comes too late as she struggles to free herself and prevent her brutal death.

Linking the false rhetoric of the Frog with the nets of the world, the *moralitas* warns against not recognizing "fals intent vnder ane fair pretence" (2917). As the narrator likens the Mouse to the human soul, we are encouraged to see the significance of the earlier fables in a larger context. By their willingness to subject their noble nature to their bodily appetites, this tale suggests, people lose not only their goods, their skins, their lives as we had seen in the earlier tales, but their very souls. The concluding stanza, like the concluding stanza of "The Cock and the Jasp," contains an implicit challenge. The narrator has taught us by his "fenʒeit fables" how to see the world, how to be prudent. Now he will say no more. As he had suggested at the outset: "Of this mater to speik, I wair bot wind, / Thairfore I ceis and will na forther say. / Ga seik the iasp, quha will, for thair it lay" (159–61). Similarly, he takes his leave abruptly at the end and leaves the final response to us. We can blind ourselves like the characters of the tales or we can seek the precious stone or the wisdom the "fenʒeit fables" contain.

In answer to Aesop's question, Henryson's *Fables* affirm the value of poetry. The *Fables* suggest that the figures of poetry provide one with a kind of prudence that enables one to see clearly in the world. Like the Mouse of the central tale who teaches the Lion to be prudent and saves him from the "net" that ensnares him, the examples of poetry provide one with wisdom in a form that the weakened human eye can consider. By teaching people to look beneath the surface of words, to distinguish between false rhetoric and the poet's "fenʒeit terms," between the nets of the world and true pleasures, poetry attempts to avert their blindness and prevent them from becoming bound by human desires. Unlike the Swallow's "preiching," poetry requires an active participation on the part of the reader to find its "sentence" and thus keeps one's mind supple and effective like the well-strung bow of the prologue. But although poetry is inherently useful, Henryson finally suggests it is up to each person to take his concluding challenge and seek the wisdom that it contains.[32]

Henryson's view of poetry as "fenʒeit fabils" finds form in a stylistic solution that is different from Lydgate's and James's. Unlike these poets, Henryson is openly wary of high style. Rather than viewing it as the medium most suitable to the poet's noble purpose, he often links rhetorical and eloquent style with the false nets of the world, as in the final fable where he warns of the deceitfulness of the Paddock's eloquence:

Ane fals intent vnder ane fair pretence
Hes causit mony innocent for to de;
Grit folie is to gif ouer sone credence
To all that speiks fairlie vnto the;
Ane silkin toung, ane hart of crueltie,
Smytis more sore than ony schot of arrow.
(2918–23)

In opposition to this style, Henryson repeatedly sets his own "rude and hamelie dite," a style that relates more directly to his meaning. At the end of the first fable, "The Cock and the Jasp," for example, the narrator juxtaposes his own plain terms with the Cock's long-winded and elaborate address to the jacinth. The difference in styles is extreme and, as we have seen, draws attention to the deceptiveness of the Cock's eloquence. His rhetoric is impressive, but as the narrator's contrasting plain style reveals, it points to a wrong view. The opposition of styles with which the fable ends forces the readers to reinterpret their initial response to the jacinth and to attempt to discern more clearly the meaning that lies under the surface of the poem's language.

The use of extreme stylistic contrast in the first of the *Fables* may be seen as an emblem of Henryson's artistic strategy not only in this work but in all of his major poems. The abrupt juxtaposition of elaborate and simple styles is one of his most characteristic techniques and serves as a means of directing the reader's attention beneath the surface of his words.[33] Unlike Lydgate's high style, which in its most effective moments impresses readers and moves them to admiration and agreement, Henryson's repeated stylistic undercutting forces the reader constantly to reinterpret the poem's apparent meaning and resolve the conflicting perspectives the juxtaposed styles afford. Although there are numerous instances of this technique in the *Fables,* for example, in the dialogue between the "Uponlandis" Mouse and the Burgis Mouse, Chantecleir and the Fox, the Fox and the Wolf, the Wolf and the Lamb, and the Paddock and the Mouse, the most striking and extended illustration is found in the *Testament of Cresseid.* The poem, in fact, may be seen as a series of startling stylistic contrasts.

The Testament is framed by the two contrasting styles of the narrator, the expansive style in which he introduces himself and eloquently laments the plight of Cresseid, his central figure, and the highly compressed moral commentary with which he ends. Within the body of the poem, Henryson structures the action around three major instances of stylistic contrast—Cresseid's lament and the lengthy planet portraits followed by the simple speech of the child, the elaborate and highly rhetorical "Complaint of Cresseid" followed by the stark address of the Leper Lady, and Cresseid's eloquent parting speech followed by Troilus's and the narrator's brief responses. In each case, the vision produced by the passages of extended high style dramatically is undercut, corrected, or qualified by the striking passages of plain style that follow. In the first instance, Cresseid turns to an expansive style to bewail the injustice of her plight:

> "Allace that euer I maid ȝow sacrifice!

> "ȝe gaue me anis ane deuine responsaill
> That I suld be the flour of luif in Troy,
> Now am I maid ane vnworthie outwaill,
> And all in cair translatit is my ioy.
> Quha sall me gyde? Quha sall me now conuoy,
> Sen I fra Diomeid and nobill Troylus
> Am clene excludit, as abiect odious?

> "O fals Cupide, is nane to wyte bot thow
> And thy mother, of lufe the blind goddes!
> Ye causit me alwayis vnderstand and trow
> The seid of lufe was sawin in my face,
> And ay grew grene throw ȝour supplie and grace.
> Bot now, allace, that seid with froist is slane,
> And I fra luifferis left, and all forlane."
> (126–40)

Her speech culminates in her elaborate eighteen-line vision of the gods that defines a universe both openly hostile and beneficient, one that at once confirms and denies Cresseid's view. In sharp contrast to these long series of stanzas is the strikingly simple speech of the child that follows:

> "Madame, ȝour father biddis ȝow cum in hy:
> He hes merwell sa lang on grouf ȝe ly,
> And sayis ȝour beedes bene to lang sum deill;
> The goddis wair all ȝour intent full weill."
> (361–64)

Innocently undercutting Cresseid's rhetoric, the child's words suggest that the gods are not to blame for Cresseid's plight, but rather it is the result of her own intent. In a similar manner, the elaborate seven-stanza "Complaint of Cresseid" with its rhetorical lament for her changed state is undercut by the response of the Leper Lady. Her terse speech suggests the inappropriateness of Cresseid's reaction and offers a more suitable response:

> Ane lipper lady rais and till hir wend,
> And said: "Quhy spurnis thow aganis the wall,
> To sla thy self and mend nathing at all?
>
> "Sen thy weiping dowbillis bot thy wo,
> I counsall the mak vertew of ane neid;
> Go leir to clap thy clapper to and fro,
> And leif efter the law of lipper leid!"
> (474–80)

Finally, Henryson closes the poem with the long speech and testament of Cresseid in which she comes to see her plight as the result of her own blindness and inconstancy. In this speech, Cresseid's style changes; it becomes plainer and less rhetorical and begins to point more directly to the "sentence" of the tale. The speech ends with the most extreme juxtaposition in the poem—abrupt silence as Cresseid dies. After a brief comment that suggests both his feeling for "fair" Cresseid and a clear recognition of her falseness, Troilus likewise takes refuge in silence: "Siching full sadlie [he] said: 'I can no moir; / Scho was vntrew, and wo is me thairfoir'" (601–2). Finally, the narrator steps forward, offers a brief parting remark, and then refuses to say anything more:

> Now, worthie wemen, in this ballet schort,
> Maid for ʒour worschip and instructioun,
> Of cheritie, I monische and exhort,
> Ming not ʒour lufe with fals deceptioun:
> Beir in ʒour mynd this sore conclusioun
> Of fair Cresseid, as I haue said befoir.
> Sen scho is deid I speik of hir no moir.
> (610–16)

As poet, he has encouraged the reader to see clearly, to cut through the "fals deceptioun" of language and life. Now he leaves the final resolution of "fairness" and "falseness" to us.

For the most part, in Henryson's work, the extreme juxtaposition of expansive and abbreviated styles is used to draw attention to the significance of his experience or the deliberate delusiveness of his rhetoric. Like the combination of fable and *moralitas*, Henryson's manipulation of styles encourages the reader to look beneath the surface of his language to its underlying meaning. It is only on rare occasions when language and meaning are in perfect correspondence, notably in prayer and in celebration, that Henryson introduces the ideal of high style without his characteristic undercutting. The most striking examples of this usage are found in two of the short poems, "The Annunciation" and "Ane Prayer for the Pest."[34] In both of these poems, Henryson builds carefully to a stylistic climax, a perfect moment of celebration and entreaty in which the narrator sees clearly the significance of his plight. The intricacy of linguistic and stylistic devices at the end of these poems, an extension of the techniques of Lydgate's aureate poems, reinforces rather than undercuts the intensity of the narrator's pleas. As the poet prays to God at the end of "Ane Prayer for the Pest," we momentarily transcend all oppositions of language and style:

> Superne lucerne, guberne this pestilens,
> Preserue and serue that we nocht sterf thairin,
> Declyne that pyne be thy devyne prudens,
> For trewth, haif rewth, lat nocht our slewth ws twyn;
> Our syte, full tyte, wer we contryt, wald blin;
> Dissiuir did nevir, quha euir the besocht
> But grave, with space, for to arrace fra sin;
> Lat nocht be tint that thow sa deir hes bocht!
> (65–72)

Although, in contrast to Chaucer, Henryson shares the fifteenth-century poets' conviction that poetry is ennobling and leads one to truth, he thus also reveals a keener sense of the poet's limits than these writers do. Like Books XIV and XV of Boccaccio's *De Genealogia deorum*, Henryson's writing defends poetry as *fabula* that conceals moral sentence beneath its pleasing surface. As Boccaccio explains:

"Fiction is a form of discourse, which, under the guise of invention, illustrates or proves an idea; and, as its superficial aspect is removed, the meaning of the author is clear."[35] Likewise, Henryson suggests both in the *Fables* and in the *Orpheus* that poetry hides under its "cloik" of fiction important doctrine.[36] But Henryson's position differs from Boccaccio's and the earlier fifteenth-century poets' in ways that are best suggested by his exploitation of the word "fenȝeit," which becomes an epithet for the fables and terms of poetry in his work. Unlike Boccaccio's recurrent metaphor of the "veil" that covers or protects the poet's meaning, Henryson's term "fenȝeit" has ambiguous connotations. The word in Middle English has both the meaning of something invented, fictitious, or created, and something that is designed to deceive, delude, or falsify.[37] In Henryson's view, unlike Boccaccio's, the surface of poetry is potentially deceptive. Readers must approach the poem as they do the world in an active effort to avoid being blinded by its appearance. The contradictory views of many of the tales, the abrupt shifts in style, and the recurrent tension in the *Fables* between tale and *moralitas* that has disturbed Henryson's critics actually becomes part of the poem's strategy. Like the "fenȝeit Foxe" with his dazzling ingenuity and wit, the surface of the *Fables* with its brilliant artifice and shifting perspectives may delude and distract us. Henryson, in fact, increases this possibility by his manipulation of his sources, characteristically reworking tales to place us in the position of the misguided characters within.[38] The surface of the "fenȝeit fabil" in Henryson's treatment is an image of the world itself with its "nets" and false pleasures, and our resource in dealing with both is "prudence," our response to the perspective of the blind beast.

"FRESCH ANAMALIT TERMES CELICALL"

In contrast to James and to Henryson who develop in different ways the fifteenth-century poets' assumptions about the usefulness of poetry, Dunbar, writing between c. 1490 and c. 1520, is less concerned with this issue than with the other important preoccupation of Lydgate's digressions on poetry, the process of "making" and the effect of the poet's craft. Like Lydgate, Dunbar begins by envisioning the poet essentially as an "enluminer" who transforms his matter with color and light. But in his writing he considers more precisely than Lydgate the way in which the poet acts upon the substance of the poem. Adopting the critical vocabulary Lydgate develops, Dunbar links and extends these terms to form a coherent metaphor for the poetic act by means of an analogy with the sun in the natural world. Like the sun which gilds and colors the landscape by its light and embellishes Nature, the poet illuminates his matter with the colors of his rhetoric. The effect of his craft, the application of color and light to the surface of the poem, is to transform his traditional matter and the impermanent event of the poem into an object or artifact that endures beyond the immediate occasion. In this process, Dunbar emerges not only as an illuminator but more precisely as an enameler who fashions an intricate surface of variegated colors that at once enhances and protects the underlying surface, the matter of the poem.

The view of poetry as a process of illuminating and enameling is developed in an extended form in Dunbar's famous dream vision, the "Goldyn Targe."[39] Unlike the majority of his poems which are occasional, the "Targe" commemorates neither a particular person nor event: instead it considers the relation between the poet and his matter that underlies most of Dunbar's other poems.[40] Dunbar's treatment of the theme of poetry in the "Targe" is a brilliant extension of the ideals inherent in the critical terms that Lydgate popularizes in English.

Although the "Targe" generally is viewed as an allegory of love in the tradition of the *Romance of the Rose* and Chaucer's early visions, Dunbar makes it clear that the poem will not be a conventional treatment of this matter. Curiously, he strips the love vision of its traditional advantages, particularly its striking psychological descriptions.[41] The poem has little exploration of the dreamer-narrator's state of mind. The garrulous Chaucerian narrator is conspicuously absent. The allegorical characters are introduced in rapid succession with little description or development. During the dream, sixty-eight figures are presented in the space of 107 lines and even the main characters of Beauty and Reason are sketched in only bare outlines:

> . . . first of all, with bow in hand ybent
> Come dame Beautee, rycht as scho wald me schent;
> Syne folowit all hir dameselis yfere,
> With mony diverse aufull instrument,
> Unto the pres, Fair Having wyth hir went,
> Fyne Portrature, Plesance, and Lusty Chere

Than come Resoun with schelde of gold so clere;
In plate and maille, as Mars armypotent,
Defendit me that nobil chevallere. (145–53)

The action itself is minimal, taking less than one fifth of the poem's
279 lines, and the dream ends abruptly without exploring the conflict
between Beauty and Reason. Although most critics agree that the
"Targe" represents a significant revaluation of its tradition, they have
not fully recognized the extent to which Dunbar employs his changed
matter and form to reconsider the nature of his poetic process. By
developing the structure of the dream vision as a triptych, Dunbar sets
up an analogy between the sun and the poet, the natural landscape and
the rhetorical that extends the implications of the view of poetry
suggested by Lydgate's terms.

In the first section of the poem, stanzas 1–5, Dunbar represents
the effect of the rising sun, "The goldin candill matutyne" (line 4), on
the landscape, emphasizing the various colors and hues created when
it illuminates the meadows below. The section begins in darkness as
Vesper and "Lucyne," the evening star and the moon, retire and
Phebus awakens. Faint hues appear in stanza 2 as Phebus greets
Aurora, the dawn, and begins to rise. In stanza 3, the sun shines its
full light on the landscape, transforming Nature into a richly enameled surface:

The rosis yong, new spreding of thair knopis,
War powerit brycht with hevinly beriall droppis,
    Throu bemes rede birnyng as ruby sperkis;
    The skyes range for schouting of the larkis,
The purpur hevyn, our scailit in silvir sloppis,
    Ourgilt the treis, branchis, lef, and barkis.
    (22–27)

In the second section, the dream, Dunbar establishes an implicit
analogy between the sun's effect on Nature and the poet's effect on his
matter, introducing parallels between the actual landscape of stanzas
1–5 and the poetic landscape of the vision by repeating lines from the
first section in the second. The first part ends with a description of
Flora's colored field; the second begins as the narrator falls asleep on
her mantle:

I saw approach, agayn the orient sky,
  A saill, als quhite as blossum upon spray,
  With merse of gold, brycht as the stern of day,
Quhilk tendit to the land full lustily,
  As falcoune swift desyrouse of hir pray. (50–54)

"Brycht as ther stern of day" (52) recalls the opening lines of the poem, "Rycht as the stern of day begouth to schyne, / Quhen gone to bed Vesper and Lucyne." The "mery foulys armony," in line 46 refers back to the description of the "mery foulis" song in stanza 1, while the "orient sky" (line 50) echoes the orient sky in stanza 5.

In stanza 2 of the dream, the analogy between Flora's meadow and the poet's is strengthened as Nature's colors are transferred to the dream figures. In the beginning of the stanza, the meadow still resembles the one in stanzas 1–5. The ship arrives "hard on burd unto the blomyt medis, / Amang the grene rispis and the redis" (55–56). But as the dream characters descend from the ship, they begin to merge with the natural landscape. In lines 58–61, for example, the one hundred ladies are described as May flowers that decorate the meadow:

Ane hundreth ladyes, lusty in to wedis,
Als fresche as flouris that in May up spredis,
  In kirtillis grene, withoutyn kepp or bandis:
  Thair brycht hairis hang gletering on the strandis. . . .

The relationship between the natural landscape and the landscape of the vision is further accentuated by the narrator's curious interruption in stanza 3 of the dream:

Discrive I wald, bot quho coud wele endyte
How all the feldis wyth thai lilies quhite
  Depaynt war brycht, quhilk to the hevyn did glete:
Noucht thou, Omer, als fair as thou coud wryte,
For all thine ornate stilis so perfyte;
  Nor yit thou, Tullius, quhois lippis suete
  Off rethorike did in to termes flete:
Your aureate tongis both bene all to lyte,
  For to compile that paradise complete. (64–72)

The sudden reference to Homer's "ornate stilis" and Cicero's "rethorike" draws our attention to the narrator's own poetic effort in the dream that follows. His artistic nervousness makes us conscious at the outset of his role in illuminating the matter of his vision. After the narrator's outburst, the natural landscape disappears completely and we view instead the dense and brightly colored surface of the allegory.

The final section of the poem, the narrator's reawakening (244–79) makes the implicit parallels between the sun and the poet, the natural landscape and the rhetorical landscape, explicit by applying the language used to describe the sun's effects to the poet's. Although Dunbar's praise of Chaucer, Gower, and Lydgate is conventional, it is loaded with echoes of stanzas 1–5 in this new context:

> O reverrend Chaucere, rose of rethoris all,
> As in oure tong ane flour imperiall,
> > That raise in Britane evir, quho redis rycht,
> Thou beris of makaris the tryumph riall;
> Thy fresch amamalit termes celicall
> > This mater coud illumynit have full brycht:
> > Was thou noucht of oure Inglisch all the lycht,
> Surmounting eviry tong terrestriall,
> > Alls fer as Mayis morow dois mydnycht? (253–61)

Like the sun which enamels the meadow with its light, Chaucer, the "lycht" of "oure Inglisch" enamels and illuminates the matter of his poetry. In a similar manner, Gower and Lydgate "ourgilt" our speech and illuminate our rude language. Without their "light," England would be bare and desolate of rhetoric and good writing:

> O morall Gower and Ludgate laureate,
> Your sugurit lippis and tongis aureate
> > Bene to our eris cause of grete delyte;
> Your angel mouthis most mellifluate
> Oure rude langage has clere illumynate,
> > And faire ourgilt our spech that imperfyte
> > Stude, or your goldyn pennis schupe to wryte;
> This ile before was bare and desolate
> > Off rethorike, or lusty fresch endyte. (262–70)

Continuing the analogy between the garden and the poem, Dunbar finally refers to his own "lytill Quair" as a garland bereft of all the "lusty rosis" of rhetoric and ends with a nice ambiguity on the word light, "Wele aucht thou be aferit of the licht" (279).

By reorganizing the dream vision in this manner, Dunbar thus explains the sense in which the poet "enlumines" his matter. While he adopts Lydgate's terms "enlumyn," "aureate," "goldyn" and "sugurit" to define the poet's effect on his matter, he links these terms by means of his analogy between the sun and the poet to form a coherent image of the poetic act. For Dunbar, as for Lydgate, the poet is essentially an illuminator who sheds light on his matter, creating a surface of splendid words and sounds. Good poetry is "illumynit full brycht" with "fresch anamalit terms celicall" (257–58). It is "ourgilt" (267) with fair speech and decorated with all the flowers of rhetoric. Bad writing is "bare and desolate / Off rethorike" (269–70) and devoid of poetic light. But by expanding the referent and correspondent of Lydgate's metaphor, Dunbar shows us in detail the gradual effect of the sun as its light hits the landscape, transforming it to a shimmering mosaic and, in the second section, the similar process of the poet adorning his verse with the light and colors of his rhetoric. In his poem, we witness the poetic process as he defines it and what had been a metaphor in Lydgate's hands becomes a reality before our eyes as Dunbar "enlumines" his vision.

Finally, Dunbar adds a pair of terms—"anamalit" and "ourgilt"—to Lydgate's coinages which point up some of the differences in the conceptions of the two poets and the directions in which Lydgate's ideal of poetic style develops in the period. Both of these terms derive from the language of the enameler's craft that flourished in the late Middle Ages. "Anamalit" refers specifically to the effect achieved when semitransparent or opaque mixtures of glass in various colors were applied directly to a metal surface and fused, creating a brilliant design in a hard veneer. Up until the end of the fifteenth century, enamels were executed in several different ways: the enamel was (1) inlaid in designs marked out by cloisonné or metal strips bent into a pattern; (2) embedded in spaces cut out of solid metal (champleve); (3) applied in a layer over gold ornaments in relief; or (4) applied like glass in windows in the interstices of outlines or frames in fine work or in bas-relief and often further embellished by inset jewels.[42]

In each case, the effect depends upon a skillful arrangement of color in perfect combination and proportion. The surface that results, in contrast to the surface of a painting, is unrivaled for its hardness and its dazzling exploitation of the possibilities of color created by the interplay of light reflected and refracted by the hardened variegated glass composition. Furthermore, the enamel design executed by these methods embodies an integral relationship between color and object as the tracery or outlines engraved in the metal provide a constant visual reminder of the underlying structure that the craftsman has embellished.

In the fifteenth century, the additional technique of painted enamel became popular. The entire surface of an object was covered with a thin layer of white enamel upon which a design was made and filled in with colored enamel set in juxtaposition. Often in the last firing the entire picture was covered or "ourgilt" with a fine layer of gold powder which gave the design added brilliance.[43] Significantly, during the same period, the term "ourgilt" became generalized in meaning in English and was used on many occasions as a synonym for "enameled," for example, in the following lines from the *Prick of Conscience* (c. 1425): "Alle þe turrettes of cristalle schene, / And þe wardes enamyld, and overgilt clene."[44]

Dunbar appears to be the first to apply these terms in Scots or in English to the poetic process.[45] Both terms suggest the way in which the poet's illuminating creates a tightly interlocked surface of words and sounds. The finished poem, in Dunbar's view, like the fine enamel is meticulously fashioned, "ourgilt" or overlaid with color to form a hard, brilliant exterior. The terms suggest that good poetry has a finely worked, jeweled quality that is not evoked by Lydgate's vocabulary. The surface fashioned by the poet is both dazzling and protective. While his enameling gives the poem a certain luster or splendor that impresses the reader, it also creates an immutable structure or artifact that survives beyond the immediate occasion of the lines. Like the enameling that enhances the structure to which it is applied, the poet's manipulation of color transforms the occasion of the poem, its underlying structure, into an event of permanence and value. The metaphor of enameling extends Lydgate's notion of "enlumyng" by defining more precisely the effects of the poet's "light" as it illuminates the variegated surface of the poem. Dunbar begins with Lydgate's description of good poetry; he then develops his terms to define an ideal that is more characteristic of his own work than of his predecessor's.

A few examples will illustrate the pervasiveness of the conception of poetry that Dunbar defines in the "Targe" in his own writing and its versatility in his hands. The official poem, "To Aberdein" (number

48), written after a visit of the Queen to praise the city for the
reception it accorded her, provides a good starting point. Dunbar
treats the poem, which contains a description of the processions and
pageants staged at the Queen's arrival, as an enamel or word painting
of the event. In describing the scene, he does not simply elevate his
style but he develops each stanza as an intricate design of words and
sounds, a finely crafted surface by means of his dense juxtapositions
of images, alliteration, internal echoing, and difficult rhyme scheme:

> Blyth Aberdeane, thow beriall of all tounis,
>> The lamp of bewtie, bountie and blythnes;
> Unto the heaven ascendit thy renoun is
>> Off vertew, wisdome, and worthiness;
>> He nottit is thy name of nobilnes
> Into the cuming of oure lustie quein,
>> The wall of welth, guid cheir, and mirrines:
> By blyth and blisful, burgh of Aberdein.
>
> . . . .
>
> Ane fair procession mett hir at the port,
>> In a cap of gold and silk, full pleasantlie,
> Syne at hir entrie with many fair disport
>> Ressaveit hir on streittis lustilie;
>> Quhair first the salutatioun honorabilly
> Of the sweitt Virgin guidlie mycht be seine,
>> The sound of menstrallis blawing to the sky;
> Be blyth and blisfull, burgh of Aberdein.
>> (1–8, 17–24)

Here, as in the "Targe," the poet functions like the experienced
craftsman to illuminate the matter of his verse and create a complex
pattern of color and imagery. The surface Dunbar fashions in "To
Aberdein" not only impresses our senses, but like a skillful enamel,
preserves the matter he embellishes in enduring form.

The same strategy of crafting a dense surface of tightly interlocked words and sounds is apparent in many of Dunbar's religious
poems of praise, for example, in the splendid Marian hymn "Ane
Ballat of Our Lady" (number 2). In this poem, Dunbar uses not only
imagery, alliteration, and rhyme, but also assonance, newly coined
aureate words, and an intricate metrical scheme to create an impressive celebration of Mary:

Hale, sterne superne; hale, in eterne,
    In Godis sicht to schyne;
Lucerne in derne for to discerne
    Be glory and grace devyne
Hodiern, modern, sempitern,
    Angelicall regyne:
Our tern inferne for to dispern
    Helpe, rialest rosyne.
Ave Maria, gracia plena:
    Haile, fresche floure femynyne:
ӡerne us guberne, virgin matern
    Of routh baith rute and ryne. (1–12)

In lines like "Hodiern, modern, sempitern," Dunbar experiments with his language, juxtaposing three startling terms which he joins to the rest of the stanza by a demanding repetition of sounds. The effect is to create a brilliant surface, the poetic counterpart of the bright veneer of the enamel. Transformed by the poet's effort, the poem becomes a tangible tribute to Mary.

The relation between the poet and his matter described in the "Targe" is not limited to Dunbar's high style, but it underlies most of the important stylistic modes of his work. Although Dunbar's vernacular style differs from poem to poem, the premise about the poetic process introduced in the "Targe," that poetry is a process of illuminating and enameling the surface of the poem, is common to most of Dunbar's works. Two examples, "Complaint to the King" and "The Tretis of the Tua Mariit Wemen and the Wedo" (numbers 45 and 14), illustrate the pervasiveness of the view of poetry developed in the "Targe" in the satires, humorous narratives, and complaints. In the "Complaint to the King," as in the more famous "Flyting," Dunbar adopts the enameled surface of the secular and religious panegyrics for the purpose of insult rather than praise. In the first section of the poem, he criticizes the injustice done to noble and well-educated men who are passed by while unqualified subjects are rewarded. As he lashes out against these subjects in the second part of the poem, he creates an intricate pattern of images and sounds, transfixing his enemies in the hard surface of his verse:

    . . . fowll, jow-jowrdane-hedid jevillis,
  Cowkin kenseis, and culroun kevellis;

Stuffettis, strekouris, and stafische strummellis,
Wyld haschbaldis, haggarbaldis, and hummellis,
Druncartis, dysouris, dyvowris, drevellis,
Mysgydit memberis of the Devillis;
Mismad mandragis off mastis strynd,
Crawdones, couhirttis, and theiffis off kynd. . . .
(15-22)

By means of his conspicuous alliteration, internal echoing, wordplay, striking coinages, and recurrent rhyme, he locks each word into place. Although the colors of the "Complaint" are harsher than those of the works of high style, the poetic principle is the same—the formation of an intricately wrought surface of words and sounds to preserve the event in a more enduring form.

Finally, in "The Tretis of the Tua Mariit Wemen and the Wedo," Dunbar takes advantage of the enameled surface for ironic effects.[46] He first presents an ornate and elaborate picture of the three "ladies" that stands out from the rest of the poem in its decorousness:

I saw thre gay ladies sit in ane grene arbeir
All grathit in to garlandis of fresche gudlie flouris;
So glitterit as the gold wer thair glorius gilt tressis
Quhill all the gressis did gleme of the glaid hewis,
Kemmit was their cleir hair and curiouslie sched
Attour thair schilderis down schyre, schyning full bricht,
With curches cassin thair abone of kirsp cleir and thin.
Thair mantillis grein war as the gress that grew in May
    sessoun.
Fetrit with thair quhyt fingaris about thair fair sydis . . .
(17-25)

Here, as in the "Targe," Dunbar borrows nature's colors to adorn his characters. The ladies are covered with the green, gold, and fresh hues of the May meadow. The gilt and splendor of the appearance, moreover, are accentuated by the conspicuous alliteration of "g" sounds in the beginning of the passage.

In the body of the poem, however, Dunbar undermines the expectations built up by the enameled style of the frame. As he allows us to see behind the glittering enamel of the opening verses, we witness a scene that is incongruous with the splendid appearance of the women.

In contrast to their outward beauty, the women are shrewd, vigorous, and even crude as they discuss the unsatisfying realities of their marriages:

> Though 3e as tygris be terne, be tretable in luf
> And be as turtoris is your talk though 3e haif talis brukill;
> Be dragonis baith and dowis ay in double forme
> And quhen it nedis 30w onone note baith ther strenthis;
> Be amyable with humbel face as angellis apperand
> And with a terrebill tail be stangand as edderis. . . .
> (261–65)

The ladies' bawdy style is the polar extreme of the idiom of the courtly dame. The contrast between frame and vision of the "Tretis" gradually defines a larger thematic opposition in the poem between what people appear to be and what they are, between the illusions of love and the actual situation, and finally between two opposing views of life. In contrast to "To Aberdein" and the "Ballat" where the "anamalit" style is used without qualification, the juxtaposition of enameled surface and bawdy subsurface of the "Tretis" underscores both the poet's power to enhance his matter and render it enduring by means of his craft and his role in translating one vision of reality into another.

The process of creating an enameled surface to transform the poet's matter has further implications for Dunbar's occasional poems. Like Lydgate, Dunbar develops this form considerably in the vernacular, turning to the occasional poem in approximately half of the works in his canon. In these poems, he treats the event or occasion as the substructure to which the colors of rhetoric are applied. Just as the process of enameling gives the metal to which the molten colored glass is fused a certain luster or splendor and enhances its value, the poet, by his "enameling," makes the underlying event of the poem more permanent and valuable. Like the artisan, the poet gives his matter brilliance and resiliency and finally creates an object that survives beyond the immediate occasion of the lines. Dunbar's metaphor thus makes explicit the positive effect of the occasional poet's role in transmuting impermanent matter into enduring form and suggests the increased significance of this genre in his hands.

A good example of the relation between Dunbar's stylistic strategy as an occasional poet and the enameler's craft is provided by "The

Ballade of Lord Bernard Stewart Lord of Aubigny," apparently written as part of the official reception for Lord Stewart when he arrived in
Edinburgh on May 9, 1508. The poet welcomes Lord Stewart as the
epitome of knightly virtues, the helper of Scotland, and commemorates his valiant deeds in service against the nation's enemies. But in
praising Stewart, Dunbar overlays the temporal event of his arrival
with an elaborate arrangement of words and sounds. In the opening
stanza, he employs the stylistic devices of the "Ballat of Our Lady"—
the dense alliteration, the internal echoing, repetition, and wordplay—hailing Stewart as "Renownit, ryall, right reverend and se-
rene / Lord, hie tryumphing in wirschip and valoure, / Fro kingis
downe most Cristin knight and kene" (1–3). In stanzas 2–4, he adds
the refrain "welcum" to his design, framing each of Stewart's attributes with this verbal repetition. The event becomes part of a large
design as Dunbar translates Stewart's achievements into a series of
conspicuously crafted stanzas interlaced by a refrain:

> Welcum, in were the second Julius,
>> The prince of knightheyd and flour of chevalry;
> Welcum, most valyeant and victorious;
>> Welcum, invincible vistour moste wourthy;
>> Welcum, our Scottis chiftane most dughti;
> Wyth sowne of clarioun, organe, song and sence
>> To the atonis, Lord, Welcum all we cry;
> With glorie and honour, lawde and reverence. (17–24)

Finally, Dunbar concludes with the most intricate stanza, an anagram
on Stewart's name, stylistically the climax of the poem's process of
translating event into artifact, a concrete representation of the man
and his attributes:

> B   in thi name betaknis batalrus
>> A   able in feild, R   right renoune most hie;
> N   nobilnes   and A   for aunterus,
>> R   ryall blude; for dughtines   is D;
>> V   valyeantnes, S   for strenewite:
> Quhoise   knyghti name   so schynyng in clemence
>> For wourthines in gold suld written be
> With glorie and honour, lawde and reverence.
>> (89–96)

Dunbar's conception of the poet as an "enameler," thus, implies a certain intricacy of form and a perfection of craft that is not emphasized by Lydgate's terms. Most of his poems are to some extent about the poet's ability to transform matter into verse and the poet's display of his craft often is more important than the underlying themes.[47] The matter becomes significant primarily as the poet-artisan gives it new brilliance and resilience through his "enameling." A striking example of this characteristic of Dunbar's work is found in his treatment of the stylistic devices he borrows from Lydgate. Although the two poets rarely are considered together, Lydgate's innovations, though not always successful, appear to have served as a catalyst for Dunbar's experimentation in some of his best poems. Two seemingly unrelated poems, Dunbar's "Ane Ballat of Our Lady" and the ending of his "Thrissil and the Rois," illustrate the way in which his poetic imagination operates, his characteristic technique of seizing upon a device of another poet and pushing it to its conceivable limits, in this case simultaneously in religious and secular terms. In both poems, Dunbar's extreme extension of Lydgate's aureate medium and his conspicuous emphasis on his craft draw attention to the underlying relation between poet and matter, giving his traditional celebrations new significance.

The inspiration for both of the Dunbar poems actually comes from Lydgate's Marian lyrics, particularly his "Ballat of Our Lady" and "Ave, Jesse Virgula." In the case of "Ane Ballat of Our Lady," the connection is well established in terms of similar excesses of aureate diction, the common refrain, and repetitive address to the Virgin.[48] But the link between these poems goes beyond the noticeable verbal connections to a larger strategy that Dunbar and Lydgate share. As we have seen at the outset of the "Ballat," Lydgate draws attention to this strategy as he defines his attempt to create a new poetic medium capable of expressing the unsurpassed praise of Mary (see discussion in chapter 2). The body of the poem is a magnificent example of his effort, a celebration of the Virgin in a style distinct from that of the "olde poets" of stanza 1, the poets of love. Repeatedly, as we have seen, Lydgate attempts to extend the Latin rhetorical traditions in which he works and create a style more dazzling than any before him by amassing striking images, epithets, and allusions, elaborate coinages from Latin, aureation, and an intricate combination of rhyme and alliteration. The first stanza with its striking use of language is typical of Lydgate's "redressed" style:

> O sterne of sternys with thi stremys clere,
> > Sterne of the see [on]-to shipmen lyght and gyde,
> O lusty lemand, moost plesaunt to appere,
> > Whos bright bemys the clowdis may not hide,
> O way of lyfe to hem þat goo or ride,
> > Haven aftyr tempest surrest as to ryve,
> > On me haue mercy for thi Ioyes fyve. (22–28)

In "Ane Ballat of Our Lady," his unique celebration of Mary, Dunbar takes the strategy of Lydgate's Marian lyrics to its absolute limits, placing an even greater emphasis than Lydgate does on the poet's role in transforming his matter into poetry. In effect, Dunbar begins where Lydgate leaves off. While he adopts the medium Lydgate develops, he makes several changes to produce a much more elaborate design of words and sounds. In the first place, Dunbar extends Lydgate's ballad stanza to a more difficult twelve-line stanza of alternating long and short lines. Within this scheme, he adds a complicated pattern of internal rhyme, alliteration, and verbal echoing, repeating, for example, the same sounds three times in lines 1, 3, 5, 7, and 11 of each stanza. Likewise, he experiments more boldly with aureate terms, reinforcing the impact of his striking language with internal echoing and alliteration. The effect of his changes is to produce an even more impressive tribute to Mary:

> Haile, bricht be sicht in hevyn on hicht;
> > Haile, day sterne orientale;
> Our licht most richt in clud of nycht
> > Our dirknes for to scale:
> Hale, wicht in ficht, puttar to flicht
> > Of fendis in battale;
> Haile, plicht but sicht; Hale, mekle of mycht;
> > Haile, glorious Virgin, hale
> > > Ave Maria, gracia plena:
> > Haile, gentill nychtingale;
> Way stricht, cler dicht, to wilsome wicht
> > That irke bene in travale. (25–36)

Lydgate's effort to develop a new medium in English worthy of
Mary's glory appears to underlie Dunbar's experimentation in "Ane
Ballat of Our Lady," but ultimately Dunbar creates a poem that is
more daring and effective and even more conspicuously crafted than
Lydgate's.

Characteristically, Dunbar also transforms the strategy of Lydgate's Marian lyrics to make it suitable for a very different kind of
purpose. A good example of his method is found in his famous
celebration of James IV and Margaret Tudor in the "Thrissil and the
Rois." While the body of this poem is derived from the dream vision
tradition, particularly from Chaucer's *Parliament of Fowls,* the magnificent song to Margaret Tudor at the end of the poem appears to be
modeled on Lydgate's celebrations of Mary.[49] Skillfully, Dunbar
adapts the same techniques, the recurrent invocation, the elaborate
wordplay, the pronounced alliteration, and internal echoing to create a
secular version of Mary's praise:

> . . . Haill be thow richest Ros
> Haill hairbis empryce, haill freschest quene of flouris;
> To the be glory and honour at all houris.
>
> . . . .
> . . . Haill, Rois, most riche and richt
> That dois up flureis undir Phebus speir;
> Haill plant of 30wth, haill princes dochtir deir;
> Haill blosome breking out of the blud royall,
> Quhois pretius vertew is imperiall. (159–68)

With a touch of wit, Dunbar turns many of the same images to his new
purpose—the "richest Ros," the "hairbis empryce," the "freschest
quene of flouris"—and in the line "Haill blosome breking out of the
blud royall," he even cleverly adapts the symbol of Mary giving birth
to the fleur-de-lis to Margaret Tudor. Thus, although seemingly unrelated, Dunbar's "Ane Ballat of Our Lady" and the end of his "Thrissil
and the Rois" both are inspired by the same source, Lydgate's Marian
lyrics. But Lydgate repeats the strategy he develops over and over
again—it underlies more than half of his Marian lyrics—whereas
Dunbar extends his techniques in two supreme examples, one religious and one secular.[50]

The two poems illustrate the way in which Dunbar develops
Lydgate's conception of the poet as an "enluminer," casting into a

new light a whole poetic tradition. Shifting his metaphor from illumination to enameling, Dunbar places more emphasis than Lydgate
on the poet as a "makar" whose craft gives the matter of the poem a
new brilliance and resiliency. Although both Lydgate and Dunbar
draw an analogy between their activities and the sun's, Dunbar's
metaphor concentrates on the way in which the poet's "light" is
reflected and refracted by the intricate design of words and sounds
fashioned on the surface of the poem. The application of rhetorical
color and sound to matter, a process analogous to the enameler's
application of color to the metal substructure, transforms the underlying occasion into an object of permanance and value. For Dunbar, the
poet's artistry is paramount and, as in the "Ballat" and the "Thrissil
and the Rois," his treatment of style underscores the poet's role in
giving traditional matter an enduring form and significance.

James I, Henryson, and Dunbar, like Lydgate, reaffirm the power
of poetry to order and ennoble humanity, to reassert the values of the
realm, and to interpret experience and transmute it into an enduring
form, yet each poet qualifies the view of poetry embodied in Lydgate's writing—James by his notion of governance, poetically as well
as morally, Henryson by his reconsideration of the Chaucerian dilemmas about the truthfulness of poetry and by his view of the
ambiguous surface of the poem, and Dunbar by his extension of
Lydgate's notion of the poet's illuminating and by his even more
extreme innovations in craft. Linked to these shifts in vision are the
particular stylistic solutions of the Scots poets—James's masterfully
governed and controlled style, Henryson's extreme juxtaposition of
styles, and Dunbar's striking stylistic experimentation and virtuousity. The styles of these poets are emblems both of their views of the
poetic process and of their efforts, like the fourteenth-century English
poets, Chaucer, Langland, and Gower, to create a vernacular of
significant literary value. The courts of James III and James IV in
Scotland, like the courts of Edward III, Richard II, and Henry IV
earlier in England, witnessed a vigorous growth of sophisticated
poetry in the vernacular, familiar with but distinct from the native
popular tradition. In several of his poems, Dunbar acknowledges this
development, presenting himself as a Scottish poet working within
his own native idiom and form. In "To the King" (number 42), for
example, he sets up a contrast between the "pyat withe the pairtie
cote" who "feynʒeis to sing the nychtengale note" and the native

birds like himself. Again, in the "Remonstrance to the King" (number 44), he notes the value of his Scots medium, its durability and resistance to "roust, canker, or corruption."[51] In this climate of a renewed awareness of a developing literary vernacular in Scotland, as in England, the relation among poet, audience, and text becomes a major thematic concern of the poems. The contribution of the Scots "makaris" to the ongoing dialogue among poets within the vernacular poetry of the period is developed with even greater theoretical vigor in the writing of Gavin Douglas and finally is absorbed again by the English poets of the courts of Henry VII and Henry VIII at the turn of the century. Contrary to the view that poetic influences traveled only in a northerly direction in the fifteenth century, the poetics of the Scots "makaris" had an impact on the discussions of poetry that emerge in the poems of Hawes and Skelton.

our

"The Man, the Sentence, and the Knychtlyke Style"

The conceptions of poetry and the ideals of poetic style defined by Lydgate and the Scots are placed in a larger context in the poems of Gavin Douglas at the end of the period. In both the *Palice of Honour* and the *Eneados* translation, Douglas treats the recurrent fifteenth-century conceptions of poetry as an aspect of the quest for a good life, the struggle to attain honor and virtue in the world. The poet's effort to illuminate matter by means of rhetoric and eloquence becomes for Douglas an image of the attempt to achieve moral goodness and honor. His progress as poet from conflict, doubt, and uncertainty to renewed creativity and confidence in the power of poetry is linked on a large scale to the journeys of the heroes within the poems. Particularly in the *Eneados* translation, Douglas represents the narrator's quest as poet-translator as a reflection of the central struggle of Aeneas to overcome the obstacles that confront him and fulfill his destiny to found Rome. The "ryall" or "knychtlyke" style that Douglas develops in both works, in the broad meaning that it acquires of ideal poetic style and moral style, becomes the verbal counterpart or emblem of the two quests.

The relation between the poet's purpose and style and the quest for honor and virtue is first articulated in the *Palice of Honour* where it serves as the central theme of the poem.[1] The poem defines the development of the narrator as man and as poet from a state of conflict, despair, and poetic dryness to inner harmony, a devotion to honor, and restored poetic power. The experience of the narrator's renewal reveals an expanding vision of the purpose of poetry and a redirection of its styles to increasingly noble ends.[2] Structurally, Douglas draws attention to this process by the intricate design of the poem. In addition to the obvious divisions into a prologue and three parts and the movement from the Courts of Minerva, Diana, and Venus, to the Court of Poetry, and the Palace of Honour, he introduces a series of five lais, stylistically set off from the rest of the poem, and a corresponding series of garden scenes that demarcate significant stages of the narrator's journey. Like the *poemae* of Boethius's *Consolation,* the lais and the garden scenes epitomize the changes in vision defined by the sections of interspersed action and debate. Finally, Douglas reinforces the poem's thematic development by a complex numerological design of stanzas and lines.[3]

Although it is impossible to consider Douglas's scheme in its entirety within the context of this chapter, two examples from the turning point and the conclusion of the *Palice* will illustrate his emphasis. The first scene, lines 772–1062, stands at the center of the poem and defines the important shift in the narrator's vision from the Court of Venus or Love to the Court of Rhetoric or Poetry. Before this point, the poet-narrator is in a state of inner dryness, out of harmony with himself and with the world and unable to find comfort from the traditional sources of wisdom, chastity, and love represented by the Courts of Minerva, Diana, and Venus. Stylistically, the narrator's first three lais, the opening lament for his loss of poetic power (91–99) and his complaints against Fortune and Venus (165–92; 606–36), disturb the order around him and reveal his lack of control over his medium as poet. Lines 722–1062 present the narrator's renewal, not through the choices afforded by the "garden of Pleasence"—wisdom, chastity, and love—but through the power of poetry, which Douglas indicates can restore one's wit and direct one to virtue. In contrast to the mutable Court of Venus, Douglas portrays the Court of Rhetoric as a constant source of comfort and pleasure, a court of "plesant steidfastnes" and "constant merines," a "facound well celestial" (837–

45). The tuneful music it produces is linked with the celestial harmony of the spheres and the narrator's restoration to its harmony at the end of the scene indicates allegorically his return to the larger order around him.

The shift from Venus to Calliope in lines 772–1062 also marks a redirection of the narrator's purpose as poet. In this scene, numerically at the center of the *Palice,* Douglas, like Lydgate in the "Ballat," calls for a new relation between the poet's style and subject distinct from that of the "olde poets," the poets of love. The poetry envisioned in this section is a

. . . Ioyous discipline,
Quhilk causis folk thair purpois to expres
In ornate wise, prouokand with glaidnes
All gentill hartis to thair lair Incline.
(846–49)

Its function is to inspire the expression of ideas in a special or heightened language; its effect to provoke the gentle heart or appropriate reader to its wisdom. In his link between purpose, style, and audience, Douglas extends the traditional combination of *dulce* and *utile* or mirth and doctrine to indicate more precisely the way in which the "ornate wise" or unique language of poetry mediates between sentence and audience and directs the reader to its meaning. As he comments in the catalogue of muses that follows, the most noble style for this purpose is the "kinglie stile" represented by Calliope, who

. . . of Nobill fatis hes the steir
To write thair worschip, victorie and prowes
In Kinglie stile, quhilk does thair fame Incres,
Cleipit in Latine Heroicus, but weir,
Cheif of all write like as scho is Maistres. (875–79)

This style, which celebrates the deeds of "Nobill fatis" and magnifies fame, most effectively draws together worthy audience and sentence and is the epitome of good poetry. The vision of the value and effect of poetry ends with the narrator's fourth lai (1015–44), an address to his "vnwemmit wit deliuerit of danger," which reveals his restored powers as a poet and his newfound order and harmony with the world.

The final section of the poem represents the fulfillment of the view of poetry defined at the work's center. The scene is prefaced in Part III with two visions that illustrate for the narrator the wrong way as poet—a hell-like picture of people suffering in pain, and a glimpse of the world as a stormy sea where the "gudelue Carwell" is tossed and ultimately wrecked. As the nymph explains, the people in the first version suffer because they merely pretend to honor but, in fact, follow pleasure, while those in the second "misknawis God" are guided by their own will. As poet, the narrator must turn from pleasure to something more enduring.

In direct contrast to these terrifying visions in the final section of the poem, Douglas introduces the dazzling sight of the Palace of Honour, the true object of the poet's attention. Allegorically, his treatment of the palace defines the poet's subject and purpose, the dedication to honor, which is not the questionable fame of Chaucer's vision, but enduring honor based on virtue. Unlike Chaucer's palace, Douglas's is set within a garden of pulchritude and perfection, a symbol of the reward of "hie honnour." Chaucer's House of Fame stands upon a rock of ice, "A feble fundament / To bilden on a place hye" (1132–33); Douglas's palace rests upon a hill of glass, a setting that is enduring and accessible only with great difficulty. Chaucer's description emphasizes the erratic and transient nature of worldly fame; the names of the famous people engraved in the hill of ice, for example, melt from the sun's heat on one side and remain undamaged on the other, the shaded side. Fame grants or rejects the petitions of the claimants according to her whim and without regard for their merit. Although the routes to Douglas's Palace of Honour differ, entrance is granted only to those who are worthy. In the outer section or "garth" (1466) the nymph shows the narrator those who have gained admission to the edge of the palace through love and then grants him a vision of the heroes of mythology and history, the subject of the muses who are assigned to the next closest area on the outside of the palace. Finally, she shows him a tabloid, carved on the gate of the palace itself of "all naturall thingis men may in eird consaue"—the elements, the spheres, the zodiac, the planets and their motions, the other important source of matter for the poet's art. The series of visions culminates with the view of the Court of Honour in the innermost hall of the palace, the "perfite Paradice" in contrast to the imperfect imitations of the earlier gardens. Enthroned in its midst is "ane God Omnipotent," that is, a god, or as the pun on "ane" suggests, the one God all powerful who is the supreme object of the poet's attention.[4]

But the narrator, still an apprentice who has been permitted only a glimpse of Honour through a "boir" (1903) or chink in the door, comically fails to understand the significance of his vision, and, overcome by the brilliance of the place, he falls into a swoon. As the nymph revives him, she teaches the narrator the proper end of his craft—honor to "this Heuinlie King"—which she distinguishes from all worldly activity or fame.

> "Honour" quod scho, "to this heuinlie King
> Differris richt far fra warldlie gouerning,
> Quhilk is bot Pompe of eirdlie dignitie,
> Geuin for estait of blude, micht or sic thing.
>
> . . . .
>
> For eirdlie gloir is nocht bot vanitie
> That as we se sa suddanelie will wend,
> Bot verteous Honour neuer mair sall end.
>
> . . . .
>
>   For vertu is a thing sa precyous
> Quhare of the end is sa delycious,
> The warld ma not consyddir quhat it is.
> It makis folk perfyte and glorious.
> It makis sancits of pepill vicious.
> It causis folk ay leue in lestand blys,
> It is the way til hie honour I wys."
> (1972–2005)

Part III closes with a final lai that links the narrator's style, subject, and purpose as a poet. In this lai, which he writes after his vision has ended, not as the naive poet-apprentice of the dream but as the narrator who looks back in retrospect and comprehends the significance of his experience, the concerns of the poem come together. The hymn, the most elaborate of the five lais, celebrates the "hie Honour" that is the object of the narrator's quest and the most appropriate to his poetry. Its style, an extension of the high style practiced by Lydgate and Dunbar, is characterized by an even more intricate arrangement of words and difficult rhyme scheme than we find in these poets' works, with increasingly intense internal echoes of two repeated sounds in

each line of the first stanza, three in each line of the second, and four
in each line of the last:

> Hail rois, maist chois til clois thy fois greit micht!
> Haill stone, quhilk schone vpon the throne of licht!
> Vertew, quhais trew, sweit dew ouirthrew al vice,
> Was ay, Ilk day, gar say, the way of licht.
> Amend offend, and send our end ay richt.
> Thow stant ordnat, as sanct, of grant maist wise,
> Till be supplie and the hie gre of price.
> Delite the tite, me quite of site to dicht,
> For I apply, schortlie, to they deuise. (2134–42)

The narrator's poetic skill, however, the theme of the lai makes clear,
is directed to the highest concern a poet might have, neither earthly
Fortune nor love, the concerns of the first four lais, but enduring
honor and virtue.

In the *Palice of Honour,* thus, Douglas views poetry as ennobling.
It revives the suffering narrator as the spring does Nature, puts him
back into harmony with the world, and leads him to honor more
effectively than the traditional paths of wisdom, chastity, and love.
His image of the gentle heart provoked to gladness and inclined to
"lore" by the poet's "ornate wise" sums up his view of the way in
which the elements of poetry work together. This conception, which
is introduced at the outset of Part II, is pivotal in the work's redefinition of poetry and marks a shift from the view of the poet as Love's
servant dominated by Venus in Part I to a higher form of poetry
represented by Calliope, the chief of the muses and the epitome of
noble poetic styles and subjects. The kind of poetry Douglas is
concerned with in the remainder of the *Palice of Honour* directs style,
subject, and audience to the goal of honor and is illustrated by the
progression of the poet-narrator's lais within the poem from the poetic
dryness of the first lai, to the uncontrolled complaints of the second
and third lais against Fortune and Love, to the renewed poetic control
in the fourth, his celebration of his revived wit, to a poetry that not
only is controlled but directs style, subject, and audience to the end of
virtue in the final lai. Likewise, the five garden scenes that punctuate
the poem emphasize the narrator's movement from a poetry linked
with love and pleasure to one directed to honor and virtue as he
progresses from the garden of pleasure of the prologue, to a hell-like

desert, the visual representation of his loss of poetic powers and the uncontrolled poetry of Part I, to the garden of the muses, the representation of the narrator's new poetic inspiration in Part II, to the garden that surrounds the Palace of Honour in Part III where he has a vision of the subject matter of poetry, to the garden of rhetoric, an image of the means to his end as poet. For Douglas in the *Palice of Honour,* the journey of the poet to restore his craft and the quest for honor and virtue finally converge.

THE *ENEADOS* PROLOGUES:
THE JOURNEY OF THE POET-NARRATOR

Douglas's translation of the *Aeneid* represents an extension of the views of poetry as a devotion to honor that he defines in the *Palice.* For Douglas, Virgil's work epitomizes the relation between subject, style, and audience that he introduces by his image of the gentle heart inclined to "lore" by the "ornate wise" of poetry in the *Palice.* As a poet-translator, Douglas experiments with the possibilities of realizing this ideal in English. His work, in the process, becomes not simply a rendering of the *Aeneid* from one language to another, but, to a certain extent, a new poem with its own audience, style, and significance. In the thirteen prologues that he adds to Virgil's text, Douglas draws attention to this shift in emphasis. Although the prologues rarely are considered together, when read sequentially as Douglas arranged them, they raise questions about the value of poetry and the relation of poetry to honor that are only partially considered in the *Palice.*[5] Together, the prologues define a journey of the narrator from conflict and doubt about his craft to restored poetic ability and a redirected style and purpose that is linked to the larger struggle of Eneas, the good man within the poem.

Prologue I, which serves as an introduction to the entire poem, outlines the terms of the narrator's conflicts. As poet-translator he lacks skill; next to Virgil's eloquent Latin, his own native Scots is deficient, and he wonders what justification he can find for so bold a venture. Second, the prologue raises the problem of the difficulty of poetry. Virgil's text is "sle"; his meaning is often obscure, and, in translating, the narrator worries how he can avoid the distortions of Caxton and even Chaucer who misrepresent Virgil's sense. Finally, the prologue questions the value of poetry for a Christian audience, acknowledging that Virgil's narrative often appears to conflict with Christian doctrine.

Douglas's response in the thirteen prologues is a defense of poetry. Following the discussions of Boccaccio, Dante, John of Salisbury, Augustine, and the medieval commentators on the *Aeneid,* he begins with a familiar justification of poetry as allegory that hides important truths under a garment of fiction (Prol. I, 193 ff.). But as Douglas proceeds to link his native Scots to his defense of his activities as poet, he adds an element that is new. Scots, though "braid and plain," has the virtue of clarifying Virgil's difficult passages and directing Douglas's new audience to the sentence of the text. It enables him as translator not to copy Virgil's excellence, an impossible task, but by uncovering his meaning, to make the greatness of the poem manifest. In his decision to translate after the sentence rather than according to Virgil's exact words, a method that is unusual for the time, Douglas also provides a resolution to his third dilemma.[6] The effect of his method will be to counter the objections about Virgil's pagan matter and point of view, for when the *Aeneid* is rendered in its entirety with careful attention to the sentence, Douglas demonstrates, it does not contradict Christian doctrine. At the end of the first prologue, he shifts his attention from Virgil to another "prynce of poetis," God, indicating that the translation is Christian in its inspiration and is directed in his own medium to an audience different from Virgil's.

The next five prologues (II–VI) define more explicitly the relation between the narrator and text that underlies the *Eneados.* Virgil's poem represents the conflict between the successful working out of historical destiny, and the personal happiness and inclinations of the individual. Douglas, in these prologues, approaches the matter of the *Aeneid,* Books I–VI, as an example of the ephemeral nature of worldly experience. The prologues, which progress from life on earth to a vision of afterlife, describe an alternation on earth of joy and woe and a corresponding involvement in the world and a poignant recognition that its pleasures are transitory. For the poet-translator, the prologues define the task of celebrating temporal happiness without jeopardizing the eternal.

Douglas strategically groups the individual prologues to dramatize these themes. Each prologue concludes with a view of the imperfection of earthly pleasure, but the prologues alternate in their emphasis on the joy and the woe in the world. Prologue II, which introduces the book that will describe the fall of Troy, is dolorous. The poet appeals to the dark muse, Melpomone, and to Saturn, father of melancholy, to guide his "tragedy" and warns by his theme that "all erdly glaidness fynsith with woe" (Prol. II, 21). Prologue III, by contrast, suggests the wonder of the adventures the narrator will encounter, the richness of narrative event in the temporal world Virgil represents. The fourth prologue again emphasizes the narrator's perception of the imperfect nature of worldly bliss and its end in woe and pain as the text contrasts two kinds of love, love of "fragil flesh" that the story of Dido in the fourth book will illustrate, and the more enduring love of God. Returning to the nine-line stanza of Prologue III, the fifth prologue celebrates the variety and allure of earthly pleasure as the narrator catalogues the diverse human activities (Prol. V, 10–19) and praises the corresponding variety he finds in Virgil, whose style may be seen as an emblem of the plentitude of the world (Prol. V, 33–36). In sharp contrast, in the last stanza, the narrator reminds himself that "erdly plesour endis oft with sorow" and prays to God to teach him how to celebrate "temporal blythness" "That our eternale ioy be nocht the less!" (Prol. V, 68).

The sixth prologue suggests a partial resolution to the poet's dilemma as Douglas turns from the alternation of joy and woe in this life to the realm after death and begins to separate himself from Virgil. This prologue, which prefaces Aeneas's descent into the underworld, is a defense of the *Aeneid* as fable, particularly of the troubling sixth book. Following the major medieval commentators, Douglas argues that Virgil's poem describes "the stait of man" if understood correctly. While the first five books represent "baith lif and ded," the sixth reveals the consequences of life on earth, the rewards of sin and virtue. In it one sees clearly the significance of the poem as an allegory of human life and the way in which Virgil, though pagan, anticipates Christian doctrine. Douglas follows Servius, Ascensius, and Landino in these views, although he makes more explicit in his defense of Book VI the power of poetry to go beyond the original sentence of an author and produce new meaning for later audiences.[7] Returning to his own struggle as poet, he makes a corresponding adjustment in vision. As he ventures, like Aeneas, into the unknown—a realm where past, present, and future meet and where one sees more clearly the significance of events—he symbolically parts company with Virgil. In an association that apparently is original with Douglas, the narrator turns from Aeneas's "Sibilla Cumane" to another sibyl, Mary, "Quha bettir may Sibilla namyt be" (Prol. VI, 140–41) to distinguish the course he will follow as a Christian poet.

Prologue VII not only is the numerical center of the work, but it represents a turning point for the narrator as poet just as Book VI, the center of Virgil's poem, marks a change in direction for Aeneas. After the waiting of the first five books and the vision of the sixth, Aeneas proceeds toward his goal in Books VII–XII. The narrator as poet makes a corresponding, though less direct, journey in the resolution of his conflicts in the remainder of the *Eneados* prologues. Although Prologue VII is most famous as one of the three nature prologues, it also represents the poet-narrator's inner state of mind by introducing a link between the natural scene, the matter of the *Aeneid,* and the poet's dilemma. Like the *Palice of Honour,* Prologue VII defines the movement from a hell-like external world and a corresponding poetic dryness to a more beneficent landscape and renewed poetic activity. Douglas, in fact, shifts the first twenty-four lines of Virgil's Book VII, which represent Aeneas still in the underworld, to the end of Book VI to underline this change.[8]

Prologue VII opens as the sun is about to set. The season is winter, "bittir, cald, and paill." As in the *Palice of Honour,* Nature takes on a hideous and unnatural form, reducing the world in the mind to "Gousty schaddois of eild and grisly ded" (Prol. VII, 46) and suggesting that, although the narrator has completed Book VI, poetically he has not emerged from his inner hell. When the narrator awakens as the sun rises, however, the atmosphere of the first half of the prologue gradually is dispelled. In the dawning sky, the narrator sees a sign, a flock of golden birds flying in the formation of a Y that is identified with the golden bough that insures Aeneas's return from the underworld.[9] This image dispels the poet's gloom and he rises, looks out, and finds the day "bla, wan, and har." As he regains his heat by the fire, he takes pen in hand and returns to his task of translating Virgil, resolving to put his neck to the "ʒok" and proceed at a good pace. Like the *Palice of Honour,* the winter prologue thus represents the renewal of the narrator "new cum furth of hell" and the recovery of his poetic powers.

Prologues VIII–XII first place the poet-narrator's conflicts in a new light and then define different aspects of a resolution. Prologue VIII translates the problem of the preceding prologues, the conflicting pulls of earthly and heavenly pleasures, into a larger context, raising the question of the value of poetry in a world that has gone awry. The prologue which stands out from all of the others by its alliterative style and dream vision form, the style and form traditionally associated with social satire, generally has been treated as a commentary on the times. But the prologue actually functions very much like the prologue to the central tale in Henryson's *Fables* in which the poet encounters his mentor, Aesop, who introduces significant questions about the power of poetry.[10] Like Langland in *Piers Plowman*, Douglas expands the medium of social satire to consider the enduring value of his activity as poet.

Douglas's prologue begins in Lent, traditionally a time for reflection. As the narrator rests in a sheltered place, he has a vision of a strange man who complains that the world is turned upside down; people are preoccupied by their desires and wickedness prevails (Prol. VIII, 79–91). Chiding the narrator for "Lurkand lyke a longeour," the strange man demands what sort of man he is, and, like Aesop in Henryson's prologue, questions the value of the narrator's endeavor. But Aesop had suggested that the world was so disordered and men were so sinful that poetry could have little effect; this strange man's reaction is even stronger: "Thy buke is bot brybry [wretchedness, triviality] said the bern than" (144). Promising to teach the narrator a lesson to ease his pain, the strange man gives him a roll on which is written all the movement of the earth, the planets, and the stars and the mysteries of life. But the narrator finds the gift only "rydlys," scorns the lesson, and, in response, the man shows him a hoard of coins that he eagerly begins to collect. When the narrator awakens, however, all of the wealth is gone and he angrily condemns dreams as "faynt fastasy."

The strange man's two lessons represent two choices or responses to the upside-down world and two matters for poetry—contemplation of God's workings or the pursuit of transitory concerns, the response of the majority of people in the world the prologue describes. The narrator, however, misses the point, both of the lessons and of the value of dreams, and, ironically, although he suggests that dreams contain no truth, Douglas changes Virgil to open Book VIII with a true dream in which the river god, Tiberinus, appears to Aeneas and prophesies the founding of the city of Alba. Finding his dream vain and seeking "nane other bute," the narrator returns to his writing, which Douglas implies might be a potential "bute" or remedy for the corrupt world the prologue describes if the slumbering poet would understand the strange man's lessons.

Prologues IX–XII reconsider the narrator's style, sources of inspiration, subject matter, and creative process. Whereas Prologue VIII concluded with the possibility of the book as "bute," Prologue IX opens with three stanzas in an explicitly moral style that suggest a remedy to the ills defined by Prologue VIII by directing the reader to follow virtue, to live honestly, and avoid idleness and duplicity. Curiously, however, the narrator suddenly interrupts himself, "Eneuch of this, we nedis prech na mor" (Prol. IX, 19) and introduces a very different style for his book in the remainder of the prologue, "the ryall style, clepyt heroycall" (Prol. IX, 21). Like Henryson who had hinted in his *Fables* that poetic style was a more effective response to the ills of the time than "haly preiching" (see chapter 3), Douglas implies by his contrast between moral and "ryall" styles in Prologue IX a similar choice of a poetic medium rather than an explicitly moral one as "bute."

But what does Douglas's phrase, the "ryall style, clepyt heroycall," mean? In the *Palice of Honour,* Douglas uses this terminology to describe the style assigned to Calliope, the chief of the muses, and to the best poets who write like her to narrate the "worschip, victorie and prowess" of "Nobill fatis" (847–49). In Prologue IX, he begins with a similar emphasis on this style as a vehicle of honor. "Ryall style" is "full of wirschip and nobilnes" (Prol. IX, 22), void of any base or empty terms. In other words, its content is honorable and morally above reproach. From this meaning, Douglas turns to style in the sense of literary effect, the second connotation of the term, and defines "ryall style" as one that avoids "all lowuess langage and lychtness" (25) and observes "bewte, sentens and grauyte" (26). Finally, he introduces a third aspect of the meaning of the phrase in terms of a correspondence between matter, language, and audience:

> The sayer eik suld weil considir thys,
> Hys mater, and quhamto it entitilit is:
> Eftir myne authouris wordis, we aucht tak tent
> That baith accord, and bene conuenient,
> The man, the sentens, and the knychtlyke stile. . . .
> (Prol. IX, 27–31)

The notion of adapting style to the subject and audience is common in classical and in medieval criticism with examples easily culled from Virgil, Horace, Geoffrey of Vinsauf, and later George Puttenham and Alexander Barclay.[11] Douglas, however, does not refer simply to the idea of decorum foremost in these passages, but, as he continues, to the way in which the poet's "ryall" style directs the audience to his sentence, or, as he had explained more succinctly in the *Palice of Honour,* to the way the "ornate wyss" or heightened language of poetry moves the "noble heart" or appropriate reader to its "lore" (835–79).

In contrast to Prologue IX, which defines the importance of the poet-narrator's redirected style, Prologues X and XI reconsider the source of his inspiration and the nature of his subject matter. Prologue X is an impressive celebration of the mysteries of the "plasmatour of thingis vniuersall" (1), the three-personed Christian God. Beginning with a tone of wonder reminiscent of the opening of Henryson's "Preaching of the Swallow," the narrator considers the artistry of God as a creator and orderer to govern the world, to control day and night and the orderly procession of seasons, and moves from these mysteries to the even greater one of God's three-personed nature and His supreme sacrifices for humanity. Contemplating the wonder of this act, he prays to God to give him the power "of this and all my warkis to mak gud end" (Prol. X, 149). With this prayer, which reapplies the language of Virgil's praise of Jupiter to the Christian God,[12] Douglas puts aside all other muses and turns to God alone as his source of inspiration, thus completing his separation as poet from his author Virgil:

From the behynnyng and end be of my muse:
All other Ioue and Phebus I refuss.
Lat Virgill hald hys mawmentss to him self;
I wirschip nowder ydoll, stok, nor elf,
Thocht furth I write so as myne autour dois.
(151–55)

Likewise, in Prologue XI, the narrator places the subject matter of his translation in an overtly Christian frame of reference. Redefining true chivalry as a battle against vice and a defense of virtue, rather than a struggle of man against man, Douglas suggests that we are to view the adventures of Aeneas, a type of Christ's more difficult struggle for our salvation, as an example of virtuous action for our own life (Prol. XI, 177–84). This larger struggle, he maintains, is the true subject matter of his poem.

The narrator's definition of the matter, style, and purpose of poetry culminates in Prologue XII, his celebration of spring. Like Prologue I, this prologue serves as more than just an introduction to a single book; it represents the completion of the entire poem as a creative act associated with the larger generative forces in the natural world. The prologue establishes a parallel between the daily renewal of life by the sun, the seasonal revitalization of spring, implicit signs of God's creative power, and the renewed effort of the poet-narrator. Like Dunbar's "Goldyn Targe," the prologue opens with a highly stylized description of the sun rising, describing as we move from night to dawn to increasingly intense light the dazzling and revitalizing effect of the sun's rays.[13] Inspired by the sun, Nature spreads her blooms with such plenitude that she creates a rich tapestry of colors and designs. Implicit in Douglas's description is the analogy with the similar activity of the poet. Prologue XII is Douglas's most conspicuously "poetic" prologue. Its diction is more noticeably aureate and crafted than in the earlier prologues; the lines more conspicuously echo literary models, and as Bawcutt points out, the natural world is repeatedly described in terms of imagery which suggests human artifacts.[14]

The second half of the prologue represents the spring season, like the sun, as a renewer of life and energy in the world. Douglas skillfully dramatizes this effect by the emphasis on procreation in the description of the animal world that follows as we move up the chain of being from plants to animals to man who is aroused by spring to love. The section ends, like Chaucer's *Parliament of Fowls,* with the impression of harmony as the birds sing in praise of May as a restorer of vitality. The last thirty-two lines of Prologue XII parallel the action of the preceding portions. Like the sun, the narrator rises and renews the life of his book, making the spring season a mirror of his own restored powers as poet. From the winter of Prologue VII, the Lenten season of Prologue VIII, and the conflicts of the earlier prologues, we move to a vision of renewed creative power and energy in Prologue XII and the completion of the narrator's undertaking as poet.

Prologue XIII forms a companion piece to the prologues in the *Eneados* proper. Although both Starkey and Bawcutt view this pro-

logue primarily as an elaborate justification for the inclusion of the
spurious thirteenth book of the *Aeneid,* the work of Maphaeus Vegius,
the prologue also introduces in different form many of the conflicts
central to Prologues I–XII.[15] But more important, the encounter
between Douglas and Maphaeus Vegius at its center, which recalls in
comic terms the similar confrontations of Henryson, Lydgate, and
Boccaccio in the *Fables,* the *Fall of Princes,* and *De Casibus,* raises a
final question that qualifies Douglas's resolution about poetry in Prologues I–XII.[16]

In response to Maphaeus's demand to translate his thirteenth book
of the *Aeneid,* Douglas reiterates the doubt that has echoed through the
prologues that the activities of the poet may be misspent time for a
Christian. Linking himself to Jerome, who was reproved for his poetry
in his famous vision, the narrator questions the usefulness of his
activity and the threat it poses to his own salvation:

> Full scharp repreif to sum is write, ȝe wist,
> In this sentens of the haly Psalmyst:
> "Thai ar corruppit and maid abhominabill
> In thar studeying thyngis onprofitabill":
> Thus sair me dredis I sall thoill a heit,
> For the grave study I haue so long forleit.
> (Prol. XIII, 125–30)

Maphaeus angrily chides the poet, reminding him of the moral value
of Virgil and his own Christian work, and then beats him, causing him
to awaken. The dream encounter, thus, serves as an emblem of the
dilemma that is central to the prologues—the value of poetry to a
Christian audience and the need for the poet to reconcile his artistic
and moral impulses to complete his poem, with Douglas taking the
skeptic's part and Maphaeus reiterating Douglas's earlier arguments
in defense of poetry. In spite of his redirected style, Christian inspiration and purpose, in his effort to be a good poet, Douglas repeatedly
must come to terms with this issue.

Prologue XIII, however, like the earlier ones that deal with these
questions, ends with a change in atmosphere and a renewed commitment to the poet's activity. In contrast to the sunset, the darkness, and
the repose of the opening of the prologue, the narrator awakens to a
new day. The "bissy lark," the harbinger of dawn, appears replacing
the bat, the creature of dusk prominent at the outset of the poem, and

awakens the world with its song. Silence and repose gave way to brilliant light and bustling activity as the day begins. The narrator, too, puts aside his doubts and returns eagerly to work, bringing his "ship" to "port" as he tells us in the *conclusio* "in sovir raid" or safe anchoring place after many storms and perils.

DOUGLAS'S "CRAFTY WARKIS CURYUS"

Although Douglas's thirteen *Eneados* prologues define a view of poetry that is linked to the fifteenth-century poets' conception of the poem as ennobling, a vehicle of truth, the prologues and the earlier *Palice of Honour* place this vision in several contexts that considerably broaden its significance. Douglas's change in focus is especially apparent in his exploitation of style, in his adaptation of the fifteenth-century critical vocabulary, and in his association of the poet's activities with the hero's. Like the fifteenth-century poets, Douglas indicates that it is the special or heightened language of poetry that draws attention to its sentence and makes it effective. But the fifteenth-century poets emphasize the poet's "enlumining," his ability to shed light on difficult matter and render it "aureate" and "goldyn"; Douglas is less concerned with the poet's elevation of style than with appropriate style as a mediator between audience and purpose. His purpose in turning to Scots is not only to make his native tongue equal to Virgil's Latin or to Chaucer's "Inglish," but to create a medium in Scots that is capable of the important role he envisions for style as the vehicle of the poem's sentence. In the *Eneados* prologues, he introduces an extreme variety of styles, each directed to a different purpose, which establish the range of possibilities of Scots as a purveyor of meaning. As we shall see, the significance of the literary language Douglas creates and its role as a mediator between audience and purpose is even more apparent in the *Eneados* translation where it often serves as a major indicator of the poem's new meaning.

The critical vocabulary that Douglas adds to the fifteenth-century terminology underscores this shift in emphasis from poetry principally as illumination to poetry as a process of mediation between audience and sentence. While Douglas follows his immediate predecessors in defining good poetry as "elloquent," "ornate," "full of rhetoric," "sweit," "sugarate," and "fresh," he adds to this cluster of terms an-

other set—"sle," "quaint," "curious," "derk," "crafty," "mysty,"
"cloudy"—which introduces an ideal of poetic difficulty absent in
the writing of the fifteenth-century poets. In his usage, these terms
define a positive ideal when applied to poetry and provide insight into
his attitude toward the poet's feigning. Before Douglas's time, one
finds only limited precedent in English for his positive exploitation of
the terms "sle," "quaint," "curious," "derk," "crafty," "mysty,"
"cloudy" to refer to poetry or speech. Generally, when the words
appear earlier in this context, they have negative connotations.[17]
Chaucer, for example, condemns the "double wordes slye" of Cal-
chas "Swiche as men clepen a word with two visages," and Henryson,
in the *moralitas* to the "Tale of the Paddock and the Mouse," warns us
to beware of "Ane wickit mynd with wordis fair and sle."[18] Chaucer
introduces the terms "crafty," "quaint," and "curious" to suggest the
overly subtle and hence potentially deceptive quality of poetry and
other arts, referring, for example, to the Canon's Yeoman's science of
illusion making as "crafty" and "queynte" (VIII [G] 752). Similarly,
Pandarus in teaching Troilus the art of letter writing warns him not to
write "scryvenyssh or craftily" (*Troilus and Criseyde*, II, 1026). The
term "derk" has even more negative connotations than "crafty" and
"queynte" in English before the fifteenth century. Chaucer, for example, introduces the word to define the "derk ymaginyng" on the wall
of the Temple of Mars in the *Knight's Tale* (1995), the "derke fan-
tasye" of the sorrowing Dorigen in the *Franklin's Tale* (844), and the
"clowdy and derk" thought of the deluded Boethius at the end of the
first book of the *Consolation* (Book I, metrum 7, 19–20).

During the fifteenth century, a change in emphasis occurs and
although the negative meanings persist, the words "sle," "quaint,"
"curious," "derk" and "crafty" also begin to appear with more
positive connotations.[19] In the first half of the century, the terms
"curious" and "crafty," for example, rather than suggesting a deceit-
ful or overly subtle quality, occasionally are introduced to draw
attention to the skillful, expert, or artistic nature of good speech or
poetry. At the outset of this period, Lydgate in the *Siege of Thebes*
praises Chaucer for the "crafty writyng of his sawes swete" (57) and
in the *Troy Book* refers to the noble stories that poets have "enlumyned with many corious flour / Of rethorik to make vs comprehende / The trouthe of al, as it was kende": (Prol., 218–20). John
Walton (c. 1450), likewise, admires the "subtle matere of Boethius,"

which he characterizes as so "hye," "so hard and curious," that it is elevated, difficult, and skillful.[20]

A more striking shift in meaning occurs in the use of the word "derk." Frequently paired with words like "hard" or "subtle," the term expresses an ideal of poetic excellence that generally is reserved for the most elevated of human experience or for divine poetry or song. At the end of the fourteenth century, for example, John Trevisa uses the term as a synonym for "figurative" and "mystic" to characterize the language used to refer to God: "Alle Godlich þinges þat beþ I seid of God haueþ figuratif mistik and derk menynge," and later in the same work, to the elusive meanings of dreams that sometimes are "I-wrappid in figuratif, mistik, and dym and derke to kenynges."[21] In a related sense, Lydgate occasionally uses the term to suggest the hidden meanings of poetry as he refers to Boccaccio in the *Genealogia* "Expownyng this derke poysye" (*Siege of Thebes*, 214). Finally, the term "derk" is introduced to define the figurative quality of scripture, particularly of the Psalms, which are praised as "ful derke in many a plae" and "derk and hard and not esli to be vnderstonde."[22]

In the *Eneados* prologues, Douglas draws together the positive meanings of the words "curious," "crafty," "mysty," "derk," sle" and "quaint," linking these separate terms to define an important ideal of good poetry, its difficulty. In his usage, the terms suggest the dense, figurative quality of poetry, its ability to embody more meaning than its surface reveals. In Prologue I, for example, Douglas praises Virgil for his "crafty warkis curyus" (11), "Sa quyk, lusty and maist sentencyus," complimenting both his stylistic skill and the depth of his sentence. Virgil's poetry is "sle" or elusive; it must be read more than once: "Consider it warly, reid oftar than anys / Weill at a blenk sle poetry nocht tayn is" (Prol. I, 107–8). Although poetry is "feigned" or fictional, it thus is not false:

> . . . vnder the clowdis of dyrk poecy
> Hyd lyis thar mony notabill history—
> For so the poetis be the crafty curys
> In similitudes and vndir quent figuris
> The suythfast materis to hyde and to constreyn;
> Al is nocht fals, traste weill, in cace thai feyn.
> (Prol. I, 193–98)

The poet's "feigning," the application of "crafty curys" and "quent figuris" to "suthfast materis," rather than being deceptive, challenges the perceptive reader to discover the poem's full meaning. Like Douglas's more obvious use of style itself, the "sle," "quaint," "curious" and "derk" surface of good poetry mediates between the audience and the purpose, the "man" and the "sentence."

In his emphasis on the "derk" and "crafty" nature of the good poem, Douglas transfers ideals from several traditions to the context of contemporary discussions of poetry. The conception of poetic difficulty was an important aspect of medieval discussions of poetry as early as the fifth century where it figured prominently in the writing of the Church Fathers, particularly Augustine upon whom Douglas draws in other contexts. In *De Doctrina Christiana,* Augustine considers the deliberate obscurity of scripture and defines a new basis of aesthetic pleasure that is distinct from classical notions. The words of scripture, and, by extension, of poetry, are signs for meanings that are contained beneath the surface of the poem. The process of penetrating this shell of figurative language to discover the sweet kernel of meaning beneath requires considerable effort on the part of the reader, which in turn produces a unique kind of pleasure. In a particularly striking passage on the Song of Songs, Augustine describes this process:

> . . . why is it, I ask, that if anyone says this he delights his hearers less than if he had said the same thing in expounding that place in the Canticle of Canticles where it is said of the Church as she is being praised as a beautiful woman "Thy teeth are as flocks of sheep, that are shorn, which come up from the washing, all with twins, and there is none barren among them?" Does one learn anything else besides that which he learns when he hears the same thought expressed in plain words without this similitude? Nevertheless, in a strange way, I contemplate the saints more pleasantly when I envisage them as the teeth of the Church cutting off men from their errors and transferring them to her body after their hardness has been softened as if being bitten and chewed . . . no one doubts that things are perceived more readily through similitudes and that what is sought with difficulty is discovered with more pleasure.[23]

Augustine's conception of the difficult surface of scripture and the importance of its figurative language had far-reaching implications for the treatment of poetry in the early Middle Ages and is reiterated in various forms in the major treatises on poetry.

With the rise of vernacular literature in the twelfth century, a new ideal of poetic difficulty evolved, at first secular in nature in the writings of the troubadours and then gradually broadened in the poetry of Dante and his successors. In its most extreme form, this ideal is manifested in the *trobar clos* of the Provencal poets, where deliberate obscurity of language and metaphor is sought, creating poems that at times are impenetrable.[24] Dante, who cites the efforts of these poets in Book II of *De Vulgari eloquentia* as examples of effective vernacular style, develops the implications of their practices into a more significant poetics.[25] In *De Vulgari eloquentia,* he establishes the vernacular as a literary language and defines a new conception of poetic style, which as Auerbach points out, differs significantly from ancient elevated style by its emphasis on two qualities—its "sweetness" and its "difficulty."[26] By an important transformation, the phrase "dulcius subtliusque," which embodies these concepts, shifts in meaning from the terms' ancient use, "sweet" and "refined," to their more resonant meanings in Dante where "subtilis" takes on the connotations of "significant," "difficult to understand," "obscure," similar to Douglas's term "derk," and "dulcius" begins to suggest a more ardent, intense quality than it had in classical usage.[27]

Equally relevant to Douglas's ideal of poetic difficulty is a third tradition represented by the numerous commentaries on the *Aeneid* that span the Middle Ages from the fourth to the sixteenth centuries. In these works, Douglas found articulated the conception of poetry that his critical terms describe as a dark and mysterious surface under which important truths are hidden. Macrobius first suggests this view in his commentary on the *Aeneid* in the *Saturnalia* as he defends Virgil as a poet who conceals important meanings in his "images and examples."[28] In the fourth century, Servius describes Virgil's poem as one that "contains truth with fiction" ("Continens vera cum fictis"), and, near the outset of his account, he introduces the term "polysemus" into the Latin vocabulary of the commentators to emphasize the difficult and many-layered nature of Virgil's works.[29] Fulgentius, in the next century, similarly, describes Virgil's words as "so bestrewn with mystical matters that in them Virgil has concealed the innermost profundities of almost every art."[30] Extending these views, Bernardus Silvestris in his famous *Commentum super sex libros Eneidos Virgili* distinguishes between the difficult outer surface of Virgil's poetry and the inner truth that it contains, arguing that his fiction does not neglect the truths of the philosophers.[31]

In his defense of poetry, Douglas draws upon the more recent commentaries of the Italian humanists Petrarch, Christoforo Landino, and Badius Ascensius. Anticipating Douglas's image of the cloudy surface of the poem, Petrarch's character of Augustine in the second dialogue of the *Secretum* observes in response to Petrarch's allegorical reading of the *Aeneid,* "Among the clouds themselves you have clearly discerned the light of truth. It is in this way that truth abides in the fictions of the poets, and one perceives it shining out through the crevices of their thought."[32] Similarly, Landino proposes to uncover in his commentary what has been darkened by "the style and figure of allegory," arguing that the reader of the *Aeneid* comes to a knowledge of "high hidden matter."[33] Although in the context of these traditions, Douglas's view of poetry as "derk," "curious," and "sle" is thus not markedly original, his discussions are important in adapting this vision to the fifteenth-century conceptions of poetic excellence. By shifting the emphasis from the poem's "enlumined" surface to its underlying meaning, the critical terms that he brings together expand and qualify the focus of the fifteenth-century vocabulary.

Finally, Douglas places the ideals of poetry he defines in the larger context of his conflicts as a Christian poet. In the *Palice of Honour,* he envisions the quest of the poet as an aspect of the more significant human journey in search of honor and virtue, which he describes ultimately as distinct from worldly fame and directed to the worship of the heavenly king. In the *Eneados,* the prologues represent the gradual separation of the narrator as a Christian poet from his model, Virgil, and his recurrent conflict about the value of poetry and the importance of his task. Skillfully, reapplying Virgil's conceptions and even at times his words, Douglas develops a new source of inspiration, subject, style, and purpose that contrasts with Virgil's and qualifies his story. His concern adds a dimension to the fifteenth-century discussions of poetry, which, though linked to traditional views, anticipates the increasing interest in the relation of poetry, honor and virtue, and the good individual in the Renaissance.

DOUGLAS'S POETIC PRACTICE IN THE *ENEADOS*

Douglas's view of poetry as "sle," "curious," and "derk" and his conception of his role as a Christian poet shed considerable light on his practice as translator and on the link he establishes in his version of the *Aeneid* between the poet and the hero within the poem. Characteristically, as Bawcutt demonstrates, Douglas adheres closely to his text and makes few changes in the *Eneados* that cannot be attributed directly to the Badius Ascensius edition of 1501 that he used, or to the mistaken interpretation of a word or a line by an earlier commentator on the text. Many of his so-called inaccuracies, in fact, are close translations of Ascensius's readings.[34]

But despite Douglas's faithfulness to his text, there are a number of important differences between the *Eneados* and Virgil's *Aeneid* that reflect Douglas's conception of his role as poet-translator. Typically, Douglas expands Virgil's poem in an effort to make its meaning clear and bring its underlying sentence to light. Thus he repeatedly explains Virgil's technical terms, geographical references, difficult words, and unfamiliar allusions.[35] Developing mere hints in Virgil's text, he attempts to eliminate ambiguity of expression and convey the full sense even of single words by considering their etymology, explaining their meaning in the translation, and, at times, by double translation, that is, by either providing both the literal and the figurative meaning of the word or by supplying both the derivative from Virgil's term and a synonym. In translating Virgil's word "oppetere," for example, Douglas explains in a note (Prol. I, 350 n.) that "quhilk to translate in our tung is with mowth to seik or byte the erd. And, lo, that is ane hail sentens for ane of Virgillis wordis," and when Virgil uses *oppetere* in Book I, 96, Douglas introduces the phrase "deit . . . bytand the erd" (I, iii, 6) to clarify the meaning in Scots. Similarly, he often provides a double translation to explain both the literal sense of Virgil's words and their sentence. In Book II, for example, before Sinon releases the Greeks from the wooden horse, Douglas translates Virgil's "flammas" ("flammas cum regia puppis / extulerat," II, 256–57) literally as "bail of fyre" and also as a signal or "takynnyng" to Sinon ("And quhen the takynnyng or the bail of fyre / Rays fro the kyngis schip," II, v, 13–14). Moreover, Douglas frequently introduces the word actually used by Virgil or a close version of the word and an explanatory phrase. Virgil's word "recentibus" (II, 395), for example, in Douglas's version is rendered as "recent . . . warm" (II, vii, 59) and later as "recent . . . fresch and callour" (VII, xii, 110) and "recent . . . newly sched" (VIII, iv, 28). And, like the commentators from whom he borrows, Douglas interpolates into the translation glosses either of his own invention or incorporated from other texts.[36]

In his effort to clarify Virgil's meaning, however, Douglas frequently changes the emphasis of his text. Although Bawcutt suggests that he merely brings out what is implicit in the *Aeneid* by developing nuances of the original meaning, the cumulative effect of his additions in many places is to transform Virgil's poem into one that is directed to a new audience and purpose. A good example of this change in emphasis is found in Book IV, one of the most controversial portions of the poem. In his book, which narrates the encounter between Dido and Aeneas, Douglas's insertions create a version of the episode that is harsher and more explicitly moral than Virgil's, with Dido emerging as a figure more contemptible than her counterpart in the *Aeneid* and her love of Aeneas being represented more explicitly as lust. As early as Book I, Douglas prepares us for his change in emphasis by subtly altering the reactions of Dido to Aeneas when she is introduced in the narrative and by prefacing the return to the Dido and Aeneas episodes in Book IV with a long prologue on the falseness of worldly love, born of "brynyng carnail, hait delyte," beginning "with a fenʒeit faynt pleasance, / Continewit in lust, and endyt with pennace."[37]

In the translation of Book IV, Douglas reinforces his emphasis on the lustful nature of Dido's love by several small changes. At the outset of the book, for example, he amplifies Dido's infatuation with Aeneas, interpolating phrases like "the blynd fyre of luve" (3) and words like "rage" (39) and "cryme" (40) which suggest the dangers of her passion, and, in chapter ii, he characterizes her feelings for Aeneas more explicitly as the "faynt lust" he describes in the prologue, inserting the heading, "Dido enflambyt in the lusty heyt, / With amorus thochtis trublys al hir spreit" and, within the narrative, expanding Virgil's

> heu vatum ignarae mentes! quid vota furentum,
> quid delubra iuvant? est mollis flamma medullas
> interea et tacitum vivit sub pectore volnus
> (IV, 65–67)

(Ah, blind soul of seers! Of what avail are vows or shrines to
one wild with love? All the while the flame devours her tender
heartstrings, and deep in her breast lives the silent wound)

to a nine-line digression that represents Dido's love as an excessive
passion that brings about her downfall:

> The blynd myndis, quhilkis na way diffynys
> The fors ne strenth of luf with hys hard bandis!
> Quhat avalyt thir sacrifice and offerandis?
> Quhat helpis to vyssy tempillis in luffis rage?
> Behald onhappy Dido of Cartage
> In this meyn sessoun byrnyng hait as gleyd:
> The secrete wound deip in hir mynd gan spreyd,
> And of hoyt amouris the subtell quent fyre
> Waistis and consumys merch, banys and lyre.
> (IV, ii, 30–38)

In the succeeding chapters, Douglas paints an increasingly negative
picture of Dido, making her more spiteful, self-indulgent, and vindic-
tive than her counterparts in the *Aeneid* and in Chaucer's versions. In
chapter vi, for example, he expands Dido's long speech to Aeneas to
emphasize her resentment (85 ff). Later in chapter vii, he exaggerates
Dido's reaction to Aeneas's impending departure (2–17) and makes
her lament in chapter x much longer and more self-indulgent than it is
in the *Aeneid*. Further, Douglas makes Dido's plea for vengeance in
chapter xii and her dying speech fiercer and more emotionally uncontrolled than it is in Virgil's version. Each of these emendations is
insignificant in its own right, but the cumulative effect of Douglas's
changes in Book IV is to introduce an emphasis on the falseness of
Dido's love that is stronger than Virgil's.

In addition to the amplification that is characteristic of many
portions of the *Eneados,* Douglas often qualifies the sentence of his
translation by another means that we have not recognized—his exploitation of style. On many occasions, although he follows his source
closely and appears to add little of consequence, he modifies Virgil's
meaning by his strategic stylistic changes. In Book II, his use of style
in the sense of his definition in the *Palice of Honour* and the *Eneados*
prologues, as the mediator between audience and purpose, the poet's
means of directing the "gentle hert" or appropriate reader to the

work's "lore," transforms Virgil's account of the fall of Troy into a compelling example of human blindness in the world.

In translating Book II, Douglas makes several changes that shape his material explicitly as a medieval tragedy. At the outset, he shifts the first thirteen lines of Virgil's Book II to the end of Book I in order to focus his account exclusively on the fall of Troy, and, within the narrative, he adds references to indicate that the events exemplify the way in which fortune acts upon men and women.[38] But more important than this change in focus is Douglas's examination of the attitudes behind the vision of tragedy and the human condition that perpetuates it. In the first four chapters of the book he introduces those concerns by manipulation of the Sinon episodes. By slight changes in wording, Douglas uses these events, which depict the immediate causes of the fall of Troy, to introduce the theme of human blindness. In contrast to Virgil, he represents Sinon explicitly as a feigner of truth, a deluder of human perception, punctuating his description of these episodes with terms that reveal Sinon's falseness. In Douglas's version, Sinon works "secretly" (II, ii, 6) to bring his "slycht to gude assay" (II, ii, 8). Whereas Virgil simply reports "accipe nunc Danaum insidias et crimine ab uno disce omnis" (Hear now the treachery of the Greeks and from one learn the wickedness of all), Douglas expands to develop Sinon's deceitfulness (II, ii, 6–15).[39] Though Sinon protests that he is "nowder lear nor fals" (II, ii, 42), Douglas, again changing Virgil's wording, underscores his acts of "fals traysoun" (II, ii, 46) and "slycht."

Significantly, it is Sinon, the feigner of truth, who introduces the style into the *Eneados* that dominates Douglas's version of Book II— the pathetic style. In both Douglas's and Virgil's accounts, Sinon seeks to elicit the Trojans' pity, but in Douglas's version his language takes on a marked pathos, characterized by more sorrowful terms and amplified passages of emotional outburst than we find in Virgil's version. After several rhetorical speeches, for example, Sinon addresses an impassioned plea to the Trojans that Douglas changes from Virgil's text to heighten the pathetic effect of the lines, translating, for example, Virgil's balanced and dignified "miserere laborum tantorum, miserere animi non digna ferentis" (II, 143–44, pity such distress; pity a soul that bears sorrow undeserved) to the more emotionally charged

Haue rewth and piete on sa feil harmys smart
And tak compassioune in thi gentill hart;
Apon my wrechit sawle haue sum mercy
That gyltles sufferis sik dyseyss wrangwisly.
(II, ii, 155–58)

In Douglas's version, it is explicitly Sinon's style, the effect of his pathetic language, that blinds the Trojans and persuades them to allow the wooden horse within their walls, thereby bringing about the fall of Troy and accomplishing what neither "fers Achilles" nor the rest of the Greeks could do in ten years of war.

In the remainder of Book II, Douglas introduces the pathetic style into the translation as a manifestation of the human blindness that underlies the tragedy of Troy. The first extended example occurs in chapter v in which Aeneas has a vision of the dead Hector. In narrating this episode, Douglas enhances Virgil's account to create one that is more sorrowful in its effect. Virgil's Aeneas reports that he sees Hector

rapatus bigis, ut quondam, aterque creunto
pulvere perque pedes traiectus lora tumentis.
et mihi, qualis erat! quantum mutatus ab illo
Hectore, qui redit exuvias indutus Achilli
vel Danaum Phrygios iaculatus puppibus ignis!
(II, 272–76)

(Torn by the car, as once of old, and black with gory dust, his swollen feet pierced with thongs. Ah me! What aspect was his! How changed from that Hector who returns after donning the spoils of Achilles or hurling on Danaan ships the Phrygian fires!)

Douglas adds the exclamation, "O God, quhat skath" (II, v, 41) and later the lament, "Ha, walloway, quhat harm and wo eneuch" (II, v, 44). He concludes the description of the wounded Hector with three lines that develop the hints of pathos in Virgil's account (II, 279–80) by means of reduplication of expression, descriptive modifiers, and intensitives: "Me thoght I first wepyng and na thing glaid / Rycht reuerently begouth to clepe this man, / And with sik dolorus wordis thus began" (II, v, 56–58). The speeches of Aeneas and Hector that follow, in Douglas's version, are characterized stylistically by more pathetic language and more uncontrolled rhetoric than in Virgil's version, as Douglas adds outbursts that draw attention to the feelings of the speakers. In Aeneas's speech, for example, he changes Virgil's "post multa tuorum funera, post varios hominumque urbisque labores" (II, 283–84, after the many deaths of thy kin, after divers sorrows of people and city) to the more intense "eftir feil slauchter of thi frendis now / And of thi folkis and cite efter huge payn, / Ouhen we beyn irkit" (II, v, 64–66) and adds the expressions of grief "allace" at the end of Aeneas's speech and at the beginning of Hector's.

In considering the purpose of Douglas's changes, it is important to recall the associations the pathetic style had in the literature with which he was familiar. Aeneas's style in Douglas's chapter v and the style of many of the speeches in Book II remind the reader of the language of the distraught Boethius at the outset of the *Consolation of Philosophy*, of Troilus as he bemoans his fate in Book V of Chaucer's poem, of the Man of Law as he laments Constance's misfortune, and of the Monk in narrating the wretched outcome of Ugolino of Pisa in Chaucer's version of the story.[40] In each of these cases, the character's pathetic style is an indication of his imperfect understanding or limited vision, his blindness to the larger design of events. As Lady Philosophy chides Boethius at the outset of the *Consolation,* he has forgotten himself in his lamenting and has clouded his vision with his tears (I, prosa 2, 22 ff). Likewise, Troilus's speeches in Books IV and V reveal him blinded by sorrow and subject to Fortune's vicissitudes, while the Man of Law's sentimentalizing of the action of his tale diverts the reader from its sentence.[41] Finally, the Monk's pathetic style, Chaucer's addition to Dante's version of the Ugolino story, underscores his limited definition of the story as tragedy, a fall from joy to woe, rather than as an example of the appropriate punishment for the sin of treachery that Dante emphasizes.

Douglas associates the pathetic style with imperfect human understanding in many of the episodes that follow in Book II to direct the reader's attention to the significance of the fall of Troy. Perhaps the best example of his treatment occurs in chapter x, which describes Aeneas's reunion with his family. The episode is preceded by the gradual revelation of the destruction of Troy to Aeneas, first his sight of the defeated Hector, then his view of the desolation of the city and the Trojan warriors, and finally his discovery of the horrible death of Priam who was forced to behold his own son's murder. As Aeneas, searching desperately for his family, unexpectedly spies Helen hiding in the Temple of Vesta, his anger flares up. His language becomes more noticeably emotional as Douglas intensifies such lines as "exarsere ignes animo; subit ira cadentum / ulcisci patriam et sceleratas sumere poenas" (II, 575–76, Fire blazed up in my heart; there comes an angry desire to avenge my falling country and exact the wages of her sin) to emphasize not only the speaker's anger, but also his grief and pain by introducing words like "teyn," "greif," "panys," "harmys smart": "My spreit for ire brynt in propir teyn / And al in greif thocht cruel vengeans take / Of my cuntre for this myschews wrake. / With byttir panys to wreke our harmys smart" (II, x, 28–31).

In the midst of Aeneas's uncontrolled sorrow, Venus appears, and, like Lady Philosophy, gradually corrects his vision, showing him what is wrong with the view his emotional language embodies. In a line that Douglas expands from Virgil, Venus tells Aeneas that his eyes are "Lyke to ane watry slowch standis dym about" (II, x, 83). She will lift the "clowd of dyrkness" so that he can understand the real significance of the fall of Troy. Neither Paris nor Helen is to blame, she reveals; rather the fall is part of a larger scheme of the gods. Aeneas's pathos and his laments for Troy, for Priam as a victim of Fortune, and for his own suffering are based on an imperfect understanding of the events. The chapter ends with Aeneas still blinded by his grief as he desperately attempts to rush into the fray, still using the pathos and inflated rhetoric of his earlier speeches as, in Douglas's version, he refers to himself as a "maste wrachit and miserabill catyve" (II, x, 167).[42]

The same pattern is repeated in the last two chapters of the book. As Aeneas and Anchises make their way out of Troy, prompted by the sign from Jupiter that confirms Venus's revelation to Aeneas, they lose sight of Aeneas's wife Creusa. Again Douglas punctuates Aeneas's speech with pathos, translating the Latin into terms that heighten his frenzied grief.[43] As he laments, Creusa appears in a vision, and like Venus in the preceding chapters, reveals the inappropriateness of his pathos. Aeneas must leave her behind with fondness not grief as he proceeds to fulfill the more important destiny she reveals to him.

The pathos that Douglas adds to his translation, thus, helps to direct the reader's attention to the underlying significance of Book II. In Douglas's treatment, this style is a manifestation of human blindness, an indication of our imperfect perception of the larger design of events. Like Chaucer's manipulation of the narrator in *Troilus and Criseyde*, Douglas's pathos is a device that encourages the reader both to sympathize with the characters in the narrative, and, at the same time, to recognize the limitations of their points of view. By drawing attention to the disparity between attachment to the things of the world and their inevitable loss, the style of the translation provides an important perspective on the action of Book II.

A second notable example of Douglas's exploitation of style as a purveyor of meaning is found in Books IX–XII. In expanding the climactic descriptions of the battles between the Trojans and the Latins in the closing books, Douglas introduces a chivalric mode foreign to the original that serves not simply to update Virgil's account but to sharpen and to qualify the significance of the action. In Books IX and X, this style defines a new context for the activity of Turnus and Aeneas and provides a point of reference for Douglas's consideration of the nature of true valor, a theme that becomes increasingly central to his version of Books IX–XII of the *Aeneid*. By his changes in these books, Douglas creates examples of "fulehardiment" and "courage," reminiscent of the examples in John Barbour's *Bruce*, which prepare for his definition of true chivalry in Prologue XI.[44]

In Douglas's treatment, Book IX offers a negative example of human valor. Changing the style of Virgil's description, he draws attention to the episodes as misguided heroic activity, the excessive courage of Turnus and the foolhardiness of Eurillius and Nysus that lead to destruction. Douglas's Turnus is a parody of the chivalric hero, a figure who is even more rash and extreme than Virgil's character. Stylistically, Douglas conveys this impression by marking the descriptions and speeches of Turnus with an excess of chivalric rhetoric. In contrast to Virgil, for example, he introduces Turnus and his forces in chapter i with the diction, imagery, alliteration, and rhythm associated with this style, translating the more stately Latin

> Iamque omnis campis exercitus ibat apertis,
> dives equum, dives pictai vestis et auri
> (Messapus primas acies, postrema coercent,
> Tyrrhidae iuvenes, medio dux agmine Turnus)
> (IX, 25–28)
>
> (And now all the army was advancing on the open plain, rich

in horses, rich in broidered robes and gold—Messapus mar-
shaling the van, the sons of Tyrrhus the rear, and Turnus their
captain in the center of the line)

into a passage laden with the language and style of the chivalric mode:

> With this the ostis all in the plane field
> Held furth arrayt, schynand vnder scheld.
> Men micht behald full mony riall stedis,
> Full mony pantyt targe and weirlyke wedis;
> Of giltyn geir dyd glytter bank and buss
> The formast batale ledis Mesapus;
> The hyndmast ostis had in governyng
> Of Tyrrhyus the sonnys or childer ʒing;
> Turnus that duke rewlys the myddill ost,
> With glave in hand maid awfull feir and bost,
> Thame till array raid turnand to and fro,
> And by the hed alhaill, quhar de dyd go,
> Hyear than all the rowt men mycht hym se.
> (IX, i, 59–71)

His change in diction, the harsh alliteration, and lines like "With
glave in hand maid awfull feir and bost," which Douglas adds,
accentuate Turnus's rage. Similarly, in chapter ii, Douglas employs
the chivalric style in his description of Turnus urging his men to battle
to underscore the excessiveness of their courage. Virgil simply reports:

> "ecquis erit, mecum, iuvenes, qui primus in hostem?
> en"—ait et iaculum attorquens emittit in auras,
> principium pugnae, et campo sese adruus infert.
> clamorem excipiunt socii fremituque sequuntur
> horrisono; Teuorum mirantur intertia corda,
> "non aequo dare se campo, non obvia ferre
> arma viros, sed castra fovere. . . ." (IX, 51–57)

("Gallants, is there one, who with me will be the first against
the foe to—lo!" he cries, and whirling a javelin sends it
skyward—the prelude of battle—and advances proudly o'er
the plain. His comrades take up the shout, and follow with
dreadful din; they marvel at the Teucrians' craven hearts,

crying: "They trust not themselves to a fair field, they face not
the foe in arms, but they hug the camp.")

Douglas translates:

"Go to, ȝyng gallandis, quhat that list," qoud he,
"That ennemyss assailȝe first with me!"
And, with that word, threw a dart in the air,
As he to geif batale all redy war,
Syne in plane feild with browdyn baneris gay
Bargane to byde drew hym till array.
Hys feris all ressauyt the clamour hie,
And followand thar chiftane, he and he,
The bruyt rasyt with grisly sound attanys.
And gan to mervell the dolf hartit Troianys,
That durst nocht, as thame semyt, in plane field
Thame self aventour, nor ȝit with sper and scheld
Mach with thar fa men in patent bargane,
Bot hald thame in thar strenthis euery ane.
(IX, ii, 41–54)

His language, particularly his addition of phrases like "The bruyt
rasyt with grisly sound attanys" and of the emphatic words—"aventour," "bargane," "strenthis"—increases the ferocity of Turnus and
his men and their eagerness to do battle, an impression that Douglas
reinforces in his translation of the Virgilian simile that follows of the
wolf stalking its helpless prey (IX, ii, 61–81) and in the violently
onomatopoetic description of Turnus burning the Trojan ships with
which the chapter concludes. Finally, in chapter iii, Douglas changes
the style of Turnus's climactic speech to his men, making it more
boastful and self-confident than the counterpart in the *Aeneid*. As he
flaunts fate, blinded by courage, Turnus echoes the language of Barbour's figure of Edward Bruce, the model of excessive valor or
"fulehardyment."[45]

This land is in our power, felt and cost;
So that thai sal na wyss eschape our brandis,
Quhou mony thousand douchty men of handis
Ar heir assumblyt, all Italyayns.
I compt na thing all thocht ȝon fant Troianys
Rakkyn thar fatis that thame hydder brocht;

All syk vayn ruyss I feir as thing of nocht,
In cace thai prowd be of the goddis answeris,
And thame avant tharof with felloun feris.
(IX, iii, 128–36)[46]

In contrast to these methods, in Books X–XII, Douglas introduces the chivalric style without undercutting it to present Aeneas and, to a lesser extent, Pallas as examples of true valor, the mean between recklessness and cowardice. The difference between his use of chivalric style to describe Turnus and Aeneas is illustrated dramatically in Book XII in the episodes that lead up to the final confrontation. In these episodes, Douglas represents Turnus's valor as extreme by adding a note of intensity and violence to his style. In his version, for example, Turnis is "smytyn so brym in fervent violens" (XIII, I, 23). Despite Latinus's and Amata's pleas for moderation, he "brynys in desyre / Of bargane into armys, hait as fyre" (XII, ii, 43–44). When Aeneas withdraws, wounded by a straw arrow, Turnus reacts hastily:

. . . for this hasty hope als hait as fyre,
To mell in feght he caucht arden desyre;
He askis horss and harnes baith atayns,
And haltandly in hys cart for the nanys
He skippis vp and musturis wantonly. . . .
(XII, vi, 37–41)

The lines become strident as Douglas underscores the wanton and excessive nature of his killing by amplifying the description and adding harsh alliteration and rough sounds, for example, in the lines "hys swift stedis hovys, quhar thair went, / Spraingit vp the bludy sparkis our the bent, / Quhil blude and brane, in abudans furth sched" (XII, vi, 57–77) which Douglas renders from Virgil's "Spargit napide ungala rores / Sanguineos" (XII, 339). In contrast, the chivalric style used to describe Aeneas is more tempered and controlled and defines an ideal of prowess directed to right rather than unmitigated rage. As Douglas describes Aeneas arming himself for his final encounter with Turnus, he provides a good example of this relationship. Virgil renders this passage with dignity:

. . . nunc te mea dextera bello
defensum dabit et magna iner praemia ducet:

tu facito, mox cum matura adoleverit aetas,
sis memor et te animo repetentem exempla tuorum
et pater Aeneas et avunculus excitet Hector.
(XII, 436–40)

(Today my hand shall shield thee in war and lead thee where
are great rewards: see thou, when soon thy years have grown
to ripeness, that thou be mindful thereof, and, as thou recallest
the pattern of thy kin, let thy sire Aeneas, and thy uncle Hector
stir thy soul!)

Douglas expands this description, introducing with words like "querrell," "senʒoery," "page," and "prowess" the diction and imagery
of the chivalric romance to define an ideal of appropriate valor.
Aeneas instructs his son:

Now sall my rycht hand thy querrell susteyn,
And the defend in batale by and by,
To mak the partis man of gret senʒoery,
Do thou siclyke, I pray the, myne awyn page,
Als fast as thou cumis to perfyte age,
Ramembir theiron, and revolue in thy mind
Thy lynage, thy forbearis, and thy king;
Exempill of prowess in the steris frendis befor,
Baith fader Eneas and thyne vncle Hector.
(XII, vii, 130–38)

The implications of Douglas's use of chivalric style in Books IX–
XII are made explicit in Prologue XI, a redefinition of "Martis
chevalry" or prowess in war. Like Barbour whom he echoes, Douglas
suggests that the ideal of worldly valor represented by the figure of
Aeneas is a mean between the extremes of foolhardiness and cowardice:

Strang fortitud, quhilk hardyment cleip we,
Abuf the quhilk the vertus souerane
Accordyng pryncis, hecht magnanymyte,
Is a bonte set betwix vicis twane:
Of quham fuyl hardynes clepid is the tane,
That vndertakis all perrellis but avice;
The tother is namyt schamefull cowardyce,

Voyd of curage, and dolf as ony stane.
(Prol. XI, 33–40)

True prowess of "moral vertuus hardyment" is directed to the ends of virtue and right rather than to strife and dissension: "Wrangis to reddress suld wer be vndertane, / For na conquest, reif, skat nor pensioun" (Prol. XI, 23–24). Finally, going beyond the sentence of Books IX–XII, Douglas reminds us that even true temporal chivalry is only a feeble imitation of "dyvyne hardyment" or the more difficult battles of the Christian knight, fought not with swords, but with the mind against evil. Set at the exact center of the four books of war, the eleventh prologue, thus, clarifies our views of the prowess of Virgil's heroes and reminds the audience, three months before the disastrous defeat of the Scots at Flodden, of an ideal higher than worldly glory.

Douglas's conception of style in the *Eneados* translation manifests itself in the broadest sense of the term in his treatment of the figure of Aeneas.[47] As he makes clear in the notes to Book I, style includes a person's or a character's style, one's social status and the unique combination of traits or virtues that establish one's identity. When Eneas makes himself known to Venus, for example, Douglas explains that he speaks in the manner in which he does, not out of arrogance, "bot forto schaw his styll, as kyng or prynce onknawin in an onkowth land" (I, vi, 125 n.). The style of his words and his actions defines his style as a prince and as a man. Likewise, Ascanius suggests this meaning of the term when he chides the Trojans for not acting according to the style that they assume: "To call ȝou men of Troy that on rycht is; / ȝe be onworthy to sa hie style to clame" (IX, x, 62–63). Often the effect of Douglas's many small changes in the literary style and the emphasis of his translation is to change the "styll" of his characters, particularly of his central figure, Eneas.

In Douglas's version of the *Aeneid,* to some extent, a different style of hero finally emerges. Whereas Virgil had rejected the traditional epic hero in his representation of Aeneas as a man who turns from the course of physically heroic behavior in his abandonment of Troy and attains greatness as a result of his inner strength and virtue he achieves on his journey, Douglas develops his Eneas more explicitly as the good man, the model for other men, who willingly undergoes hardship and suffering. In the prologue and notes to Book I, he prepares the reader for this view, introducing Eneas not as a perfect man but as one whose actions bring together the possibility of nobility.

For euery vertu belangand a nobill man
This ornate poet bettir than ony can
Payntand discryvis in person of Eneas—
Not forto say sikane Eneas was
ȝit than by hym perfytely blasons he
All wirschip, manhed and nobilite
With euery bonte belangand a gentill wycht,
Ane prynce, ane conquerour or a valȝeand knycht.
(Prol. I, 325–32)

In his note to the first line of the translation, Douglas indicates that Virgil does not name Aeneas but calls him "the man" to underscore his role as "most soueran man" or model. Following Landino, he introduces the view of Aeneas's actions as an allegory of man's effort to attain "soueran bonte and gudnes" in life, and, without making this sentence explicit in the text, draws attention to the interpretation of the medieval commentators as an important context or perspective on Aeneas's significance as hero. In his notes, Douglas concentrates on the consistency of character we may expect in the representation of Aeneas. Throughout the work, his actions define him as a man of virtue, particularly in piety and devotion, ideals anticipated by but not fully embodied in Virgil's poem.

ȝe sal ondirstand Virgill in all partis of his process,
quhat maner of fasson he discrivis ony man at the begynnyng,
sa continewys he that samin person all thro, and Eneas in
all his wark secludis from all vylle offyce; bot as twychand
materris of pyety or devotion, thar laborwris he euer wythn
the first, as ȝe may se in the beginyng of the vi buke.[48]

In the translation, Douglas places an increased emphasis on certain aspects of Eneas's character, particularly on his compassion as an important feature of his "style" as a hero. Among the many examples of his reshaping, two instances at climactic points in the narrative, the descent to the underworld in Book VI and the final encounter with Turnus in Book XII, illustrate the centrality of this virtue to Douglas's conception of Eneas. In contrast both to Virgil's account and to the other medieval versions of Book VI, Douglas reworks Eneas's journey to illustrate his innate qualities of pity and sympathy. In the famous encounter with Dido in chapter vii, he expands Eneas's grief at seeing the former queen, rendering Virgil's "talibus Aeneas ardentem et torva tuentem / lenibat dictis animum lacrimasque ciebat" (VI, 468–69, with such speech amid springing tears Aeneas would soothe the wrath of the fiery, fierce-eyed queen):

> With sik wordis Eneas, full of wo
> Set him to meyss the sprete of Queyn Dido,
> Quhilk, all inflambit, full of wreth and ire,
> With acquart luke glowand hait as fyre,
> Maid him to weip and sched furth teris wak.
> (VI, vii, 89–93)

When Dido departs, Douglas translates Virgil's couplet (VI, 475–76) into a passage double in length in which Eneas, moved by pity and brooding over his distress, pursues the fleeing shade:

> And, netheless, fast eftir hir furth sprent
> Ene, perplexit of hir sory cace,
> And weping gan hir follow a weil lang space,
> Regratand in his mynd, and had piete
> Of thie distress that movit hir so to fle.
> (VI, vii, 104–8)

Similarly, Douglas emphasizes Eneas's compassion in the meeting with Anchises in the concluding chapters of this book, adding to Virgil's account lines which underscore Eneas's concern about finding his father (VI, x, 110–11, 118). When Anchises greets the weeping Eneas, Douglas emphasizes that it is Eneas's qualities of "piete" and "kyndness" that moved him to undertake the treacherous journey to the underworld, rendering Virgil's "pietas" as "gret piete, amd kyndnes weil expert"; "Thou are cummyn at last, my deir child! / Thy gret piete, and kyndnes weil expert / Onto thy fader, causyt the and gart / This hard vayage venquyss and ourset" (VI, xi, 16–19).[49] Amid his vision of his past, present, and future, Eneas, somewhat more humanized in Douglas's version, pauses to pity those whom he has made suffer.

The relation of the quality of compassion to Eneas's character as a hero is defined even more clearly in the second episode, the encounter with Turnus in the last scene of the epic. In the translation, Douglas changes Virgil's text to add several lines that accentuate Eneas's concern for his defeated enemy. In response to Turnus's plea for mercy, for example, Douglas interrupts Virgil's account to describe Eneas's sympathy. Virgil remarks that Aeneas paused and might have weakened, for "flectere sermo coeperat" (XI, 940, these words began to sway him), but Douglas introduces a more significant conflict:

> Eneas stren in armys tho present
> Rolland hys eyn toward Turnus dyd stand,
> And lyst nocht stryke, bot can withdraw hys hand,
> And mor and mor thir wordis, by and by,
> Begouth incline hym to reuth and mercy,
> Abydand lang in hovir quhat he suld do. . . .
> (XII, xiv, 124–29)

In Douglas's version, it is explicitly Eneas's "reuth and mercy" that makes him hesitate. But unlike the "reuthful" figure of Book II, blinded by his pity for the Trojans, Eneas in this scene finally combines compassion with his concern for justice as he spies the dead Pallas's belt on Turnus' body:

> . . . eftir that Eneas with hys eyn
> Sa cruell takynnys of dyseyss hes seyn,
> And can sik weid byreft thar aspy,
> And full of furour kyndkys he inhy, . . .
> (XII, xiv, 139–42)

In addition to heightening Eneas's compassion and pity, Douglas tempers his physical prowess more completely than Virgil does. In his notes to Book I, he goes out of his way to stress the limitations of unqualified valor and to distinguish this trait from the prowess Eneas exhibits. To the line "Belive Eneas membris schuk for cald" in the description of his shipwreck, for example, Douglas adds a gloss explaining that this "cald" comes from fear, "nocht that Eneas dred the ded, bot this maner of ded," and he goes on to note the importance of fear in distinguishing the hardy from the reckless: "alsso he that dreddis na thyng, nor kan haf na dred, is not hardy, but fuyll hardly and beistly" (I, iii, i n.). Likewise, he glosses Neptune's angry threat to "chastyss" the winds by warning against hasty vengeance. "Heir is an notabyll doctryn, than nan nobill man suld hastely reveng him eftyr his greif" (I, iii, 69 n.) but should wait until the heat of his anger had passed. In the translation, Douglas reinforces the view of "hardiment" he defines in the notes and in Prologue XI, as we have seen, by heightening the contrast Virgil introduces between Aeneas and the men of arms, particularly Turnus, in Books IX–XII where he makes Turnus's rage more violent and represents Eneas's prowess more clearly as a desirable mean between the extremes of recklessness and cowardice. As in the last scene of the epic, he emends Virgil's lines by small but significant changes to present Eneas's valor as reasoned and deliberate and checked by his wisdom and compassion.

The aspects of Eneas's character that Douglas highlights are summed up by his translation of Virgil's epithet "pius." This word in the *Aeneid* generally has the meanings of "good" or "dutiful." Douglas, however, draws attention to the four ideals embodied in his translation of the term—"rewth," "devotion," "pyete" and "compassion." As he explains in his note to I, vi, 125, which refers to Eneas's style as a man, Eneas was called by common voice "Enease full of pyete." Douglas says, "And for that Virgill clepis hym swa all thro this buyk, and I interpret that term quhylys for 'rewth,' quhis for 'devotion' and quhilis for 'pyete' and 'compassion.'" These terms define Eneas's relation as a hero to other men and to his country. As Douglas comments, "3e shall knaw that pyete is a vertw or gud deid by the quhilk we geif our dylligent and detfull lawbour to our natyve cuntre and onto thaim beyn coinonyt to vs un neyr degre" (I, vi, 125 n.). "Pyete" in its various senses thus is the quality that joins men with other men and involves one in a larger cause.

Both in rendering Virgil's word "pius" and in instances where the term is not used in his sources, Douglas works these ideals into his translation. A good example of his method is found in his introduction of the character of Eneas in Book I. Virgil uses the epithet "pius" only three times in the opening book to refer to Aeneas and its related form "pietate" two additional times.[50] Douglas exploits the epithet or various translations of it almost twice as often, introducing the term to characterize Eneas in each of his major appearances in the book. Amplifying Virgil's "insignem pietate virum" (I, 10), he presents Eneas at the outset of the epic as "A worthy man fulfillit of piete" (I, i, 17) and raises the question of why such a man must suffer. In Douglas's version, Eneas's suffering and his concern for the suffering of others, his "piete" in the sense of "pity" or "sympathy" as well as "piete" in the sense of devotion becomes an important aspect of his style as a hero. When Eneas appears for the first time amid the storm in chapters iii and iv, Douglas translates the epithet "pius" as "pietefull" to accentuate these qualities, making more explicit in his lines than in Virgil's the meaning "sorrowful" as he renders Virgil's "praecipue pius Aeneas nunc acris Oronti" in the translation as "Bot principally the pietefull Eneas / Regratis oft the hard fortoune and cace / Of stern Orontes new drownyt in the sey" (I, iv, 105–7). When Eneas reappears at the outset of chapter vi, Douglas likewise translates the epithet "pius" (I, 305) as "reuthfull" (I, vi, i) to underscore Eneas's role as a suffering hero, and, within the chapter, he renders the line that Virgil's Aeneas uses to characterize himself to his mother Venus, "sum pius Aeneas," (I, 378), generally translated by modern editors as "I am Aeneas the good," or "the good devoted man," as "Rewthfull Ene am I" (I, vi, 125), shifting the emphasis to Eneas as a man who endures suffering and care, the quality defined by the account of his past hardships that appears in the next fourteen lines.

Douglas qualifies Eneas's last appearances in the book, his encounters with Dido, by three further uses of his terms for "pius." The first occurs as the Trojans introduce themselves to Dido and Eneas's men describe his "style" as king:

> To ws was kyng the worthy Eneas,
> Ane iustar man in all the warld nane was,
> Nor mair reuthfull, nor wisar into weir,
> And mair valiant in dedis or armys seir.
> (I, vii, 89–92)

In contrast to Virgil's "pietate" (I, 545), Douglas's translation "reuthfull" in the context of these lines draws attention to the combination of justice, wisdom, valor, and the capacity to sympathize and suffer he introduced at the outset of the book. In Douglas's version, it is not only Eneas's goodness that makes him heroic, but also his ability to endure hardship patiently, a trait that Douglas often underscores by coupling the epithet "reuthfull" with the word "pacient" to translate Virgil's "pius" (see, for example, XII, vi, 1). In his remaining uses of the terms for "pius" in Book I, which he adds to his source, Douglas suggests two additional aspects of Eneas's character—his compassion and his piety. When Eneas first presents himself to Dido near the end of the book, she addresses him with the question, "Art thou not theilk compacient Eneas . . ." (I, ix, 69), drawing attention to his reputation for being concerned with others. Although the commentator Ascensius adds to Virgil's "tune ille Aeneas" (I, 617) the word "nobilissimus," Douglas further emends to "compacient" to point explicitly to the quality of pity for the suffering of others he repeatedly attributes to Eneas. Finally, Douglas introduces the epithet to show Eneas's piety or devotion to the ideals underlying his struggle and to others. After Dido has welcomed the Trojans, Douglas, following Virgil, suggests that Eneas is unable to rest until his son Ascanius is reunited with him. In Book I, 643–44, Virgil comments, "Aeneas (neque enim patrius consistere mentem passus amor)" (for a father's love did not suffer his heart to rest); Douglas changes the word "amor" to "piete" in the sense of "devotion," linking it more directly to the cluster of virtues he attributes to Eneas (I, ix, 115–18).

Douglas's small changes in the "style" of Eneas have the effect of replacing the earlier medieval figures—the courtly lover of the *Roman d'Eneas* and the betrayer of women in Caxton's and Chaucer's translations—and also the Virgilian great man with a hero who is more human and compassionate, the good man who undergoes suffering and hardship. Our involvement with this figure, Blyth suggests, often has less to do with the fact that he is an epic hero, the founder of the Roman Empire, than with the feeling we are encouraged to have for a fellow human who willingly accepts hardship.[51] The qualities of "rewth," "devotion," "pyete," and "compassion" that Douglas emphasizes in his representation of Eneas thus give an additional meaning to his journey, making it not only an account of the direction of an individual will to a larger national destiny but, to some extent, a model for the lives of all humanity. Although Douglas does not impose the allegory of the commentators on Virgil's poem, the "style" of his translation in many places subtly reminds the reader of this interpretation.

Douglas's *Eneados,* thus, embodies two journeys, that of Eneas within the poem both in its Virgilian sense and with the additional meaning Douglas introduces and that of the narrator as poet in the thirteen prologues who overcomes conflict and uncertainty to complete his translation. In several senses one struggle complements the other. The poet-narrator's conflicting responses to earthly experience in Prologues I–VI, his struggle between his involvement in the world and his awareness as poet of its transitory nature, mirror Eneas's effort in the first five books to put aside the worldly attachments that divert him from his larger journey as hero. The sixth book and surrounding prologues, which deal with Eneas's descent to the underworld and the narrator's similar movement from a hell-like external world and a corresponding poetic sterility to a more beneficent landscape and renewed poetic activity, mark a turning point in both struggles. The remaining portions define the redirection of the narrator's and the hero's efforts to their higher goals, the narrator's as a Christian poet and Eneas's as the hero destined to found Rome. Both journeys are at once national and universal; Eneas's represents both the struggle to build a new nation and the quest of the good man, and the poet-narrator is introduced in the double role of Scots "makar" who seeks to extend the limits of his native medium and as poet in a broader sense who attempts to defend the value of his art. But more important, the two struggles, the effort of the poet to produce a worthy poem and the journey of Eneas to fulfill his destiny and found Rome, define different aspects of the quest for honor and virtue, which Douglas introduces in the *Palice of Honour* as the highest human goal in the world. In his consideration of the relation of the poet's activity to the hero's journey, the narrator's definition of the good poet and the value of poetry in the thirteen prologues becomes the artistic counterpart of Eneas's representation of the good man in the body of the poem. Douglas's defense of poetry in the *Palice of Honour* and the analogy between the poet and the hero that he establishes in the *Eneados* ultimately place the earlier fifteenth-century poetic ideals in the context of a complex of concerns that are increasingly important in the Renaissance—worldly piety, honor, and fame.

ive

From "Enluminer" to "Vates"

The writing of Stephen Hawes at the outset of the sixteenth century
represents a transformation of the ideals of good poetry and the
relation between poetry and high style that dominates the fifteenth
century. A courtier and suitor for preferment in the reigns of Henry
VII and Henry VIII, Hawes begins with the attitudes of the fifteenth-
century poets, but during the course of his career, he moves from their
conceptions to a vision of poetry that is quite different from his English predecessors'. Although critics have paid only scant attention to
his writing, principally as a potential source for Spenser's poetry, his
three long poems—*The Example of Virtue* (1503–4), *The Pastime of
Pleasure* (1506–7), and *The Conforte of Louers* (1510)—provide an
important link between medieval and Renaissance poetics. An ad-
mirer and self-styled disciple of Lydgate, Hawes retains in his early
poems the view of poetry as a vehicle of truth, the vision of poets as
"enluminers" who shed light on their matter by means of rhetoric and
eloquence, and a belief in the power of poetry with its heightened
language to ennoble and to civilize human beings and to bring order to
the state. Like Douglas, he places these ideals in the larger context of

the quest for honor and virtue in the world, linking the journey of the poet with that of the good man to create an expansive and occasionally unwieldy model of human aspiration. But his perspective gradually shifts from the notion of the poet as an "enluminer" and a corresponding ideal of eloquence to a vision of the poet as "vates" or prophet and a conception of style almost entirely devoid of the features of fifteenth-century style. While he adopts the familiar critical terminology of the fifteenth-century poets, to a considerable extent, he changes its meaning.

Hawes's shift in perspective evolves gradually in this three allegorical poems—*The Example of Virtue, The Pastime of Pleasure,* and *The Conforte of Louers.*[1] Curiously, these poems, which, he suggests, unlike his other works, were written with his "right hand" or with his full poetic power, appear to be different versions of each other, drawing upon similar sources—Lydgate's *Pilgrimage of the Life of Man* and *Temple of Glas,* the *Courte of Sapyence,* the *Assembly of Ladies,* the *Margarita Philosophica,* among other works—and exhibiting marked similarities of theme, structure, character, and imagery.[2] In an interesting process of revision, Hawes develops increasingly complex and significant perspectives on his themes—the worldly quest of the narrator for love, honor, and renown. As the three versions evolve, the role of poetry and the activity of the poet become central to the work's meaning.

The Example of Virtue, the earliest of the three poems, is the least ambiguous.[3] Drawing upon the *Courte of Sapyence* and Lydgate's *Pilgrimage of the Life of Man,* the allegory, with little personal or topical allusion, defines the worldly course to salvation through the marriage of Virtue and Cleanness. The protagonist, who comes to represent virtue, is unnamed at the outset and appears only briefly in the guise of the poet in the prologue to protest his lack of poetic skill and to suggest that, like Paul, he writes for "oure document" (21). In a September dream vision, the season of the waning of one's life, Discretion appears to the narrator and warns him of the transitory nature of the world. As guide, she shows him various aspects of earthly experience in the figures of Hardiness, Sapience, Fortune, and Nature. After discovering the limitations of each of these characters, the narrator sets out on a quest to win the Lady Cleanness or earthly perfection to whom Dame Sapience directs him. First, he must overcome all worldly temptations, the Sea of Vainglory, the alluring ladies

Sensuality and Pride, the three-headed dragon who represents the world, the flesh, and the devil; then he joins the company of "Perceueraunce," Charity, Prayer, and "Lowliness" who attend the lady; and finally, with little difficulty, the narrator wins the lady and Virtue and Cleanness are wed. The elaborate ceremony with which the poem closes dramatically represents the significance of this marriage as a means of salvation. The wedding takes place in a chapel set within an earthly garden of paradise, a figure of the celestial garden the lovers will reach later. Attending the couple as the King of Love, the father of Cleanness, presides, are the various virtues and the most noble of the saints. The ceremony culminates in a feast "moost swete and precyous / To fede the soule with dyuyne comfort" (1857–58). The couple gracefully age and, after a vision of hell and heaven, attain their place in the celestial garden to dwell in eternal joy.

At first glance, *The Pastime of Pleasure* appears to be simply a longer reworking of the theme of *The Example*—the worldly quest for salvation.[4] At the outset of the poem, the narrator again meets a female figure who instructs him and initiates his journey over the sea to an allegorical lady whom he hopes to wed. Like his predecessor in the *Example*, he is introduced to various aspects of worldly experience before he is forced to overcome several obstacles to his quest, including a similar three-headed dragon. The journeys in both works raise questions about the relation of earthly activity to salvation and end with a wedding, the aging of the narrator, and the view that the human world is transitory. Finally, the language and the topoi of the *Pastime,* for example, the introduction of the Nine Worthies, the descriptions of the three castles, the extended rhetorical complaints based on the anaphora "wo worth," echo *The Example of Virtue.*[5]

But the emphasis of the *Pastime* differs substantially from that of the *Example,* particularly in its concern with worldly pursuits and with the narrator's activities as poet. The poem presents us with a quest of the narrator for Fame through love, knightly achievement, and poetry, and, at the same time, affords a vision of the limitations of this quest. The first hint of change is provided by the work's title. In contrast to *Example of Virtue,* which prepares us for an allegory of the attainment of virtue, *Pastime of Pleasure* suggests a poem that will be concerned with earthly pursuits, the qualities represented by the figure of Dame Pleasance in *King Hart.* As the *Pastime* opens, these expectations are confirmed by the narrator's explicit choice of the active life, the way of worldly pleasure and fame. The names of the central characters, Grand Amour and La Bel Pucell, rather than Virtue and Cleanness, indicate a similar shift in focus from a quest for perfection to a worldly quest. Finally, the proportions of the quest reinforce this change in emphasis. The main action of the *Example,* the narrator's pursuit and winning of the lady and their wedding feast, occupies only a small segment of the narrative in the *Pastime* and these events are framed by more than 4,000 lines which deal with the education of the narrator as man and as poet in the Towers of Doctrine, Chivalry, and Correction and his dialogues with Time and Eternity at the end of the poem in which Pucell is forgotten entirely. Although the *Example* is concerned principally with overcoming worldly interests, the body of the *Pastime* deals with perfecting these talents. Thus, it is Fame in the *Pastime,* rather than Sapience or Wisdom, who initiates the narrator's quest, and, although she awakens the narrator from sloth by the sound of her horn and gives him the greyhounds Grace and Governance, she points the way neither to perfection nor to salvation as her predecessor, Sapience, in the *Example* did.[6] Rather, she promises the endurance of the narrator's name and the reward of La Bel Pucell at the end of the quest. In this context, the quest itself, which introduces the narrator in the triple stance of poet, lover, and knight, becomes a model of human aspiration in the world.

While much of the material Hawes incorporates in the quest in the *Pastime* is conventional, his effect is not. The narrative, like many of the inclusive fifteenth-century visions, begins with the hero's education in the seven liberal arts of the Trivium and Quadrivium, the standard curriculum of the medieval university. But again, the proportions of the account are revealing. Of the seven arts represented in the Tower of Doctrine, Hawes devotes the greatest amount of attention to rhetoric, and within this category, to eloquence, which together include more lines than all of the remaining arts. In contrast to his counterparts in the other fifteenth-century versions, the narrator in the *Pastime* is educated conspicuously and self-consciously as poet.[7] Hawes's treatment of the seven arts is further distinguished from his sources by the introduction of several related themes in this section— particularly the association of the arts and good government and the civilizing effect of poetry.

By establishing a link between the correct use of words and the well-ordered state, in his discussion of the Trivium, Hawes develops Lydgate's view of the poet as a reformer and civilizer. Following Lydgate, he indicates that grammar is the base of all other arts, the first means of human order in the world. Like God, who created the world by the word and by the word restrained chaos, people in ancient times by the power of language established prudent government:

Who knewe gramer / without impedyment
Shoulde perfytely haue intelleccyon
Of a lytterall cense / and moralyzacyon
To construe euery thynge ententysly
The worde is gramer / wel and ordynatly

By the worde the worlde / was made orygynally
The hye kynge sayde / it was made incontynent
He dyde commaunde / all was made shortly
To the worlde / the worde is sentencyous Iugement. . . .
(598–606)

Grammar is the original source of order in the world, but rhetoric, which Hawes conceives of as being developed by Reason, enables one to continue to govern "well and prudently" (692).

Before the lawe / in a tumblynge barge
The people sayled / without parfytenes
Throughe the worlde / all aboute at large
They hadde none ordre / nor stedfastnes
Tyll rethorycyans / founde Iustyce doubtles
Ordenynge kynges / of ryghte hye dygnyte
Of all comyns / to haue the souerainte. . . .
(876–82)

Finally, music keeps concord among the arts so that they may work to human benefit.

The poet as the person who exploits words most effectively and hence most closely approaches God's perfect power of language emerges as an ideal in this section of the *Pastime*. The poet's role is fundamental to the other roles the narrator as quester will assume. Essentially Hawes's vision of the poet in this work is derivative and like the majority of medieval writers, he represents good poetry as allegory, the cloaking of truth with feigned fables:[8]

It was the guyse in olde antyqyute
Of famous poetes / ryght ymagynatyfe
Fables to fayne / by good auctoryte
They were so wyse / and so inuentyfe
Theyr obscure reason / fayre and fugratyfe
Pronounced trouthe / vnder cloudy fygures
By the inuencyon / of theyr fatall scryptures. . . .
(715–21)

Under the surface of this fiction is a reasoned sentence, and Hawes, like Dante and Boccaccio, argues that it is precisely the rational underpinning that one may uncover beneath the fiction of the poem that distinguishes poetry from other writing.[9] The fable is the poet's invention, his means of embodying truth, and his language is the cloak or cloud that at once protects and reveals its sentence. An imitation of God's language, it represents the distillation or purification of human speech. Echoing Lydgate, whom he ranks even higher than Chaucer as a model of excellence, Hawes defines the process of transmuting ordinary speech into poetic language:

As we do golde / from coper puryfy
So that elocucyon / doth ryght well claryfy

The dulcet speche / from the langage rude
Tellynge the tale / in termes eloquent
The barbary tongue / it doth ferre exclude
Electynge wordes / which are expedyent
In latyn / or in englysshe / after the entent
Encensynge out / the aromatyke fume
Our langage rude / to exyle and consume. . . .
(916–24)

Although he preserves Lydgate's conception of the appeal of poetic language as "swete and dylycyous," and splendid or "depaynted with golde," Hawes changes his emphasis. In contrast to Lydgate's ideal of amplification, Hawes stresses the hardness of the surface of the poem, an efficiency on the poet's part in refining and purifying his medium. And, like Douglas, he suggests that the poet's language has a difficult, subtle, or covert quality that is linked directly to its allegorical purpose.

For Hawes, the effect of good poetry is threefold. Most important, it leads one to truth by "couert lykeness" (775). Developing Lydgate's notion of the poet's "enlumynyng," he suggests that poets are like "Carbuncles / in the most derke nyght" whose light preserves one from ignorance:

Carbuncles / in the most derke nyght
Doth shine fayre / with clere radyant beames
Exylynge derkenes / with his rayes lyght
And so these poetes / with theyr golden streames
Deuoyde our rudenes / with grete fyry lemes. . . .
(1128–32)

Specifically, their stories teach people to govern themselves well and to live without strife or "myschiefe" and to follow the way of "vertue / welthe and stablenes" (1119). Second, in an important departure from his English predecessors, Hawes argues that poetry preserves fame and insures that the honor of the worthy endures. In contrast both to Chaucer who parodies this notion in the *Hous of Fame* and to Douglas who rejects worldly honor, Hawes develops this theme for the first time in English explicitly as a positive motive for the poet-narrator's quest and thus provides a significant and generally overlooked link to the Renaissance poets.[10] Third, Hawes indicates that poetry is the ground of all knowledge, the source of "connynge," wisdom, and skill. Science, learning, and pleasure derive from an understanding of the poets' fables: "For you therof / were fyrst orygynall grounde // And vpon youre scryptue / our scyence ensueth" (787–88).

In educating Grand Amour in the seven liberal arts, explicitly as poet, Hawes emphasizes the importance of this role as the basis for human activity in the world. Buckner, in fact, argues that the entire section of *The Pastime of Pleasure* may be seen as an allegory of Hawes's quest for poetic renown:

Educated in rhetoric in the Tower of Doctrine, instructed in chivalry and the ways of the world by a benign Melyzyus (Henry VII), he achieves success at court in spite of the rancor, envy, and vice of his fellow courtiers, who may be visualized in the monsters who obstruct Amour's way. His enemies and detractors (the monsters) are slain and his poetic rivals who scorn traditional methods (Godfrey Gobylyve) are put to humiliating punishment.[11]

Though many elements of personal allegory are present in the poem, particularly the description of the narrator's ambition as poet, his relationship to King Melyzyus or Henry VII, and his harassment by various enemies, this interpretation is too limiting in the final analysis. The narrator's quest in the *Pastime*, rather than simply representing Hawes's own aspirations as a poet, is a larger emblem of worldly ambition, a quest that includes Hawes's personal allegory but goes beyond it. In educating the central figure first as poet in the Tower of Doctrine, then as knight in the Tower of Chivalry, and finally as lover in the Tower of Correction, Hawes draws together the principal aspirations of one engaged in the active life of the world, the path the narrator had chosen at the outset, and, by his treatment of the allegory, he indicates that the objects of these quests are interrelated. Poet, knight, and lover are aspects of the same narrator who combines in one figure the experiences of the dreamer in the *Romance of the Rose,* Dante's poet in the *Vita Nuova* and *Commedia,* Boccaccio's narrator in the *Amorosa Visione,* and the questers in the *Courte of Sapyence* and Lydgate's *Pilgrimage of the Life of Man.*

At several points in the narrative, Hawes emphasizes the links among Grand Amour's three roles. It is only after his instruction as poet, for example, that the narrator first gains sight of Pucell and his education in the Tower of Doctrine is interrupted for several hundred lines (1456–2403) as he reveals his love to his lady. The poet's newly acquired powers of language first secure the lady's affections and turn her from adversary to friend. Finally, Hawes repeatedly echoes the experiences of the narrator in one guise in another section. The battles the narrator fights in the Tower of Chivalry incorporate numerous echoes of his experience of poet in the Tower of Doctrine while the object of his quest, Lady Pucell, is characterized in language that recalls the earlier descriptions of poetry.[12] In contrast to the *Palice of Honour* where Douglas's narrator moves from the influence of love to that of poetry, Hawes represents a fusion of the concerns of poet, knight, and lover in the *Pastime,* placing the poet's activity in the context of human striving in the world.

While in the Tower of Doctrine the narrator is instructed in the seven arts, the foundation of knowledge, and particularly the power of language to order worldly experience; in the Towers of Chivalry and Correction, he is taught by experience the knowledge essential to his quest in the world. Again, in contrast to *The Example of Virtue,* Hawes focuses on perfecting rather than abandoning worldly concerns, with reestablishing the ideals of chivalry and love, which like the ideal of poetry considered in the Tower of Doctrine, have degenerated since ancient times. Allegorically, he presents both the negative and the positive conceptions of each role. By his treatment of the figure of Mars, Hawes first introduces the view of chivalry as success in battle, a source of fame. The narrator sees represented on the temple walls scenes of the destruction of Troy and the renown of its heroes and prays to the god of war for similar courage and fame:

> O prynce of honoure and of worthy fame
> O noble knyghtes of olde antyqyute
> O redouted courage the causer of theyr name
> Whose worthy actes fame caused to be
> In bokes wryten as ye may well se
> So gyue me grace ryght well to recure
> The power of fame / that shall longe endure. . . .
> (3046–52)

But, reminding the narrator and Mars of her higher power over human destiny, Fortune immediately qualifies this view. Both arguments and the conception of chivalry as a quest for fame are superseded by Minerva's larger definition of knighthood as a devotion of arms to truth and to honor, an ideal represented by the Court of King Melyzyus (Henry VII) to which the narrator gains admission.

Similarly, Hawes introduces both a negative and a positive vision of the lover's quest in the contrasting experiences of Godfrey Gobylyve and the narrator. Godfrey, the misshapen and foolish dwarf, seeks a wife but can find no woman who is not a shrew. In an attempt to divert the narrator from his quest, he bitterly chronicles the falseness of women and the disappointments of love. The narrator, in contrast, pursues his quest for ideal earthly love in Pucell, a love that Venus defines as true and stable with the object of procreation under the sanction of Dame Nature. Finally, like Minerva, Dame Correction rejects the false version of the ideal and reaffirms its more noble aspect as she shows the narrator the punishment of Godfrey Gobylyve or False Report and the others who have misrepresented the value of love.

The testing of the narrator that follows demonstrates that the obstacles to his quest as poet, lover, and knight are internal. In contrast to the three-headed monster of the *Example,* an image of the world, the flesh, and the devil, the beasts in the *Pastime* allegorically represent inner failings, particularly human perversions of truth by false use of language or false vision. The first of the monsters, the three-headed giant, is an image of falsehood, imagination, and perjury. His first head works to remove love "by a grete yllusyon" made with subtle fraud, deceit, and variance (4319–32). The second, "ymagynacyon," brings truth into jeopardy by "fals wytte," while the third, perjury, creates discord between lovers by false swearing (4333–60). The second monster, the seven-headed giant, Variance, is an allegory of the narrator's conflicts and uncertainties. The seven heads—"Dyssymulacyon," "Delay," "Dyscomforte," "Varyaunce," "Envy," "Detraccyon," and "Doubleness"—suggest a wavering on the part of Grand Amour in his quest and his subsequent discouragement, a more dangerous threat than illusion. Finally, the fire serpent or monster of the seven metals is the most insidious of the beasts. Fashioned by "Strangeness" and "Disdain," it represents a secret malice or the inner treachery that works to diminish Grand Amour's desire for Pucell. As Hawes shows, the narrator cannot rely on his own resources, the understanding and prudence that enabled him to defeat the other monsters, to overcome this beast, but must seek the aid of Minerva, the goddess of wisdom. In a curious passage, in which he describes the narrator's appeal to Minerva as being "in englysshe," and Minerva's response, which reveals the remedy for the monster's operation, as verses of "crafty eloquence," Hawes suggests by his language a link between her power and the vernacular poet's:

> And all in englysshe with longe cyrcumstaunce
> She shewed vs all the hole condycyon
> Of the meruayious serpentes operacyon
> And dyde shewe vs a perfyte remedy
> To withstand all the craft of sorcery

> And in lykewyse as the maner foloweth
> In depured verses of crafty eloquence
> Euery thynge vnto vs she sheweth
> And fyrst of all with all our dylygence
> These verses we sayd vnto her excellence

But she with craft verses eloquent
Gaue vs an answere full expedyent. . . .
(4979–90)

In her ability to arm Grand Amour against malice and illusion by her poetry, Minerva, who like the narrator speaks in the vernacular and in verse, becomes an image of the poet whose eloquence leads one from falsehood and variance to wisdom and truth.

In the Castle of Pucell, the various meanings of the narrator's quest come together as Hawes gathers up hints of earlier scenes to make Pucell's significance explicit. In her several aspects, she is an image of the narrator's devotion to the world in its most splendid form. More obviously, Pucell represents noble earthly love, the highest form of worldly pleasure. Dwelling within a jeweled "place of pleasure" that seems more like a "place celestyal," Pucell, "the moost fayr creature / Of ony fayre erthely persone lyuynge" (5216–17), dazzles the narrator by her appearance and noble qualities and inspires him to love. As she begins to speak, Pucell also is seen as a symbol of knightly achievement, the narrator's reward for his worthiness in his adventures in the world. As she reminds him, "for my sake you haue had often wronge / But your courage so hardy and stronge / Hath caused you for to be vyctoryous / Of your enemyes so moche contraryous" (5225–28). Finally, Hawes treats Pucell as an image of the power of poetry itself. Echoing earlier descriptions of the Fountain of Helycon and the Fountain of Rhetoric, he reunites the narrator and Pucell before a similar fountain, "which dyde spoute out the dulcet lycoure / lyke crystall clere with aromatyke odoure" (5199–5200), suggestive of the language of rhetoric and poetry. The description of Pucell's speech, likewise, recalls the earlier references to poetry:

Her redolente wordes of swete influence
Degouted vapoure moost aromatyke
And made conuersyon of my complacence
Her depured and her lusty rhetoryke
My courage reformed. . . . (5264–68)

Like the true verse to which the narrator aspires, Pucell has the power to reform and ennoble humankind.

But unlike Cleanness in *The Example of Virtue,* Pucell remains a worldly and hence an ambivalent figure. Her palace, however splendid, is still a transitory "place of pleasure and delectacyon" (5244) and, as the object of the narrator's quest, she represents explicitly earthly and unenduring rewards. The limits of her significance to worldly aspiration are made clearer by the description of the wedding with which the narrator's quest ends. In contrast to the similar scenes in the *Example,* in this wedding the couple is attended by secular rather than spiritual virtues and its outcome is the payment of the debt of nature rather than salvation. The wedding feast is the high point of the *Example,* occupying about a fourth of the entire poem, but Hawes devotes only forty-two lines to it in the *Pastime,* and after these lines, Pucell drops out of the story entirely. The whole episode is anticlimactic and calls into question the validity of the narrator's goals as poet-knight in search of renown.

In the final section, Hawes qualifies his earlier vision with another as Time and Eternity step forward to replace Fame, the original guide for the narrator's quest. Under their tutelage, Grand Amour, now aged and at the point of death, recognizes the vanity of his aspirations:

> . . . my selfe called la graunde amoure
> Sekynge aduenture in the worldly glory
> For to attayne the ryches and honoure
> Dyde thynke full lytell that I sholde here ly
> Tyll dethe dyde marke me full ryght pryuely
> Lo what I am and where to you must
> Lyke as I am / so shall you be all dust
>
> Than in your mynde inwardly dyspyse
> The bryttle worlde so full of doublenes. . . .
> (5481–89)

While Time suggests the limits of Fame's power, Eternity steps forward and reveals the only enduring fame where time gives way to everlasting time in God's realm. Worldly success and joy, the objects of the poet-narrator's quest, are now seen as vain pursuits with no certainty (5775–81).

The *Pastime* thus presents us with two visions, a worldly quest of the narrator for Fame through love, knightly achievement, and poetry and a vision of the limitations of this quest. In contrast to the *Example,* it suggests both the appeal of the world and the transitoriness of its pleasure. The education of the narrator as a poet, in a sense, becomes an emblem of this dilemma, a more significant version of the conflict of every human being. In the *Pastime,* the narrator is fashioned as poet by means of worldly arts, the seven sciences of the Trivium and Quadrivium. His medium is refined and purified language, more perfect than ordinary speech, yet mutable, while his matter is earthly action, fables and stories of noble deeds that are seen as allegories of more permanent truths. The poet's role as an orderer and illuminator of experience requires an involvement in the world despite a recognition of its insubstantial nature. As a means of civilizing and governing humankind, poetry is ennobling, and like the carbuncle, it protects from darkness and ignorance. Yet from the perspective of eternity, it is "but a blast of wynde" (5777).

In his last allegorical poem, the *Conforte of Louers,* Hawes discovers a solution to this dilemma that distinguishes his vision of the poet from his fifteenth-century predecessors' and anticipates some of the concerns of the Renaissance poets.[13] His solution is reflected both in the changed style of the poem and in its curious treatment of allegory. To some extent, Hawes's final vision of poetry is anticipated by the critical vocabulary of the *Pastime.* In this poem and also in the *Example,* Hawes introduces the familiar terminology of the fifteenth-century poets which characterizes the poet as a skilled rhetorician whose "colours" and "floures" of eloquence and "swete," "dulcet" terms illuminate and transform his matter.[14] Like Douglas, he qualifies this vocabulary by a second cluster of terms—"crafty," "sle," "subtle," "derk," "clowdy," "mysty," and "covert"—which draw attention to the difficulty of the good poem.[15] The surface of poetry is "mysty," "derk," "subtle," and "couert." The poet's fables are hidden under "clowdy colours" and "derk" fictions. As he explains in the *Pastime,* poets write "In an example / with a mysty cloude // Of couert lykenesse" (981–82), concealing "the sentence / vnder mysty fygures // By many coloures" (922–33). At the outset of the *Pastime,* he praises Lydgate for his "fyccyons" "grounded on reason with clowdy fygures" and apologizes for his own lack of ability to "cloke" or hide his matter "with a mysty smoke" or under "couert colour" (34–42).

Hawes adopts the critical vocabulary of the fifteenth-century poets, yet he changes the meaning of some of the most important of their terms and introduces new words which reveal a shift in attitude toward the poet's craft. A good example of this process is his exploitation of the term "fayne" and its forms "fayned" and "faynynge," which he purges of negative connotations, particularly of the implication of falsifying or creating deceptive illusions. Henryson and Douglas use this word in an ambivalent sense, suggesting both the poet's power to imagine and the potentially deceptive nature of his fables, whereas Hawes consistently introduces "fayne" when it refers to poetry with the positive meaning "to create" or "to imagine."[16] At the outset of the *Pastime,* for example, he praises Lydgate for his "ryght famous bokes . . . if his faynynge with termes eloquent" (31–32), using the term in the sense of inventing or imagining. Dame Rhetoric praises the noble poets of antiquity for being "ryght ymagynatyfe / / Fables to fayne / by good auctoryte / / They were so wyse / and so inuentyfe" (716–18), again introducing the word with the meaning of "invent" or "imagine." Later, in defending poets for the purposefulness of their writing, she observes, "They fayned no fable without reason" (953). Finally, Hawes underscores the positive meanings of the term when he criticizes modern poets for failing to "create" or "invent" fables: "They fayne no fables / pleasaunt and couerte / / But spend theyr tyme / in vaynfull vaynte" (1389–90). In Hawes's treatment, the term "fayne" no longer suggests the fictional and potentially deceptive nature of poetry but refers unambiguously to its imaginative and invented quality.

Even more significant than this shift in meaning is Hawes's addition to the fifteenth-century vocabulary of two critical terms—"fatall" and "scryptures"—which define an aspect of good poetry not found in the conceptions of his English and Scots predecessors. "Fatall" in Middle English had a range of meanings—"predetermined," "predestined," "fated" or "fatefull."[17] In applying the term to poetry, Hawes calls attention to the prophetic nature of true poetry, its power to anticipate the future and embody figures of events to come. This use is apparent in the *Example of Virtue* when he commends poets and philosophers for their prophetic wisdom, philosophers for their prudence in founding the seven sciences, and poets for their ability to foresee truth: "also poetes that were fatall / Craftely colored with clowdy fygures / The true sentence of all theyr scryptures" (901–3). In the late Middle Ages, "scryptures" refers both to the sacred writing of the Bible and, in a general way, to "inscriptions" or "writings."[18] Often linking this term with "fatall," as in the earlier passage, Hawes uses "scriptures" to describe the poem as "true writing." He reveals this emphasis, for example, in his praise of famous poets at the outset of the *Pastime* as men who "Pronounced trouthe / vnder cloudy fygures / / By the inuenuyon / of theyr fatall scryptures" (720–21). By his application of the terms "fatall" and "scryptures" to poetic writing, Hawes suggests a link between poetry and prophecy and underscores the good poem's power to embody enduring truths. The poet's "faynyng" or creation is a type of God's creation and like the divine prophecies, his fables contain sacred truths under their mysterious surface. In Hawes's view, the poet does not merely "enlumine" or shed light on the world as Lydgate conceives, but the poet is a prophet whose meaning transcends the worldly medium and whose activity, though human, is divinely inspired.

The conception of poetry as "fatall" or prophetic is developed more explicitly in Hawes's final allegory *The Conforte of Louers.* Despite its brevity, this poem resembles the *Pastime* in many ways. Most conspicuously, the cast of characters is the same—Grand Amour and La Bel Pucell. The narrator of the *Conforte* again appears in the guise of the poet and, after being educated by various allegorical figures, sets out in quest for the lady who again represents the triple reward of love, renown, and poetic excellence. Grand Amour and Pucell engage in dialogues similar to those of the *Pastime* and the *Conforte* is laced with echoes of the earlier poem. In the body of the *Conforte,* we find a similar fusion of concerns, the relation of worldly success as poet, lover, and member of court to the larger issue of the transitory and often ambiguous nature of human experience.

But these features are shaped to a different vision in the *Conforte* which reveals Hawes's changing conception of the poet and his solution to the dilemmas of the *Pastime.* The poem is Hawes's most interesting treatment of the themes of the three long works, and, though brief, his most ambitious experiment with allegory. In the *Conforte,* one immediately notes a changed atmosphere. The narrator opens the prologue with a discussion of the difficulty of poetry, "Harde is to construe poetycall scryptures" (3), and from the outset the surface of the poem is more allusive and mysterious than it was in the *Pastime,* with the action being marked by riddles, complicated symbols, and numerous personal allusions that are not easily deciphered. The quest is truncated drastically and the major portion of the narrative focuses on the description of the three symbolic mirrors that the narrator finds as he begins his search for Pucell and the lengthy dialogue between Grand Amour and Pucell at the end. The allegory is at once more personal and internal and more universal. In contrast to the *Pastime,* Grand Amour is presented more explicitly both as the poet Hawes and as a figure for the conception of the poet in general, while Pucell, who, in contrast to the experience of the *Pastime,* now is the final goal of the quest, is drawn both as a particular woman and as a symbol.

On one level, the *Conforte* presents a detailed allegory of Hawes's hopes for preferment in Henry VII's court, where he served as one of the grooms of the Chamber and was the recipient of occasional payments for his "ballets," and the court of the new King Henry VIII. The poem is simultaneously a defense of his practices as poet and a bid for recognition. Although these concerns are introduced in the *Pastime,* they do not dominate the narrative as they do in the *Conforte.* At the outset of his vision, the narrator emphasizes this aspect of the allegory as he explains to his guide that he has written many books in the past, "vnder coloure" to a lady, who may perhaps be identified with Mary Tudor (1496–1533) who was at that time promised to a "myghty lorde" (861), Charles of Castile, later Emperor Charles V, and whom Hawes describes in the "Joyfull Meditatioun" in terms similar to the description of Pucell in the *Conforte.*[19] Because of his devotion to her, he had been subjected to sorrow and pain. For three years, the period between the *Pastime* and the *Conforte,* he was forced to bind his right hand, that is, he was prevented from writing allegorically and hence in a manner that is "clowdy" or figural and might be misconstrued politically. During this time, he was beset by numerous enemies, who "dyde me touse and rent // Not longe agone / delynge moost shamefully // That by theyr tuggynge / my lyfe was nere spent" (163–65). Because of his enemies' hatred of his lady's father or Henry VII, he feared for his life, but nevertheless he remained true "thoght that my body had but lytell rest" (173). Hawes describes the various forms of torment he was made to endure and suggests that his enemies harassed him because they have misconstrued the meaning of his allegories:

Some[e] had wened for to haue made an ende
Of my bokes / before [t]he[y] hadde begynnynge
But all vayne they dyde so comprehende

> What they of them lacke vnderstandynge
> Vaynfull was & is theyr mysse contryuynge
> Who lyst the trouthe of them for to ensu[e]
> For the reed and whyte they wryte full true.
> (183–89)

As poet, he insists, he is loyal to the "reed and whyte," the dynasty of Henry VII. The lady assures the poet that his books are pleasing to the king who perceives their true meaning and she anticipates his preferment. Advising him by "wytte" to make friends of foes and let God avenge his wrong, she reinforces the earlier hope that the narrator had expressed in his prophecy of better fortune to come.[20]

The guide directs the poet-narrator to a tower, symbolically decorated with greyhounds, "many lyons" of gold and "dyuers sondry dragons," the heraldic symbols of Henry VII and Henry VIII, where he may gain sight of his lady and learn of his fate as poet.[21] In three mirrors within the tower, he witnesses his past, present, and future and receives the sword and shield destined for the chosen knight. Shortly afterward, Grand Amour gains sight of his lady and reveals his dedication to her. From reading *The Pastime of Pleasure,* she recognizes the strength of his love, but she warns him of her friends' disapproval and her promise to another lord. Finally, the lady is moved by his plea and promises "grace after gouernance." Like the guide, she insists that his wisdom is his best defense against his enemies, and, in a very difficult stanza, the narrator responds that he has suffered well "the phyppe" and the net of his enemies and anticipates the aid of God in overcoming his foes and in winning his lady's love.[22]

Although most of the attention devoted to the *Conforte* has been directed to the historical allusions and to the personal allegory in the poem, Hawes exploits these events as a vehicle for introducing a number of more significant themes. Like Dante in the *Vita Nuova* and James I in the *Kingis Quair,* he expands our perspective on the personal to reveal the universal. Developing the implications of his critical terms, "fayned" and "fatall," he makes the narrator in search of preferment beset by enemies, a type of the poet-David of the *Canticles,* the divinely inspired prophet who writes sacred songs in God's praise despite harassment by his enemies. The association between the narrator's quest and David's introduces a vision of the

poet that enlarges the views of the fifteenth-century writers and resolves the conflict of the *Pastime* between the poet's involvement in
the active life in the world and his recognition of its transitory nature.
The poet's divinely inspired words contain truths that transcend the
misguided responses of human beings and the ravages of time, and,
like the sacred writings of the Psalmist, become an emblem of God's
mysteries.

By his double emphasis on the power of God to prophesy and to
protect the righteous and on the stance of the narrator as poet persecuted in the world, Hawes introduces the context of the *Canticles* at
the outset of the *Conforte*. Like David, Grand Amour asserts his
devotion and his recognition that God will defeat the enemies of those
who are dedicated to him:

> To god I sayd / thou mayst my mater spede
> And me rewarde / accordynge to my mede
> Thou knowest the trouthe / I am to the true
> what that thou lyst / thou mayst them all subdue
> . . . .
> who dyde preserue / Ionas and moyses
> who dyde preserue yet many other mo
> And as the byble maketh mencyon doub[t]les
> who dyde kepe Charles frome his euyll fo
> who was he / that euer coude do so
> But god alone / than in lyke wyse maye he
> Kepe me full sure / frome all inyquyte.
> (39–56)

As he outlines his plight to his guide in the vision proper, his language
recalls many of the themes and images of the Psalms. Grand Amour
presents himself as sorrowing lover and as poet alone among enemies
awaiting God's aid:

> Thretened with sorowe / of ma[n]y paynes grete
> Thre yeres ago my ryght hande I dyde bynde
> Fro my browes for fere / the dropes doune dyde sweet
> God knoweth all it was nothynge my mynde
> Vnto no persone / I durst my hert[e] vntwynde.
> (134–38)[23]

Echoing David's words, he describes his enemies as wolves who tear
apart and devour him (163), as cruel tormentors who attack him

continually with their "falshode" and "subtylte" (169), and as evil
men who set nets, snares, and traps for him (407).[24] He lives in
"meane seson" and feeds on "grene grasse" (204–5). Although the
narrator has little relief from this torment, his heart remains true to his
lady and to God as he awaits their grace. Reiterating the words of
many of the Psalms, the guide urges reconciliation rather than violence and assures him of God's power and certain aid if he endures
these trials, "It is oft stedfast / and wyll long endure // Yf always
malyce / they wyll put in vre // No doubte it is / tha[t] god so hygh[e]
and stronge / Ful meruaylously / wyl soone reuenge theyr wronge"
(214–17).[25]

Hawes's association of Grand Amour's quest with the plight of the
poet-David in the Psalms has further implications when considered in
the light of medieval and early Renaissance interpretations of this
figure. In contrast to Lydgate's Amphion who civilized men and
brought order out of chaos by the power of his words, David in both
Christian and in Jewish traditions has a mission that is not only
political but also sacred as God's chosen king whose offspring will
redeem and rule over Israel. A simple shepherd anointed by the Lord,
he endures exile and temptation, even the betrayal of one of his sons,
before he finally witnesses the fulfillment of God's promise. Whereas
Amphion's eloquence is the gift of Mercury and subdues dissension
and strife, David's Psalms are born of suffering and are a testimony of
God's power and the just man's devotion. His words are both prayer
and promise, and as poet, he is at once a model for man and a prophet
whose writing contains sacred truths.

In medieval commentary, David generally is treated from one of
two points of view.[26] The majority of writers, following Augustine,
allegorize him as a figure of Christ and his Psalms as prophecies of
New Testament events and teachings. In the *Enarrationes in Psalmos*
(A.D. 392–418), Augustine approaches the *verba et gesta Davidis* as
sacramentum that contain deeper layers of meaning when the hidden
senses of the words are revealed.[27] For Augustine, David is variously
a type of Christ and a figure of the Christian church. This interpretation is illustrated effectively by his treatment of Psalms 54–56 upon
which he builds some of his most elaborate allegories.[28] Literally, the
Psalms contain David's account of his flight from Saul into the city of
Gath. Distressed by the betrayal of his friend, which is more torturous
than the stratagems of his enemies, David turns to God in whom he

puts his trust. As he suffers the torments of the Philistines, he takes refuge in "the shadow of [His] wings," till "the storm of destruction pass."

For Augustine, David's torture at the hands of the Philistines and his ultimate escape are a veiled foreshadowing of the crucifixion and resurrection of Christ. Surrounded by enemies who refuse to accept him as king and who contrive his death, David is an image of Christ among the Jews who betrayed him. As Augustine explains, the word "gath" means a press-room, in which one finds a wine press, an image of the passion of Christ:

> Ergo David nostrum Dominum Jesum Christum natum ex semine illius David, non solum tenuerunt, sed et tenent adhuc Allophyli in Geth. Geth diximus quod civitas sit. Interrogata autem interpretatio hujus nominis, indicat Torcular. Christus secundum quod caput Salvator corporis, ille natus ex virgine crucifixus, qui jam nobis exemplum resurrectionis nostrae in resurrectione suae carnis ostendit, qui sedet ad dexteram Patris, et pro nobis interpellat, est et hic, sed in corpore suo quod est Ecclesia.[29]

This press is not harmful as we might suppose, for when it squeezes the grape, it produces wine or the essence of the fruit. Similarly, Christ's crucifixion in the "torcula" of his enemies bore the fruit of his resurrection and our redemption:

> Tenetur in torculari corpus ejus, id est ecclesia ejus. Quid est, in torculari? In pressuris. Sed in torculari fructuosa pressura est. Uva in vite pressuram non sentit, integra videtur, sed nihil inde manat: mittitur in torcular, calcatur, premitur; injuria videtur fieri uvae, sed ista injuria sterilis non est; imo si nulla injuria accederet, sterilus remaneret.[30]

Further developing this image, Augustine suggests the faithful, the body of Christ, are also in "Gath" and instructs true Christians to endure the suffering and persecution of their enemies in the world, and, like Christ, await their deliverance. The Old Testament David as king and priest, thus, for Augustine represents the New Testament Christ and Church and his words reveal mysteries that the original readers did not understand.

In contrast to the view of David as a type of Christ, other commentators, placing more emphasis on the historical meaning of the Psalms, approach this figure not only as a veiled representation of Christ but as a man of faith who is worthy of imitation in his own right by Christians under the New Law. As Gosselin points out, this position is developed significantly in the *Postilla super totam bibliam* (c. 1322–31) of the fourteenth-century commentator, Nicolaus Lyra.[31] Considering the immediate context of the Psalms, Lyra treats David as a multidimensional figure, at once prophet and type of Christ, spokesman of the Christian church, figure of the good prelate and king, and as a model of the Christian man. The last two categories, particularly, modify the principally christological conceptions of David. For Lyra, David's persecutions become an image not only of the persecution of Christ and of the early church but also of the harassment of the medieval church and the shameful occupation of the Holy Land by the Muslims. In his commentary on Psalm 5, for example, Lyra's emphasis is not on the attack on David by his enemies and his plea to God as a prophetic figure of the Church triumphant in the heavenly kingdom, but rather as an example of the experience of the Church in the world, while in Psalm 19, he treats David's prayer as that of the Church for the Christians who are about to confront the Infidel.[32] Thus, as Gosselin emphasizes, for Lyra, David as prophet is not defined once and for all figuratively by the events of the time of Christ, but he is a model that accrues relevance in later times.[33]

This ongoing significance of David manifests itself also in his role as example for the individual Christian. In Lyra's *Postilla,* David becomes a model not only of the virtuous believer, beloved of God, but also of the Christian who falls into sin, a *viator* poised between the beatified and the damned. Through his own free will, David succumbs to the temptations of Bathsheba, strays from God, and jeopardizes his salvation. Finally recognizing and repenting his sin, he receives God's mercy and thus by his actions offers hope of God's promise to the individual in tribulation. In interpreting Psalm 85, for example, in which David prays to be freed from the persecutions of Saul, Lyra suggests that the Psalm may be read as the prayer of any just person who is tormented by the devil or wrongdoers, and who, like David, relies on God's mercy.[34] Likewise, although he allegorizes Psalm 26 more elaborately than some of the other Psalms, he envisions David at the beginning of his reign over the tribe of Judah after the death of Saul, the situation the Psalm describes, essentially as a man of faith amid his worldly pilgrimage. Morally, he suggests the kingdom over which David is about to reign is his own spiritual state, threatened by various dangers, and more exactly, the Psalm provides an image of the pious man's passage from adolescence to adulthood, undertaking the task of controlling his passions or the "agitations" of his soul:

> Psalmum istum literaliter exponi de statu David quando, post mortem Saul in Ebron, ascendit et cepit regnare super tribum Juda quamvis eius adversarii adhuc assent in multitudine magna. Moraliter autem exponi potest de quolibet fideli ad estatem adultam veniente, tunc enim debet regnum suum incipere bene regendo motus animae. Et quoniam in hoc difficultatem patitur, rogare debet Fominum ut ab eo dirigatur. . . .[35]

In two interesting historical applications, Lyra even links the persecuted figure of David in the Psalms with the twelfth-century martyr Thomas à Becket betrayed by Henry II (Psalms 70 and 116) and with Saint Hilarion and Saint Francis in their effort to escape the temptations of the world (Psalm 63). For the Christian, David becomes an example to be imitated in his own right, a model of the just man's struggle and of his hope in God's promise.

The commentaries of the Protestant reformers develop this view of David by linking him as a man of faith with their own true followers. Interpreting the history of the Christian church as a process of rise, decline, and rebirth, they define a parallel between David's restoration of the true Church and doctrine and their own struggle as a "faithful remnant." For the reformers, David is not simply an example of a mouthpiece through which God speaks, but one of the elect, a man sanctified by the Holy Spirit and given the gift of wisdom. In their writings both Luther and Calvin suggest a personal model in David, a sense of historical identity in their efforts for their faith. As Preus demonstrates, Luther, in his lectures on the Psalms written between 1513 and 1516, gradually comes to a new understanding of the faith of the Old Testament and a sense of the anguish and hope of David as a type of his own, whereas Calvin states his identification with David explicitly in the preface to his *Commentary on the Book of the Psalms:*[36]

In considering the whole course of the life of David, it seemed to me that by his own footsteps he showed me the way, and from this I have experienced no small consolation. As that holy king was harassed by the Philistines and other foreign enemies with continual wars, while he was much more grievously afflicted by the malice and wickedness of some perfidious men amongst his own people, so I can say as to myself, that I have been assailed on all sides, and have scarcely been able to enjoy repose for a single moment, but have always had to sustain some conflict either from enemies without or within the Church.[37]

The Psalms are important because they portray the plight of the just and faithful not only in David's time but in all times, and provide an example for God's followers of how to avoid despair. As Calvin advised his readers, they should turn to the Psalms in order to find consolation and encouragement in their present adversity.[38]

In the *Conforte,* written on the eve of the Reformation, Hawes applies many of these associations with David, God's chosen king, to himself as poet, considerably extending the fifteenth-century conceptions of this role. The link between David and the poet occurs both in literary and in artistic traditions in the Middle Ages in terms of a recurring analogy between Orpheus and David.[39] Yet Hawes's emphasis is not on the power of David's song prominent in these treatments, but on his role as a persecuted and misunderstood follower of God. Although he undoubtedly also knew Lydgate's representation of David in "Misericordias Domini in Eternum Cantabo" as a model of sacred eloquence or the perfection of song that Lydgate as a newly dedicated religious poet hopes to attain, he does not develop this aspect of David but turns to him as a more complex figure of the poet in historical, political, and moral terms.[40] For Hawes, David represents the poet as "vates" inspired by God, given the gift of prophecy, yet harassed and tormented by unjust enemies. His trials are a test of his calling and distinguish him from ordinary men while his mysterious language, like the words of the Psalms, reflects the impenetrable wisdom of God. But more important, Hawes's figure of David is an emblem of the poet's plight in the active life in the world and brings together the main concerns of the questers in his three allegorical poems, linking his own personal situation to the larger thematic questions he considers.

In the *Conforte,* these associations broaden the significance of the narrator's traditional love quest. The comfort he seeks is at once his lady's and God's; he is both love poet and poet of prophetic wisdom, political man and the chosen knight of the Lord. The central section draws together these concerns to redefine the relation of the various kinds of allegory in the poem. Within the tower where he parts company with his guide, the narrator in search of comfort discovers not the lady he seeks, but three mirrors "made longe ago to be memoryall" (313), which reveal past, present, and future and clarify the poet's role. In the first glass, under which is written "Beholde thy selfe / and thy fautes" (315), the narrator sees an image of his past life, a pursuit of pleasure and willful deeds without regard for virtue, an image of the action of the *Pastime.* Above this mirror is an unsheathed sword perilously hanging by a silken thread, point downward, ready to chastise those who incline to sin. Echoing the *Canticles,* the narrator emphasizes the sword's power to revenge those who resist God and resolves to correct his past errors.

The second mirror, which reveals the narrator's present experience in the world, provides an image of the prudence and virtue that one may attain by one's own efforts. Over the mirror hangs a flower of fine gold, bordered with diamonds, set with a spectacular emerald, and attached to the wall "by a ryght subtyll gynne // With a chayne of yron / and many a pryue pynne" (356–57). The legend in the table of gold beside the mirror bids the narrator know himself and prepare for what is to come by laboring to get the flower and the comfort it will bring. The stone within its midst is both a symbol of prudence and a test of faithfulness. One of the twelve jewels upon which the heavenly city of Jerusalem rests in the Apocalypse, in lapidary tradition the emerald has many powers. It sharpens human sight and enables one to foresee future dangers and, finally, inclines one to goodness and virtue. As Bartholomaeus Anglicus remarks, it

> sheweth fygures ymages & shapes of thinges that ben nyghe
> thereto. And hath of yefte of kynde a goodnes of vertue to saue
> & to hele dyueres syknesses & euyiles. Dyas[cordes] sayith it
> encreasyth riches: & maketh men haue good wordes; & fayre
> euydence in cause & in plee. Yf this stone be hanged abowte

the necke it heleth Enutricem & the fallyng euyl & saueth &
comfortyth feble syght. And chasteth lecherous meuynges &
maketh good mynde: and helpyth also ayenst all fantasyes &
Iapes of fendes And sesseth tempeste: & stauncheth blood.
And it is sayd that it helpyth them that vse to dyuyne & gesse
what shal befall as it is sayd in Lapidario.[41]

Hawes assigns many of these qualities to the emerald, and in his
vision he links its strengths directly to faithfulness in love, warning
that if Grand Amour is untrue, the stone will break apart and shatter.
Specifically, the emerald will protect the narrator from the dangers he
beholds in the second mirror, the "subtyll engynes" and "trappes" of
his enemies. It is by his own "wit" and "prudence" as a man that the
narrator finally is able to undo the chain and obtain the stone:

> . . . after this to the yron gynne
> I wente anone my wyte to proue
> By lytell and lytell // to vndo euery pynne
> Thus in and out / I dydde the chayne ofte moue
> Yet coude I not come / vnto myne aboue
> Tyll at the last / I dyde the crafte espy.
> (428–33)

The acquisition of the emerald in Hawes's treatment, thus, becomes a
sign of the narrator's intelligence and prudence (440), the most noble
of his human attributes.

The third mirror, in contrast, represents the powers that derive not
from one's own abilities but from God. In the mirror the narrator sees
an image of the Holy Ghost burning in flames, and the verses underneath describe the mysterious nature of God who neither enters one's
eyes, nor ears, nor is apprehended by any of the senses, focusing
particularly on His ability to give humans language and inspire them
to spiritual understanding and to prophecy. Words are the gift of the
Holy Ghost who "ryght ofte inspyre / Dyuers creatures with spyryt-
uall knowynge" (457–58). Appearing at the feast of Pentecost to
Mary and the Apostles on the third of His visitations, He inflamed the
human heart with virtue so that we could penetrate the meaning of the
Gospel, and by the same power, enable the faithful to understand His
prophecies.

The poet-knight of the *Pastime* is formed by worldly education in the Tower of Doctrine and by his quest for honor to win Pucell; the poet of the *Conforte,* like the Psalmist David, is presented explicitly as the chosen one of God and his ability is seen not as something learned or acquired by human effort but as a divine gift. The symbolic sword and shield that hang above the third mirror make this shift in the nature of the poet-knight clear. The sword may be handled only by "one persone / chosen by god in dede" (506) and descended from the "grete lady" who inscribed its handle a hundred years ago. Its virtues enable man to win right and increase truth and amity; the shield, "Perceverance" or understanding, protects and strengthens him against enemies. The description culminates with a vision of the firmament in the third mirror and a marvelous star that the narrator recognizes as a sign of the "resynge of a knight," the image of God drawing His chosen one to Him, like the upright man of the *Canticles,* out of the fury of the wrongdoers:

> This sterre it sygnyfyeth the resynge of a knyght
> The bowynge beame agayne so tournynge
> Betokened rattonnes of them whiche by myght
> wolde hym resyst by theyr wronge resystynge
> The beame towarde Phebus clerely shynynge
> Betokened many meruaylous fyres grete
> On them to lyght that wolde his purpose lete.
> (547–53)

The apocalyptic vision and the lines from Psalm 129 that follow underscore the poet-knight's elevation. The verses that Hawes quotes, "Sepe expugnauerunt me a iuuentute mea; et enim non potuerunt mich," and "Supra dorsum meum fabricauerunt peccatores prolongauerunt iniquitatem suam," come from the beginning of the Psalm, a song of ascents, which sum up both the trials and endless suffering of the faithful and God's power to defeat their enemies. Though short, the Psalm epitomizes the recurrent themes of David's songs and provides, if one completes the lines the narrator introduces, a prophecy of the just man's triumph. As Augustine remarks, the words of this Psalm are few, but their meaning is great: "sic et iste psalmus, si verba numeres, brevis est; si sententias appendas, magnus est."[42] In his commentaries, Psalm 129 is treated as an emphatic statement of God's commitment to the faithful and His power to defeat the wicked. Augustine points out in his *Enarratio* that the

Psalm is addressed to those who persevere in bad times and attend to the words of God.[43] Members of the true Church, like the faithful of the Old Testament and the evangelists of the New, they need not fear the repeated evils of the wicked, but should consider the goodness of God's creation and His work and be consoled. God tests those He has made to separate the just from the evil, the saved from the damned. The words of the Psalm finally promise certain torment to the wicked, types of antichrist, and a passing from this life to God for the faithful.[44]

Similarly, Rolle treats the Psalm as a consolation of Holy Church to the feeble but good man who endures suffering.[45] Reminding him of the torment she had undergone since she first began to love God, the Holy Church stresses the powerlessness of the wicked to harm him. God will defeat those who hate the faithful, shaming them "when thei see thair owne dampnacyon" and the "vnspedful" end of their life.[46] Calvin interprets Psalm 129 in his commentaries as a model of God's testing and unwavering commitment to the faithful:

> This psalm teaches, in the first place, that God subjects his Church to diverse troubles and afflictions, to the end he may better prove himself her deliverer and defender. The Psalmist, therefore, recalls to the memory of the faithful how sadly God's people had been persecuted in all ages, and how wonderfully they had been preserved, in order by such examples to fortify their hope in reference to the future. In the second part, under the form of an imprecation, he shows that the divine vengeance is ready to fall upon all the ungodly, who without cause distress the people of God.[47]

In the concluding section of the poem, Hawes attempts to draw together the triple aspects of the narrator's quest in search of comfort in the world. Approaching the mirror, he reaches for the sword that hangs above it. The handle quakes and then gradually slides out of its sheath, validating the narrator's role as chosen poet and knight. Holding the emerald flower, shield, and sword, he immediately thinks of his lady whom he likens to the bright daystar that shines before the rising of the sun, echoing the image of the poet-knight's elevation. In turn, he links the lady to his books, which privately greet her and by their mysterious prophecies anticipate their meeting. As the lady suggests, poet, lover, and knight are joined in Grand Amour's quest.

His success in attaining the flower, the sword, and the shield reveal him as a knight who has proven himself to be worthy of love and of important destiny while his devotion makes his role as poet possible, for as the lady recognizes, had he not been in love, he could not have written the *Pastime of Pleasure* which she admires. In the context of their concluding debate, the double sense of the title of the poem clearly emerges as comfort from the lady and from God.

In his effort to link his personal allegory with the poet-knight's love quest and the experience of the just man of the *Canticles,* Hawes goes further than Douglas in placing the role of the poet in a broad context of human pursuit. Douglas ultimately considers the poet's quest as an aspect of the search for honor and virtue in the world; Hawes enlarges this vision to define the importance of the poet in political, moral, artistic, and religious terms. No longer simply an "enluminer," who in Lydgate's view civilizes and inspires humanity to wisdom by the power of words, the poet in the *Conforte* is at once a particular man and a "vates" chosen by God, whose verse embodies His mysteries. The poet's words, unlike the carefully crafted language of the Scots "makaris," the epitome of human artistry, are the gift of the Holy Ghost, and, rather than imitating the power of the sun, God's creative force in the world, which in the earlier fifteenth-century visions is an emblem of the poet's relation to his matter, they are the direct instrument of God's revelation of truth. But although the poet in Hawes's view is a prophet or sayer of truth, his verse is not necessarily effective. Although the poem is both a testimony to and a revelation of God's wisdom, it is misconstrued and scorned by the ignorant who continually assail the poet.

Although Hawes's treatment of poetry in the *Conforte* considerably expands the fifteenth-century poets' conceptions of the poem as ennobling, a vehicle of truth, in practice his effort is not entirely successful. Frequently in the *Conforte* there is a tension between the kinds of allegory, and the meaning becomes impenetrable. This problem is particularly apparent at the end of the poem when Hawes attempts to join the various strands of allegory. In response to Pucell who withholds her love and bids the narrator to hold out against his enemies by governing himself well, for example, Grand Amour reveals:

Surely I thynke / I suffred well the phyppe
The nette also dydde teche me on the waye

But me to bere I trowe they lost a lyppe
For the lyfte hande extendyd my Iournaye
And not to call me for my sporte and playe
Wherfore by foly yf that they do synne
The holy goost maye well the batayle wynne.
(890–96)

But the private allusions in the passage obscure rather than reinforce Hawes's meaning, and as at the conclusion of Chaucer's *Parliament of Fowls,* we end with a deferred decision, the submission of the narrator's fate to Venus and Fortune, and the poet's reawakening.[48]

Hawes's changing conception of poetry manifests itself in the stylistic development of his three long works. Although he repeatedly presents himself as a disciple of Lydgate, *The Example of Virtue, The Pastime of Pleasure,* and *The Conforte of Louers* represent a movement away from the earlier fifteenth-century ideal of high style and "depured eloquence" (*Example of Virtue,* 1–9) and rhetoric to a plainer style later associated with the Protestant reforms, and, finally, to a new stylistic solution. The shift from an eloquent to a plain style first is apparent in the *Example* where Hawes introduces an unadorned medium that points more directly to the work's allegorical meaning. Although several prolonged sections of Lydgatian eloquence remain, notably at the outset of the poem, in the encounter with Dame Sapience, in the description of the lady, and the wedding of Virtue and Cleanness, these passages are surrounded by stanzas of conspicuously plainer style that direct attention to the significance of the events, for example, in the descriptions of Dame Nature, Fortune, Hardiness, and Wisdom and their instructions to the narrator, in the account of the narrator's journey to find Lady Cleanness, and in his battle with the dragon. In the *Pastime,* the plain mode predominates, punctuated by intermittent rhetorical elaboration, for example, in the praise of famous poets in the Tower of Doctrine, the description of Pucell, and in the passionate address of Grand Amour to his lady, and also by the comic banter of the Godfrey Gobylyve section. In contrast to the *Example,* which concludes with an elevated celebration of the union of Virtue and Cleanness and an eloquent prayer to God, to Prince Henry, and to Hawes's masters Chaucer, Gower, and Lydgate, even the ending of the *Pastime,* which, with its catalogue of the Nine Worthies and the vision of Fame, would provide a perfect opportunity for stylistic elaboration, is straightforward and understated.[49]

In the *Conforte,* Hawes abandons the mixture of plain allegorical and rhetorical styles of the *Example* and the *Pastime* as his principal mode and introduces a medium that is a strangely discordant combination of stylistic features from the dream vision tradition, the love allegory, the long didactic narrative, and the *Canticles.* The shifts from one style to another often are unexpected and abrupt, as in the dialogue between Grand Amour and Pucell at the end of the poem where we move from the lover's passionate complaint (778–84), to a discussion of his books (792–98), to the lady's moral instruction (869–75), to his veiled allusions to his own troubles (890–910). In these passages, Hawes often appears to be manipulating style to create a deliberate obscurity or mystery, to form the "derk," "clowdy," and "sle" surface that he defines as a quality of the good poem. Speaking "vnder parable" (171) in the concluding dialogue, he prompts his audience by his "clowdy" words to seek his meaning:

> The snares and nettes / set in sondrye maner
> Doone in tyme past / made many abyrde a dawe
> But euermore it is an olde sayd sawe
> Examples past dooth t[e]che one to withdrawe
> Frome all suche perylles / wherefore than may I
> By grace of god / beware fulyy parfytly.
> (904–10)

In the *Conforte,* this use of style reinforces Hawes's conception of the poem as a prophecy that contains hidden meaning under its words. As the letters engraved on the walls of the buildings the narrator views embody prophecies of his life and his lady's that "agreynge well / vnto my bokes all" (293), the poet's words, the gift of the Holy Ghost, conceal "many meruelous thynges" (795) of life and love and fate. The language of the *Conforte,* in contrast to the style of the earlier long poems, corresponds to Hawes's changing conceptions of the poet from that of "enluminer" or craftsman, skilled in the arts of rhetoric and eloquence, to the view of the poet as "vates" or sacred instrument of truth and brings to its outer limits the fifteenth-century vision of the poem as ennobling and the heightened language of poetry as a source of truth.

_ix_

"Poets Are Few and Rare"

In John Skelton's writing (1483–1528), we witness the dissolution of
the vision of poetry that dominates the fifteenth century. Like Hawes,
Skelton begins with the fifteenth-century conception of the poet-
craftsman who illuminates his matter, turning out several skillful
poems in a rhetorical and eloquent high style. But he moves rapidly
away from this vision of poetry, questioning and finally rejecting the
assumptions that underlie the fifteenth-century views of poetry and
the role of poetic style. His disillusionment with the practices of his
predecessors is apparent even in his early poems and is voiced explicitly in "The Bowge of Courte" (1498) and "Phyllyp Sparowe"
(1508), although the bases for the fifteenth-century views are most
effectively challenged in the poems between 1521 and 1528, particularly in "Speke Parott," "Collyn Clout," "The Garlande of Laurell," and "A Replycacion." In these works, Skelton questions the
ability of the heightened language of poetry to order and to civilize
humanity and lead one to truth, indeed to provide any meaningful
statement or point of stability in a world marked by an increasing
decay of authority. Experimenting with and rejecting both the high

styles of Lydgate and his followers and the "mysty," "clowdy," and "derk" style of Hawes, Skelton searches for a new medium and stance as a poet.

In the lyrics written between 1483 and 1496, Skelton introduces the assumptions of the fifteenth-century poets as the underlying matrix of his verse, borrowing both the critical terminology and the stylistic modes of these poets. The ideal he articulates is a poetry that is "polished," "aureate," and "ornate," in which the poet turns his eloquence to the "illumination" of his matter and the celebration of the values of the realm. In his poem on the death of the Earl of Northumberland, for example, Skelton echoes the fifteenth-century poets as he apologizes for his "homely rudnes" and strives for the "ellumynynge" or "aureat poems" worthy of the earl's noble acts.[1] Like Douglas and Hawes, he suggests that the poet work "craftily" concealing important truths under the "derk" and "subtle" surface of his verse. As he reminds us in the prologue to "The Bowge of Courte," the great poets, of authority "full craftely, / Under as coverte termes as coude be, / Can touche a troughte and cloke it subtylly / Wyth fresshe utteraunce full sentencyously" (9–12). Finally, like Hawes, Skelton maintains that the reward of these poets is eternal fame, a renown that "maye never dye."[2]

In many of the early poems, diction is a central concern, for Skelton, like Lydgate, Dunbar, Douglas, and Hawes, envisions the poet's role essentially as that of developing a medium worthy of his noble subject. In his poem "Upon the Dolorous Dethe and Muche Lamentable Chaunce of the Moost Honorable Erle of Northumberlande," for example, he imitates the rhetoric of Geoffrey of Vinsauf's famous lament for Richard I, a passage that was frequently anthologized as a model of eloquence in the later Middle Ages:[3]

Alas for pite that Percy thus was spylt,
The famous Erle of Northumberlande;
Of knightly prowes the sworde, pomel, and hilt,
The myghty lyoun doutted be se and sande;
O dolorous chaunce of Fortuns fraward hande!
What man, remembring how shamfully he was slayn,
From bitter wepinge hym self kan restrayne?

O cruell Mars, thou dedly god of war!
O dolorous Teusday, dedicate to thi name,

When thou shoke thi sword so noble a man to mar!
O grounde ungracious, unhappy be thy fame,
Whiche wert endiyd with rede blode of the same
Mooste noble Erle! O fowle mysuryd grounde,
Whereon he gat his fynall dedely wounde. (106–19)

Interrupting his lament, he indicates that the poet's eloquence enables him to be true to his subject. In this case, his aureate language is the instrument that preserves the earl's fame. Beseeching aid not only of Clio, the muse of history, but the "hole quere of the Musis nyne" (156) and the "blast of influence dyvyne" (158), Skelton suggests that his task may be above the realm of human language. Finally, he turns from his effort to establish the earl's mortal fame to his eternal renown as he prays to the "perles Prince of hevyn emperyall" (190), the model of perfect language, who "with one worde formd all thing of nought" (191) to receive Percy in his company.

Like Lydgate, Dunbar, and Douglas, Skelton extends the conception of the poet as illuminator and enameler to his nonaureate verse. In the poems, "On Time" and "Knolege, Acquayntance, Resort, Favour with Grace," for example, he develops discrete units of language in the manner of Dunbar's enameling in order to create a dense verbal pattern to embellish his subject. In the stanzas on Time, his repetitions demarcate an elaborate design of images; in "Knolege, Acquayntance, Resort, Favour with Grace," the lines create a word-painting of their subject and finally form an acrostic on her name, Kathryn.

Even in these early poems, however, Skelton reveals an incipient dissatisfaction with the conceptions of poetry he has inherited from his fifteenth-century predecessors. Like the best of these poets, he repeatedly builds up expectations by his exploitation of traditional styles and forms, only to deflate or undercut these expectations with sudden reversals as in "My Darling Dear, My Daisy Flower," with the subtle sexual innuendos of "The Auncient Acquaintance" that qualify his courtly praise, and other similar devices. But more important, in these lyrics, Skelton begins to question the effectiveness of the predominant fifteenth-century styles and the role of the poet as the illuminator and embellisher of matter. In many of the poems, unexpected stylistic modes intrude to draw attention to the limits of his principal style as a purveyor of meaning, for example, the alliterative lines of the "Lament for the Erle of Northumberlande" which introduce a perspective alien to the aureate celebration. In some poems like "Knolege, Acquayntance, Resort, Favour with Grace," Skelton shifts in the concluding stanzas from his eloquent high style to a plainer style in an effort to interject the emotion the aureate mode conceals. The poem ends with a conflation of the two styles, neither of which presents a complete vision of the reality of the lady. Similarly, in "The Auncient Acquaintance," his contrasting aureate and bawdy modes underscore the incomplete perspective of each. Like Henryson's sudden shifts from rhetorical to plain styles and Dunbar's juxtaposition of aureate and bawdy, Skelton's stylistic manipulation draws attention to the limits of the poet's traditional modes as vehicles of truth.

In "The Bowge of Courte" and "Phyllyp Sparowe" Skelton makes explicit his reconsideration of the fifteenth-century ideals and assumptions about poetry. The two poems question the poet's power to illuminate human experience and to provide any stable vision of reality in a world where truth is undermined by deceit, language veils meaning, and words falsify. In both poems, the reassessment of the poet's role finds form in the manipulation of language and the vacillation between rhetorical and plain styles. In "The Bowge of Courte," Skelton introduces a poet figure who is an emblem of the uncertain position of poetry in the world. Aptly named Drede, the poet-narrator finds himself in an atmosphere of mutability and unsteadiness.[4] As poet, Drede articulates the fifteenth-century view of poetry as a process of "illuminating" and of a poem as "craftily" and "subtily" cloaked with "covert terms" and fresh utterance." His companion Ignorance reveals that he is too uncertain and dull to master this art.

The world of the dream vision in which Drede finds himself underscores his dilemma as poet. Reminiscent both of the Ship of Fools, familiar to his audience in Sebastian Brandt's *Das Narenschiff* (1494) and J. Locher's Latin translation of 1497, and of the experience of Langland's narrator, Will, in Books VIII–X of *Piers Plowman,* the narrator's adventure under the rule of Fortune, who guides the "Bowge of Courte," defines the plight of the poet with no source of authority or certain vision of truth. Langland's narrative suggests the poet-narrator's ineffective pursuit of truth by means of his intellectual faculties—Thought, Wit, Study, and Learning—but the situation in Skelton's poem is much worse. The poet in "The Bowge of

Courte" confronts a cast of characters—"Favell," "Suspect," "Dis-
dayne," "Ryote," "Dyssymulation," and "Disceyte"—who represent not a limited use of one's intellectual faculties, but a perversion
of emotional stability and a disordering of perception. As the action
unfolds, the poet has increasing difficulty apprehending reality. The
characters appear in confusing disguises that progress from the rela-
tively obvious appearance of Flattery, to the hooded dress of "Dis-
dayne," to the torn and ragged cloak of "Ryote," to the double-faced
guise of "Dyssymulation," to the stealthy figure of "Disceyte" who
sneaks up from behind and frightens the narrator.

Even more dangerous than their disguises are the perversions of
language that these characters introduce. Flattery "feeds" the poet a
surfeit of false words, insisting all the while that his style is the plain
style of unadorned truth: "I can not flater, I muste be playne to the"
(164). "Suspect" offers few words and plain speech but his verbal
economy is based upon dangerous insinuation and doubt, while the
crafty Hervy Hafter's idiom is full of contradiction and sudden shifts
of purpose. The order of language breaks down entirely with the characters of "Ryote," "Dyssymulation," and "Disceyte," who speak respectively in nonsense, opaque allusions, and riddles (393 ff, 477 ff,
512 ff). The effect of this verbal misrule is to produce false and
terrifying images in the narrator's mind and the vision ends as he
jumps overboard for fear of his life. As poet, Drede can only write
what he remembers, bidding us to construe it as we will, for sometimes dreams are found true. From the perspective of Drede's experience, "The Bowge of Courte" is thus less important as the unconven-
tional treatment of the dream vision form, as critics have judged it,
than as a significant statement about the plight of the poet in a world in
which his medium and vision of reality are in jeopardy.

In "Phyllyp Sparowe," Skelton introduces a fuller consideration
of the limits of the fifteenth-century vision of poetry. The relation of
the two parts of the poem, Jane's 844-line lament and epitaph for the
death of her sparrow and Skelton's "Commendacions" of Jane, raise
questions about the stance of the poet as an illuminator of experience
and the ability of his poetic language to deal with reality.[5] Like Caxton
who is distressed by the "dyversite chaunge of langage" and the
failure both of "rude" and of "curious" English to convey meaning,
Skelton in this poem vacillates between aureate and plain styles as
poetic choices. For Caxton, the dilemma is a practical one:

For in these dayes every man that is in ony reputacyon in his contre. wyll utter his commynycacyon and maters in suche maners and termes that fewe men shall understonde theym And som honest and grete clerkes have ben wyth me and desired me to wryte the moste curyous termes that I coude fynde And thus bytwene playn rude and curyous I stande abasshed.[6]

For Skelton as poet, the issue takes on serious moral and intellectual dimensions.[7]

The persona of Jane, which Skelton develops in the first part of the poem, comically reassesses the position of the poet as the embellisher of matter. As Jane moves between Christian liturgy and classical myth, the language of the Psalms and the speech of the rhetoricians, she articulates many of the assumptions of the fifteenth-century poets toward their craft. The poet's effort is primarily one of finding the eloquence worthy of the subject. The poet's role is to amplify and elevate matter and insure its fame. In this case, Jane suggests, her object is so noble that even the most skillful of writers cannot report its virtues:

> . . . after my dome,
> Dame Sulpicia at Rome,
> Whose name regystred was
> Forever in tables of bras,
> Because that she dyd pas
> In poesy to endyte
> And eloquently to wryte,
> Though she wolde pretende
> My sparowe to commende,
> I trowe she coude not amende
> Reportynge the vertues all
> Of my sparowe royall. (147–58)

Although, echoing the humility topoi of her predecessors, she protests that she lacks the ability to use the high style her subject demands, she proves to be a master of the devices of amplification characteristic of the fifteenth-century poets, expanding and elaborating the event with rhetorical outbursts, numerous digressions, allusions to classical stories, lengthy catalogues, and an impressive survey of her reading both in ancient and modern texts. Like the best of these poets, she is a skillful rhetorician, simultaneously exploiting the liturgy and classical sources for the framework of her poem.

But Jane's effort, although masterful, reveals several problems that underlie the fifteenth-century conception of poetry as a process of illumination or embellishment of matter. From the outset, her subject, the death of Philip Sparrow, encompasses both the serious dimensions of Matthew 10.29, "Are not two sparrows sold for a penny? And not one of them will fall to the ground without your father's will," and the lascivious and humorous possibilities of a mock heroic work. Teetering between these extremes, her account exaggerates the incongruity between word and deed, language and reality inherent in the poet's activities. The medium that she has available to her, in the first place, is inadequate to express her emotion. Her digressions, catalogues, and allusions, in fact, dispel rather than reinforce our sense of her "sorrowful heaviness." More seriously, Jane suggests, her words do not effectively preserve Philip's image and fame. Thus, longing for some of Medea's art, she attempts to reconstruct his image in a sampler (210–18). But the extreme realism of his picture is too distressing. In her attempt as poet to do justice to Philip's death and her own grief, she can find no useful models and her extensive reading merely exaggerates her dilemma. The ancient poets are "to diffuse" (768), and she suggests the three great English masters, Chaucer, Gower, and Lydgate, no longer are understood and appreciated (795–818). The situation of the English language is antithetical to the use of an effective high style. As Jane observes:

> Our naturall tong is rude,
> And hard to be enneude
> With pullysshed termes lusty;
> Our language is so rusty,
> So cankered and so full
> Of frowardes, and so dull,
> That if I wolde apply
> To wryte ornatly,
> I wot not where to fynd
> Termes to serve my mynde.
> (774–83)

She thus abandons English for Latin "playne and lyght" and resolves her dilemma as poet by engraving Philip's image in her heart where it will be preserved, "enneude" by emotion rather than inadequate language:

Semper erunt nitido
Radiantia sydera celo;
Impressisque meo
Pectore semper eris.
(830–34)

(So long as the stars shine in the sky, will your image be graven on my heart.)

Jane's observations about the poetic process are tempered by her characterization as an inexperienced and innocent young maid; however, the outlook changes sharply in the second part of the poem, Skelton's "Commendacions." Drawing upon many of the same sources, these lines echo, exaggerate, and even parody Jane's views. In contrast to Jane's humble stance, Skelton presents himself as an experienced and self-conscious poet, the devotee of the muses and Apollo in eloquence:

That my pen hath enbybed
With the aureat droppes.
As verely my hope is,
Of Thagus, that golden flod,
That passeth all erthly good.
(872–76)

His purpose is to register Jane's name in the Court of Fame so that she "floryssheth new and new / In bewte and vertew" (896–97).

Although Jane's treatment hints of a disparity between poetic language and object and the inability of traditional styles to deal with emotion, Skelton's commendation exaggerates this dilemma as, courting blasphemy, he inappropriately applies sacred and secular modes to her praise. In contrast to Jane's use of the Psalms to intensify the description of her loss at the death of Philip, Skelton's reworking of Psalm 118, a celebration of the relation of the faithful to God's law and part of the *Ordo Commendationis Animae* of the burial service, underscores the distance between the two objects of praise. The

disparity between language and object increases as Skelton turns to
the literary devices of secular praise: "For to compyle / Some goodly
style; / For this most goodly floure" (987–88). Aureate and plain
styles clash as the colloquial style and the realm of reality it represents
invades his elevated and artificial description of Jane's beauty:

> The Indy saphyre blew
> Her vaynes doth ennew;
> The orient perle so clere,
> The whytnesse of her lere;
> The lusty ruby ruddes
> Resemble the rose buddes;
> Her lyppes soft and mery
> Emblomed lyke the chery,
> It were an hevenly blysse
> Her sugred mouth to kysse.
>
> Her beautye to augment
> Dame Nature hath her lent
> A warte upon her cheke,
> Who so lyst to seke
> In her vysage a skar
> That semyth from afar
> Lyke to the radyant star,
> All with favour fret,
> So properly it is set:
> She is the vyolet,
> The daysy delectable,
> The columbyn commendable
> The jelofer amyable.
> (1031–53)

Similarly, unpleasant sexual innuendos, carefully kept in check in
Jane's portion of the poem, invade the remote world of poetic illusion.
The contrasting endings of the "Commendacions" and the "Addition" underscore the rift between style and subject, the poet's aspirations and his achievement. The former ending assumes the eternal
fame of Jane and her poet:

> Per me laurigerum Britonum Skeltonida vatem
> Laudibus eximiis merito hec redimita puella est:

Formosam cecini, qua mon formosoir ulla est;
Formosam potius quam commendaret Homerus.
Sic juvat interdum rigidos recreare labores,
Nec minus hoc titulo tersa Minerva mea est. (1261–66)

(Through me, Skelton, the laureate poet of Britain, this girl is
deservedly crowned with choice praises. I have sung of the
beautiful girl than whom there is no one more beautiful; a
beautiful girl preferable to any Homer might commend. Thus,
it is pleasant occasionally to refresh hard labours; nor is my
wisdom any less brief than this inscription.)

The latter provides a vision of shame and envy in which even Jane
shuns her bard. Thus the poem concludes without resolving the dilemma it introduces.

The poems between 1521 and 1523 reveal Skelton's increasing
disillusionment with the ideals of the fifteenth-century poets—the
vision of poetry as ennobling and the poet as an "enluminer" and
enlightener, the effort to develop a high style in English, and the belief
in the power of this heightened language to lead one to truth, the
effectiveness of the poem in civilizing mortals and bringing order and
harmony to the state. These poems, "Speke Parott" (1521), "Collyn
Clout" (1522), and "Why Come Ye Nat to Courte?" (1523), question
the bases of fifteenth-century poetics in eloquence, rejecting both the
persuasive power of rhetoric and the "derk" styles of Douglas and
Hawes, the examples of Amphion and of the poet-prophet David, as
viable stances. The terms, which Skelton used seriously in the early
poems, now appear in ironic contexts and underscore his shift in
vision. This process is apparent as early as 1516 in the play "Magnyfycence," where Skelton exploits the fifteenth-century critical terms
to characterize Courtly Abusion (Courtly Deceit) who, along with
Crafty Conveyance, Delusion, and Cloaked Collusion, leads the
prince Magnificence astray. Echoing the fifteenth-century poets, Magnificence praises Courtly Abusion's language: "with pleasure I am
supprysyd / Of your langage, it is so well devysed; / Pullyshyd and
fresshe is your ornacy" (1529–31). Courtly Abusion responds with
the wish that he could be "crafty" and "eloquent" enough to please his
prince (1550–51). The poems between 1521 and 1523 turn from the
"eloquent" and "crafty" modes to the plain style in an effort to reunite
language and truth, style and meaning. In contrast to the early poems,

these poems describe the responsibility of the poet to communicate and to assume a role that confronts the encroaching reality of the world around him.

Several events, alluded to in "Speke Parott," "Collyn Clout," and "Why Come Ye Nat to Courte?" appear to have influenced Skelton's changing vision of poetry. In the period between 1521 and 1523 when these poems were written, Skelton was with the Howard family, probably in Yorkshire as tutor to young Henry Howard.[8] After a number of years as "orator regis" in which he composed several official poems, Skelton began in 1516, both in "Magnyfycence" and in the short poem "Against Venomous Tongues," to express his concern about the increasing influence that Cardinal Thomas Wolsey and the trends he represented were exerting in England.[9] Specifically, he objected to Wolsey's swift rise to power in a single decade from a member of the King's Council to a cardinal to lord chancellor.

Between 1520 and 1522, the situation seemed threatening to Skelton and to the noble families like the Howards whose society he frequented and whose support he received, as Wolsey initiated a number of policies reprehensible to this group. In August through November of 1521, Wolsey launched a diplomatic campaign in Calais, the subject of the caustic envoys of "Speke Parott," which purportedly was to resolve the rival claims of Francis I of France and Emperor Charles V, but actually was designed to advance Wolsey's own career in the church by attempting to insure the emperor's support for his candidacy at the next papal election.[10] Wolsey not only left England with a huge retinue at great expense, but he took with him the Great Seal, effectively paralyzing the business of the realm in his absence.[11]

Second, during the years 1519–23, Wolsey was instrumental in bringing about changes that Skelton viewed as damaging to the traditions and the order he valued. Not only was Wolsey's concentration of power as chancellor and cardinal politically dangerous, but it represented an alliance which, in Skelton's view, was inimical to the feudal system upon which England's power has rested for centuries. A striking example for Skelton of the breakdown of the old order was Wolsey's effort in 1520 to establish a professorship of Greek at Oxford and his support of the new educational practices that were under dispute in the Grammarians' War of 1519–20.[12] As a firm adherent of the Old Learning, Skelton found Wolsey's patronage of the new trends and the values they implied disturbing. In the social and political setting of 1520–23, the solutions of the fifteenth-century poets no longer were viable for Skelton.

Finally, the period immediately preceding the writing of "Speke Parott," "Collyn Clout," and "Why Come Ye Nat to Courte?" was one of great controversy about the role of language and its status among the arts of the Trivium. As Struever points out, among the transitional writers, the Janus-like figures at the end of the Middle Ages and the beginning of the Renaissance, one notes an assertion of the independence of grammar from logic and a shift from the importance of dialectic to the importance of rhetoric as the dominant mode. In the histories of the early Renaissance that she considers, this shift marks a new concern with change rather than permanence, with participating in the sphere of flux rather than attempting to escape or transcend it.[13] At the same time, these writers emphasize the active, independent power of language as a mediator of reality and the shaper of experience.

Related concerns are apparent in the theological disputes in northern Europe in the period between 1510 and 1525. Working from the perspective of translator rather than historian, for example, Erasmus, whom Skelton admired, in his series of prefaces to his translations of the Bible, reasserts the primacy of grammar as the basis for theological study.[14] Lamenting the neglect and disrepute of this art, he demonstrates that only the appropriately correct word can produce true theology. In contrast to the members of Plato's Republic who attempted to apprehend reality without language, he argues, the Christian seeks truth through the word, the human imitation of the divine Logos. As Christ is the enactment of God's word on earth, Himself a divine language and an example of God's eloquence, human discourse is an analogous version of this relationship. Boyle sums up Erasmus's arguments:

> The same divine *ratio* and its expression in *oratio* which describes the relationship of the Son to the Father is copied analogously in the relationship of the sons to the Father. The Father's generation of the Son is complemented in creation by the human mind: "What in divine affairs is the Father generating from himself of the Son, is in us the mind, the seat of thought and speech (sermo)." The Son's being born is comple-

mented by human discourse: "What in that case is the Son being born from the Father is in us speech (oratio) issuing from the spirit."[15]

These parallels have far-reaching implications for the Christian writer. If Christ, oratory incarnate, the enactment of divine eloquence on earth, could by His words redeem and reconcile humanity to God, the Christian orator might by imitation reconcile individual to individual and redeem the commonwealth. The refusal to speak or the use of incorrect or inappropriate words thus becomes a sin against God and a defiance of humankind's sacred obligation. The choice of vocabulary, the discovery of the appropriate word, in this context takes on primary significance for Erasmus. His change of the traditional Latin text of John: "In principio erat verbum" to the reading "In principio erat sermo" in the second edition of his translation of the Bible and the controversy that ensued brought dramatic attention to his views.[16]

In Skelton's later poems, many of these issues coalesce in his search for an appropriate style and stance as a poet. His choice of words becomes an emblem of his dilemma as poet in a troubled and fallen world. In "Speke Parott," his most vehement attack on the ideals of the fifteenth-century poets, Skelton places himself in the tradition of the misunderstood prophets who speak to a world that neither understands nor attends their message (115–20). As his mouthpiece, Parrot is a complex image of the poet, linked by his mythological and literary inheritance both to the Ovidian parrot of Corinna, the master mimic who uncomprehendingly chronicles scraps of wisdom, stories, and events, and to the tradition of the semidivine hero of Boccaccio's *Genealogia,* the son of Deucalion, who survived the flood and saved humankind by his faith, and the grandson of Prometheus, who in old age prayed to be removed from human affairs and was transformed into the Parrot and in later tradition, placed in heaven.[17] Parrot's vacillation between these stances colors his role with a troubling ambiguity. Although a "byrd of paradyse," as he reveals at the outset, he has been forced to return to the world of sixteenth-century England where he is alternately caged and pampered by "greate ladyes of estate" and prodded to "speak." He both disdains his prison and embraces it as a safe refuge from the disorder of a world that seems to invite its own destruction. From his mistress, Dame Philology, Parrot has received verbal gifts, and like the Apostles with their gift of tongues, he has the ability to speak and understand all language.[18] His words, smatterings of English, Latin, Greek, French, Castilian, Dutch, and German, shift from statements of great wisdom to the verbal undercutting and misrule of "The Bowge of Courte" and "Magnyfycence." "Parlez bien," Parrot advises, "ou parlez rien." "*In Salve festa dies, toto* theyr doth best" (on holiday it is best to go the whole hog, 49), he suggests, "*Moderata juvant* [moderation delight us], but *toto* doth exede," he warns.

His veiled allusions to the outrages of Wolsey and the relation of Wolsey and Henry VIII link contemporary London with the biblical Heshbon, in need of being reclaimed from the enemies who lead its people to destruction, and his own sadness as witness with that of Jeremiah, Rachel, Moses, and Gideon.[19] As in the earlier "Bowge of Courte" and "Magnyfycence," Skelton makes it clear by his references to the issues of the recent Grammarians' War that the social and political abuses he chronicles are linked to a more insidious verbal corruption. The instruments of human speech and learning, the faculties that ennoble humans and set them off from beasts, are in jeopardy. Language is separated from reality and word from meaning as the new scholars of Greek, the ancestors of Alexander Pope's Dunces, make havoc of ancient texts and produce a diction that ignores the world around them. As Skelton slyly remarks, "our Grekis theyr Greke so well haue applyded / That they cannot say in Greke, rydynge by the way, / 'How, hosteler, fetche my hors a botell of hay!' " (145–47).[20] These scholars set "theyr myndys so moche of eloquens / That of theyr scole maters lost is the hole sentens" (181–82).

Skelton taunts us with the possibilities of Parrot as satirist, seer, lover, the redeemer who would defend Israel (England) from the enemies which surround her, as his "own dear heart," as one's soul or better part that does not putrify. Finally, as Edwards and Brownlow suggest, Skelton appears to link Parrot with the poetic faculty itself. Parrot, Brownlow argues,

> is a symbol of the transformation of the poet into his poems, both the speaker and the thing spoken, both that which prompts speech and the speech itself. Like the philosophers' stone, he is both the cause and effect of a transformation. It is in this sense that Parrot is incorruptible. The voice briefly contained in the

poet's body will die with it, but changed into the enduring form
of poetic speech it will live as long as there are texts and
readers.[21]

Parrot is created by "that pereles prynce," made "of nothynge by his
magistye." His words, inspired by God, have the potential to bring
comfort to humans on earth and direct them to a more enduring life:

> For that pereles prynce that Parrot dyd create,
> He made you of nothynge by his magistye;
> Poynt well this probleme that Parrot doth prate,
> And remember amonge how Parrot and ye
> Shall lepe from this lyfe, as mery as we be;
> Pompe, pryde, honour, ryches and worldly lust,
> Parrot sayth playnly, shall tourne all to dust.
> (218–24)

Echoing 1 Thessalonians 4.18, "Itaque consolamyni invicem in ver-
bis istis" (Wherefore comfort one another with these words), which
follows the description of God's redemption of the living and the dead
who "shall be caught up together with them in the clouds to meet the
Lord in the air," Skelton warns us to cherish Parrot.[22]

But although Parrot's words have the potential of transforming
individuals, their effect in the world the poem represents is uncertain.
Each of Parrot's roles, to some extent, is undercut by his antics and by
the difficulty of speaking. As poet, he vacillates between involvement
and rage at the events he witnesses and the profound detachment of
his cage. Stylistically, his uneasy stance is represented by his lack of
an appropriate medium. Although he is equally skilled at aureate,
prophetic, and satiric modes, none of these styles allows him to deal
effectively with the world around him. Like the quester of T. S. Eliot's
Waste Land who shores up his fragments against ruin, Parrot, the
polyglot who speaks in different tongues and styles, gathers together
"shredis of sentence" from which he produces learned arguments in
the poets' sacred school ("Unde depromo / Dilemata docta in ped-
agogio / Sacro vatum," 95–97). Boldly linking the mirror that he
"toots" in with the description of our vision in 1 Corinthians 13.12
("For now we see in a mirror dimly, but then face to face"), Parrot
suggests that, for some, his poetry, "*Confuse distrybutyve*" (methodi-
cal confusion, 198) will seem "*confuse tantum*" (so much confusion,

196). Dodging responsibility, he advises each man to take what he can from it, for allegory is his protection and his shield:

> Let every man after his merit take his parte;
> For in this processe, Parrot nothing hath surmysed,
> No matter pretendyd, nor nothyng enterprysed,
> But that *metaphora, allegoria* withall,
> Shall be his protectyon, his pavys, and his wall.
> (199–203)

The dialogue between Galathea and Parrot in Part II draws attention to the limitations of this solution. Refusing to accept Parrot's aloofness, Galathea, the object of the lover's complaint in the twelfth-century pseudo-Ovidian *Pamphilus de Amore,* demands from him a similar "moan." But, in contrast to the straightforward seduction of Pamphilus, Parrot's response is a conglomerate of stances and corresponding styles, each of which Galathea rejects as inadequate. The allegorical and prophetic modes dominate his song to "Bess" and the series of envoys that appear in the British Library Manuscript Harleian 2252 of the poem. Parrot's song has the air of a popular ballad, but as Edwards points out, the lines contain a clear allusion to a well-known moralized ballad that represents Bess as Mankind wooed by Christ.[23] Similarly, Pamphilus, glossed in contemporary texts as *totus amor,* the all-loving, is a type of Christ declaring his love for Mankind. Although Parrot may speak profound truths, the difficulty is that to some his words will seem to "hang togedyr as fethyrs in the wynde" (293), a line that the confused character, Magnificence, had used earlier to describe Folly's speech (*Magnyfycence,* 1842).

The style of the envoys that follow is even more "derk." As Nelson has demonstrated, these passages contain a tissue of references to Wolsey's activities between August and November of 1521 during his expedition to Calais.[24] The relation of the envoys to the monostichons that follow, however, introduces an increasing tension that draws attention to Parrot's dilemma as poet. While Parrot reminds us in each envoy of the "fruitful mater" under his confusing words and urges us to consider his lines carefully, "For trowthe in parabyll ye wantonlye pronounce, / Langages divers, yet uydyr that dothe reste / Maters more precious then the ryche jacounce" (364–66), the monostichons, with increasing urgency, demand a different style. Parrot must be a truthful messenger; he must "turn back the shafts of fatuity" ("Fatuorum tela retundas"); he must go in haste and "reprove the evil tongues" ("I, properans Parrote, malas sic coripe linguas"): he must moderate his wit, for "scarce will they understand you who read you and your writings" (I, volitans, Parrotte, tuam moderare Minervam: / Vix tua perceipient, qui tua teque legent"). In the context of these pleas, Galathea's recurrent demand, "Speke Parott," becomes less a command to speak and more an urgent request to change styles as poet and speak plainly. Moving from the very obscure style of the first envoy to the thinly veiled allegory of the last, to the less obscure "complaint" style of the passages that follow, to the alternation of plain and parabolic styles, Parrot, in response to Galathea's strongest and final pleas to "speke owte," to "sette asyde all sophysms, and speke now trew and playne" (7–8), offers the unadorned and vigorous medium of the concluding stanzas as the tentative resolution of this poem.

Skelton's final stance as poet in "Speke Parott" thus represents a qualification not only of the aureate and allegorical styles of the fifteenth-century poets and the visions they embody, but it also contains an implicit rejection of Hawes's "derk" style and his stance of the poet-prophet in *The Conforte of Louers*. Skelton's position at the end of "Speke Parott," his shift from obscure to plain styles, and his recognition of the need to communicate to the world recall the teaching of Paul in 1 Corinthians 13–14 that it is better to interpret than to speak allegorically:

> One who speaks in a tongue speaks not to men but to God; for no one understands him, but he utters mysteries in the Spirit. On the other hand, he who prophesies speaks to men for their upbuilding and encouragement and consolation. He who speaks in a tongue edifies himself, but he who prophesies edifies the church. Now I want you all to speak in tongues, but even more to prophesy. He who prophesies is greater than he who speaks in tongues, unless some one interprets, so that the church may be edified.

In the Heshbon of contemporary London, it is not sufficient for poets to remove themselves and elaborate God's mysteries; they must speak to redeem fallen humankind.

Although Skelton returns to the plain style and the vision of the poet involved in the world that it implies in all but one of the poems written after "Speke Parott," his stylistic solution is a qualified one. In "Collyn Clout," and "Why Come Ye Nat to Courte?" Skelton emphasizes even more strongly than in "Speke Parott" the responsibility of the poet to address the corruption that surrounds one in the world. The lines that he quotes from Psalm 94 as an epigraph to "Collyn Clout" introduce this problem in emphatic terms: "Quis consurget mihi adversus malignantes, aut quis stabit mecum adversus operantes iniquitatem? Nemo, Domine!" (Who will rise up with me against evildoers, or who will stand up with me against the workers of iniquity? No one, O Lord!). In their context in the Psalm, these lines, without the response "Nemo, Domine!" that Skelton adds, provide the climax of the poet's call for God's vengeance against the wicked who spurn Him and challenge His power. Immediately following his questions, the narrator answers, "If the lord had not been my help, my soul would soon have dwelt in the land of silence" (Psalms 94.17). God, his consolation, his refuge, and his stronghold, will punish the evildoers. In contrast to the Psalmist, Skelton at the outset of his poem is uncertain. His response, as Atchity points out, comes from the account of Christ's encounter with the scribes and Pharisees who have challenged him to condemn an adulteress:[25]

> So when they continued asking him, he lifted up himself, and said unto them, He that is without sin among you, let him first cast a stone at her.
>
> And again he stooped down, and wrote on the ground.
>
> And they which heard it, being convicted by their own conscience, went out one by one, beginning at the eldest, even unto the last: and Jesus was left alone, and the woman standing in the midst.
>
> When Jesus had lifted up himself, and saw none but the woman, he said unto her, Woman, where are those thine accusers? hath no man condemned thee?
>
> She said, No man, Lord. And Jesus said unto her, Neither do I condemn thee. . . . (John 8.7–11)

Skelton's allusion to this passage suggests that there is no one without sin in the world the poem represents who may speak out. By casting the first stone, the narrator, Colin Clout, reminds us both of his own culpability and his inescapable responsibility as poet to respond to the evil around him. The members of the clergy, the proper spokesmen, have ignored their role and no one is left to restore order. As the lines from John imply, each person must first address his or her own sins before the commonwealth may be redeemed. Like Christ with the adulteress and like Will at the end of *Piers Plowman,* Colin Clout reminds us of this responsibility.

But like Drede and Parrot, Colin is uneasy about the ability of poetry to make readers heed his message. Opening the poem proper with this dilemma, he asks what effect poetry can have:

> What can it avayle
> . . . .
> To ryme or to rayle,
> To wryte or to indyte,
> Other for delyte
> Or elles for despyte?
> Or bokes to compyle
> Of dyuers maner style,
> Vyce to revyle
> And synne to exyle?
> (1–12)

The problem, as in the earlier books, is also one of style. If the poet is elaborate, then people say "he gloseth and he flatters" (25); if he speaks plainly, then "he lacketh brayne, / He is but a foole" (27–28). In the world of the poem, Fish points out, "Colin is no more able to forge the perfect diction than he is to discover the perfect authority."[26] His compromise is to shake out his "conning bag" and offer his jagged and torn rhyme. Although the effect of his poem is uncertain, Colin resolves to persist in his effort, "Tyll my dyenge day / I shall bothe wryte and say" (506–7). Like the prophets of old who were scorned, he refuses to be silenced:

> Howe may we thus endure?
> Wherefore we make you sure,
> Ye prechers shall be yawde;
> Some shall be sawde,
> As noble Isaias,
> The holy prophet, was;
> And some of you shall dye,
> Lyke holy Jeremy;

Some hanged, some slayne,
Some beaten to the brayne;
And we wyll rule and rayne,
And our matters mayntayne
Who dare say there agayne,
Or who dare dysdayne
At our pleasure and wyll.
For, be it good or be it yll,
As it is, it shall be styll.
(1202–18)

Anticipating the moment when Christ will draw His ship out of this storm and send grace "to rectyfe and amende" (1263) the evil he witnesses, Skelton concludes with the troubling prayer that "the rewards may exceed the punishment" (prestet peto premia pena). This resolution to write at all costs again underlies the excesses of "Why Come Ye Nat to Courte?" which is a longer and even more explicit condemnation of Wolsey, written, Skelton indicates, "Quia difficile est / Satiram non scribere" (because it is difficult not to write satire, 1216–17). His stance at the end of "Collyn Clout" is reiterated in the short poem "Calliope," supposedly written in response to the question of why he wore a robe with the word Calliope embroidered in gold letters. Placing himself in the company of poets, Skelton vows to remain Calliope's servant, "Maulgre touz malheureux" (25), despite the misfortune and unhappiness this role involves.

In "The Garlande of Laurell," his final long poem, Skelton returns to the dilemmas he defines in his earlier poems—the stance of the poet in a world where order has broken down, where truth has lost its hold, and where people appear to court their own destruction; the search for a style that mediates between the aureate and the plain and the visions of reality they imply; the responsibility of the poet, though a culpable man, to communicate, in Paul's terms to speak in order to edify rather than to speak in tongues. Although many of the same dangers exist that trouble Skelton in the earlier poem—the weakness of justice, truth, and reason, and the difficulty of being heeded as poet in the world—in the "Garlande" they are less terrifying. The poem, with its catalogues and allusions to earlier works, sums up Skelton's efforts and suggests a new resolution. It is not only the laurel but also the olive that is the poet's tree; his mission is not only fame but also peace. His style is not a single mode, but a mixture of styles that, in its juxtaposition of one realm of vision with another, hints of a complete perspective. The poem is at once a bold self-advertisement and tribute to poetry and a comic assessment of its limitations. Parodying his own achievements while defending his right to the garland of laurel, Skelton produces a work that emphasizes both the necessity and the folly of his endeavor.

Skelton's perspective in "The Garlande of Laurell" is underscored by a comparison with his earlier dream poem "The Bowge of Courte." "Garlande," in contrast to the "Bowge," is written under the secure patronage and protection of the Howards at Sheriff Hutton Castle.[27] The poem opens not in the mutable and discordant world of the "Bowge," with Luna "smylynge halfe in scorne / At our foly and our unsteadfastnesse" (5–6) and Mars arming for war, but in a more temperate atmosphere as Mars disarms and puts away his sword "for he cowde make no warre" (5) and Lucina shines fully. While the fame of the narrator of the "Bowge" is uncertain and the mood of his vision anxious, the renown of the poet in the "Garlande" is anticipated in hyperbolic terms in the opening epigram:

Eterno mansura die dum sidera fulgent,
Equora dumque tument, hec laurea nostra virebit:
Hinc nostrum celebre et nomen referetur ad astra,
Undique Skeltonis memorabitur alter Adonis.

(While the stars shine with eternal day, and while the seas swell, these our laurels shall be green; our illustrious name shall be translated to the sky, and everywhere shall Skelton be renowned as another Adonis.)

Finally, in contrast to the tavern setting, an image of the discordant world in which the narrator of the "Bowge" falls asleep, the oak stump against which the narrator of the "Garlande" rests before his own dream provides both a symbolic suggestion of the immortality of poetry and a reminder of its present blasted state.

The vision of poetry in the dream proper reiterates and qualifies the emphasis of Skelton's earlier poems. At the outset of the dream, Pallas, like the narrators of "Speke Parott," and "Collyn Clout," define the poet's dilemma in terms of a search for a suitable medium. While Fame demands that the narrator adhere to the fifteenth-century ideals of poetic excellence and produce a quantity of aureate verse sufficient to ensure his reputation, Pallas reveals the limitations both of this stance and of his other stylistic possibilities—the plain and the parabolic or prophetic—indeed of any solution the poet might find:

> . . . if he gloryously publisshe his matter,
> Then men wyll say how he doth but flatter.
>
> And if so hym fortune to wryte true and plaine,
> As sumtyme he must vyces remorde,
> Then sum wyll say he hath but lytill brayne,
> And how his wordes with reason wyll not accorde.
> Beware, for wrytynge remayneth of recorde!
> . . . .
> A poete somtyme may for his pleasure taunt,
> Spekyng in paroblis, how the fox, the grey,
> The gander, the gose, and the hudge oliphaunt,
> Went with the pecok ageyne the fesaunt;
> The lesarde came lepyng, and sayd that he must,
> With helpe of the ram, ley all in the dust.
> Yet dyuerse ther be, industryous of reason,
> Sum what wolde gadder in there conjecture
> Of suche an endarkid chapiter sum season.
> How be it, it were harde to construe this lecture;
> Sophisticatid craftely is many a confecture;
> Another manes mynde diffuse is to expounde;
> Yet harde is to make but sum fawt be founde.
> (83–112)

Similarly, Pallas emphasizes the limitations of Skelton's earlier conception of fame as the personal renown and enduring reputation he sought at the outset of "The Bowge of Courte." Echoing Chaucer's *Hous of Fame,* she suggests that this sort of fame is ephemeral, of little more value than noise.

The response to the dilemmas that Skelton defines in the "Garlande," however, is more tempered than his earlier positions. The allegory of the center of the vision provides a definition of poetic activity that includes both optimistic and pessimistic views. Skelton introduces his perspective symbolically by his exploitation of the

myth of Daphne and Apollo with which he prefaces the catalogue of
poets in the garden of poetry. The myth, which explains the significance of the laurel, the reward of poets, emphasizes both the pain and
personal sacrifice that underlie the poetic process and the immortality
of the poem produced by the transformation of experience into art. As
Apollo indicates, it is in remembrance of Daphne's metamorphosis
and his own sorrow that "all famous poetis ensuynge after me / Shall
were a garlande of this laurell tre" (321–22). The catalogue of poets
that follows represents Skelton's relation with tradition, particularly
his position as heir to an English that has been "ennewed" by the
earlier poets' mastery. At the same time, his comic intrusions, for
example, his amusing description of the prolix Lydgate's silence, hint
of the distance between him and the poetry Chaucer, Gower, and
Lydgate represent.

The allegory of the garden defines a role for Skelton as poet that
replaces both the fifteenth-century conception of the poet-illuminator
and Hawes's view of the poet-prophet. The poet in this vision is
guided by Occupation, who in troubled times saved his "storm-driven
ship" from destruction (540–46). He enters the garden through the
gate labeled "Anglia" with a fierce leopard above it, that is, as an
English poet in service to Henry VIII.[28] Inside the garden, which he
points out is situated on the estate of the Countess of Surrey (766–70),
he is protected by its walls from the abusers of language, the "Fals
flaterers that fawne the, and kurris of kynde / That speke fayre before
the and shrewdly behynde" (619–20) who inhabited the world of
"The Bowge of Court" and "Magnyfycence." Finally, the garden
encloses three symbols within its midst that sum up the poet's powers
in their ideal form. In the herber, he discovers:

> . . . growyng a goodly laurell tre,
> Enverdurid with levis contynually grene;
> Above, in the top, a byrde of Araby,
> Men call a phenix; her wynges bytwene
> She bet up a fyre with the sparkis full kene
> With braunches and bowghis of the swete olyve,
> Whos flagraunt flower was chefe preservatyve
>
> Agenynst all infeccyons with cancour enflamyd,
> Agenynst all baratows broisiours of olde,

It passid all bawmys that ever were namyd,
Or gummis of Saby so derely that be solde.
(665–75)

While the laurel in Skelton's account of the myth of Daphne and
Apollo reminds us of the pain and the immortality of poetry, the
phoenix, a more optimistic version of the bird which does not putrify
in "Speke Parott," suggests poetry's power to regenerate from its
own ashes, to create new visions out of "shreddes of sentence." The
symbol of the olive adds a new element to the image of the poet. The
emblem of peace, the "chefe preservatyve / Agenynst all infec-
cyons," the plant suggests the poet's stance not as the satirist or critic
of "Collyn Clout" or "Why Come Ye Nat to Courte?" but as a
peacemaker or reconciler of men.

Although these symbols define an ideal of poetic activity, Skelton
reminds us that this vision is nurtured in a poetic paradise, a place of
"contynuall comfort" (710) and joy remote from the pressures of life.
His style in this section, the aureate style of the fifteenth-century
poets, suggests an artificial and enclosed world of the poet's creation.
Although Skelton is cheered by this garden and chooses "here to
inhabite and ay for to dwell" (719), he hints, by the intrusions of the
real world that interrupt the vision, that this wish is not possible, and
the satiric style replaces the aureate as Skelton denounces his detrac-
tor Roger Stratham. The remainder of the poem contains a mixture of
styles that remind us both of the vision of the garden and the less
perfect world that surrounds it. In the eleven lyrics in praise of the
Countess of Surrey and her ladies, Skelton demonstrates his ability to
fulfill the standards of Fame and write in the manner of the fifteenth-
century poets, and by undermining this mode with comic and ironic
intrusions of reality, he rejects Fame's narrow dictates and the remote
world they imply. The catalogue of his works that follows, in its
omission of the most controversial of his satires and its concern that
his poems do not offend, anticipates Skelton's new role as peacemaker, the poet who will later praise his old enemy, Wolsey, in his
envoys.[29] But it is the figure of Janus, the double-faced character,
which Skelton sees when he awakens from his vision that best embodies his stance in the "Garlande." Consult your mind, he advises,
"Emula sit Jani, retro speculetur et ante" (Let it emulate Janus,
looking behind and before, 1520). As poet, Skelton both anticipates

his fame as the radiant light of the Britons, the English Catullus, Adonis, and Homer, and the possibility of his position among the exiled poets Virgil and Ovid. Celebrating the enemy he had condemned, he emulates Janus in his role as a type of Prudence who looks before and behind. Standing "twene hope and drede," Skelton takes leave of his poem.

Skelton's concluding stanzas indicate that the world is still the same. Justice is dead; Truth is asleep; Right and Reason have "gone to seke hallows" and no one will undertake to set things right. But, in contrast to many of the earlier poems, the "Garlande" balances this picture with the vision at its center of the laurel, the phoenix, and the olive. The poet's stance is still a difficult one, but his dilemmas in this poem are comic as well as serious. Similarly, although no one poetic style proves adequate to deal with the world the "Garlande" represents, the poem's juxtaposition of styles suggests the possibility of a more complete perspective.

In his final poem, "A Replycacion," Skelton provides a good example of the stance that he develops in the "Garlande." The poem, written at the request of Wolsey, reveals his effort to join forces with the opposition and fulfill the role of peacemaker and defender of order suggested by the olive branch in the "Garlande." In the world of the "Replycacion," the triumph of authority is uncertain. The heresy that the two scholars, Thomas Bilney and Thomas Arthur, practice, Skelton suggests, has its foundation in an insidious misuse of their intellectual faculties:

A lytell ragge of rethorike,
A lesse lumpe of logyke,
A pece or a patche of philosophy,
Than forthwith by and by
They tumble so in theology,
Drowned in dregges of divinite,
That they juge them selfe able to be
Doctours of the chayre in the Vyntre.
(1–8)

Their abuse of language, like the deceptive speech of the characters in the "Bowge" and "Magnyfycence," "disorder all things" and distort human vision, a degeneration reflected in the breakdown of the Skeltonics at several points in the description of their activities.[30]

In opposition to the heresy Bilney and Arthur represent, Skelton places his poetry. Boldly defending his effort against detractors, he indicates that the poet's words, like the songs of David, are divinely inspired. Inflamed by the heat of the Holy Ghost, he is compelled to write:

> Sometyme for affection,
> Sometyme for sadde dyrection,
> Sometyme for correction,
> Sometyme under protection
> Of pacient sufferance,
> With sober cyrcumstance
> Our myndes to avaunce
>
> . . . .
>
> Agaynst these frenetykes,
> Agaynst these lunatykes,
> Agaynst these sysmatykes,
> Agaynst these heretykes. . . .
> (389–403)

The poem ends with the most extreme statement of the dilemma that Skelton's narrators have confronted. The reality of the world is that "heresy wyll never dye" (408). Yet the poet must continue to speak out against the abuses that threaten the order around him. As Skelton concludes, "poets are few and rare":

> Innumeri sunt philosophi, sunt theologique,
> Sunt infiniti doctores, suntque magistri
> Innumeri; sed sunt pauci rarique poete.
> Hinc omne est rarum carum: reor ergo poetas
> Ante alios omnes divine flamine flatos. . . .
>
> (Infinite, innumerable are the sophists, infinite, innumerable are the logicians, innumerable are the philosophers and the theologians, infinite in number are doctors, and masters; but poets are few and rare. Hence all that is precious is rare. I think, then, that poets before all others are filled with the divine afflatus.)

Skelton effectively sums up his changing course as a poet by his recurrent use of the ship metaphor in his poems. At the outset of his career, he introduces the metaphor in "The Bowge of Courte" as an emblem of the poet in a world of uncertain order and reward, subject to the whim of Fortune. The ship that the poet discovers in his dream is rich in appearance and is "fraghted with plesuer of what ye coude devyse" (42). But Lady Fortune is its helmswoman and those who would have its merchandise "muste paye therefor dere" (53). As Bon Aventure advises the narrator, "how ever blowe the wynde, / Fortune gydeth and ruleth all oure shyppe: / Whome she hateth shall over the seeboorde skyp" (110–12). In "Collyn Clout," written twenty-four years later, Skelton, although in a world that is even more disordered and perilous than the setting of the "Bowge," envisions his eventual passage as poet out of these turbulent waters to a calmer sea. In his mind, his ship will slip "out of the wawes wodde / Of the stormy flodde" (1253–54), anchor and wait until the coast clears and the lodestar appears. His destination is the port of Christ who will rectify and amend the troubled conditions he leaves behind. Although the hope in "Collyn Clout" is for a future safe port, the ship metaphor in the "Garlande" suggests not an eventual but an immediate voyage. In both instances when the metaphor is used in this poem, it emphasizes, in addition, the effort of the poet on his own behalf to traverse the troubled waters around him. The first example of the ship metaphor in the "Garlande" looks back to the narrator's early activities as poet, replacing the image of the ship governed by Fortune of "The Bowge of Courte" with a vision of Occupation, the poet's dedication or effort, repairing his battered barge. As Occupation reminds the narra-tor,

> . . . when at the port salu
> Ye fyrste aryvyd; whan broken was your mast
> Of worldly trust, then did I you rescu;
> Your storme dryven shyppe I repared new,
> So wel entakeled, what wynde that ever blowe,
> No stormy tempeste your barge shall overthrow.
> (541–46)

It was his own effort and the act of writing itself that rescued the poet. Finally, before he presents his poetic offering to Fame—the eleven lyrics in praise of the Countess of Surrey and her ladies and his catalogue of his writing—Skelton likens his experience as poet to that of a mariner caught by surprise in a "stormy rage" who nevertheless is driven to hope "that the tempestuos wynde wyll aswage" (831). Comforting himself within his heart, he cuts the cable rope from his anchor and sets his ship out to sea, praying as he begins his journey for Christ to be his guide. In contrast to his stance in "Collyn Clout" where he hopes for future calm, in the "Garlande" the poet, though committing his fate to God, makes the gesture that preserves his barge and sets it to sea. He finds comfort within although the outer storm persists.

Although Skelton's critics have judged him to be unique as a poet, stylistically and metrically distinguished from other writers by his striking innovations,[31] his poetic stances and styles more accurately represent a response to the visions of the fifteenth-century poets. Skelton's poems reiterate, confront, reject, and finally qualify the assumptions about poetry that these poets articulate in their poems. His journey from the early aureate poems and the vision of the poet as the illuminator of matter to his rejection of the artificial and enclosed world of these poems and the poetic and social order they imply in the poems between 1521 and 1523 to the paradoxes and resolutions of the "Garlande" and the "Replycacion," provides a final coherent statement of the fifteenth-century ideals and an important example of their limitations in the new social, political, and religious setting of the early Renaissance. Skelton's poetry represents a deconstruction of fifteenth-century poetics and an effort to reconstruct a viable medium and form in a world that renders such an act difficult.

Skelton defines his development as poet away from the fifteenth-century visions symbolically by the changing personae of the narrator and the corresponding poetic styles he introduces in his poems. In "The Bowge of Courte," he replaces his early poet-illuminator figures with Drede, the uncertain poet in a world of disorder and change where false uses of language dominate and where it is difficult to distinguish true order from the characters' distorted versions. Drede's successor, Parrot, vacillates between detachment and involvement in the world of the poem and among aureate, prophetic, and plain styles, formal meters and seemingly formless Skeltonics, accentuating, by his changing stances and his stylistic uncertainty, the dilemma of the poet who finds his predecessors' poetic solutions inadequate responses to his concerns. Colin Clout, the figure of the poet as the just man who is committed to speak out against the corruption he witnesses, develops the plain style that Parrot concludes with as a possible resolution to the dilemma. As a poet, he will continue to write, to shake out his "conning bag," despite the difficulties, misfortune, and unhappiness that ensue. Though a culpable man, he will speak in order to edify rather than speak in tongues. Finally, the narrator of the "Garlande," the figure of the poet Skelton in suit of Fame, is a poet who recognizes both the folly of his effort and the importance of the possibilities it represents. His style, a mixture of opposing styles, hints of the limitations of all style and yet suggests a larger perspective that emerges from the interrelation of his disparate modes.[32] Paradoxically, he suggests, the poet must speak although his medium is limited.

In his resolution in the "Garlande" and in "A Replycacion" to persist as poet, Skelton concludes with a vision of poetry that differs both from his fifteenth-century predecessors' and from the solution of Hawes. Although, like Hawes, he moves gradually away from the conception of poetry as the illumination of matter and the poet as one who is capable of ennobling and enlightening humanity by his heightened language, he finally qualifies Hawes's vision of the poet as "vates" beset by enemies who writes his "derk" and "mysty" verse as a token of his faith in God and a message to the faithful few. Skelton turns from the "derk" and obscure style to an uncertain mixture of styles, from an effort to allegorize to an effort to communicate, from the stance preeminently as prophet to an acknowledgment of the poet's humanity as culpable man. Anticipating T. S. Eliot at the end of the *Waste Land*, who senses he must "at least set my lands in order" and who shores up the "fragments" of his literary past "against my ruins," Skelton's poet gathers "shredis of sentence, strowed in the shop" ("Speke Parott," 92) and scraps of meter from which he produces his poems.[33] As poet, he relies on his own resources, the dedication and effort that the figure of Occupation in the "Garlande" represents. Although he commits his work to God and defends the process of poetry in "A Replycacion" as divinely inspired, he recognizes his own responsibility to speak despite the difficulties, to make the gesture that initiates the poem, or, to borrow his metaphor, that cuts the cable rope and sets the ship out to sea. Two lines from his final poem, "A Replycacion," epitomize his position: "heresy wyll neuer dye," and "Poets are few and rare" ("sunt pauci rarique poete"). The poet's struggle is continual both because it is difficult to apprehend the truth and because it is difficult to communicate it.

even

Conclusion

Skelton's abandonment of the stylistic and formal solutions of the fifteenth-century poets marks the end of a century of significant redefinition of the poetic process within the thematic framework of the poetry itself. Introducing their self-conscious assessment of the value and effect of poetry and their roles as poets as central themes, the fifteenth-century poets articulate the shared assumptions and poetic ideals that underlie much of their poetry. The ongoing dialogue between poets from Lydgate to Skelton about these concerns suggests the beginning of a criticism in English earlier than the formal treatises of the Elizabethans who usually are credited with the inception of a poetics in English. The revaluation of the poetic process in the fifteenth-century poems also reveals an infusion of continental theory earlier than we had recognized, particularly in the discussions about the noble mission of the vernacular and the relation between the poet, eloquent language, and the state in such works as Dante's *De Vulgari eloquentia, Convivio,* and *Commedia* and in the defense of poetry as a means of ennobling humanity as articulated in Boccaccio's *De Genealogia* and other texts. Skelton's shifting stances as poet from "enluminer" to "makar" to "vates" to the common man, Colin Clout, in search of a voice exemplify the changing vision of the fifteenth-century poets. His ultimate rejection of their attitudes and his new approaches in the "Garlande" and "A Replycacion" presage the renewed search and the definition of the "true and rare" poet, the "laureate" of the Renaissance, a descendant of the fifteenth-century poets, but clearly a representative of the new generation.

Even more significant than the new poet's genealogy in terms of his specific links to the late medieval poets, is his broader inheritance. Although the various fifteenth-century poetic solutions break down with Skelton, the profound changes in the literary process this period introduces cannot be revoked. The fifteenth century represents a broad secularization of poetry, manifested in a shift from a salvation-oriented literature to a literature that focuses on this world; in the turning away from the quest for Truth, to the quest for wisdom and political order; in the shift from God's Word to the poet's language as a manifestation of order; in the increasing professionalism of the poet's role and the turning from the poet as an "enluminer" to the poet as a "makar," a master craftsman, public servant, and good man; and, finally, in the change from the rejection of worldly fame to the poetic pursuit of fame and the creation of "monuments of eternity."

The transition from a salvation-oriented context to the pursuit of worldly perfection is underscored by the differences in the dominant modes of the periods. In the thirteenth and fourteenth centuries, one of the most conspicuous literary forms is the pilgrimage. Defining the potential path from the "dark woods," the garden of fallen man and woman, the imperfect city, the worldly court, the "field full of folk," to the perfect garden, the higher court, the pure joy of the redeemed, and the vision of God's order, the pilgrimage underlies works as disparate as Dante's *Commedia*, Guillaume de Lorris's and Jean de Meun's *Romance of the Rose*, Laurent de Premierfait's *Pélerinage de la vie humaine*, *Sir Gawain and the Green Knight*, Langland's *Piers Plowman*, and Chaucer's *Canterbury Tales*. It encompasses both the temptations of the attractive world and one's struggle to extricate oneself from these temptations and turn one's attention to more enduring concerns, recognizing as Chaucer's pun suggests that "al nys but a faire / This world, that passeth soone as floures faire."[1] Although the pilgrimage survives in the fifteenth century in works like Hawes's three long poems and Douglas's *Eneados,* it is neither as pervasive a form nor as salvation oriented as it was before Chaucer. Hawes's *Pastime,* for example, devotes the bulk of its 5,800 lines to the education of its hero in the active pursuits in the world as lover, poet, and knight with only 500 lines for the salvation-oriented ending; in contrast to the interpretation of the medieval commentator, Douglas treats his *Eneados,* Books I to XII, as a model of the good man in the world. At the same time, other forms that reflect the increasing focus on earthly concerns begin to appear with frequency, particularly the occasional poem, by then a form common to most poets of the period, and the manual for princes, both in its explicit form in texts like Hoccleve's *Regiment of Princes* and in the reworking of classical matter in poems like Lydgate's *Siege of Thebes* and *Fall of Princes.* In the sixteenth century, the dominant mode is the model, the self-conscious creation of the poet offered for our study and aspiration. This mode, which directs attention to the possibilities of "self-fashioning," cuts across the genres and types of the period with examples in Edmund Spenser's "gentleman," Baldassare de Castiglione's Courtier, the Lover of Shakespeare's and Philip Sidney's sonnet cycles, Machiavelli's Prince, and Shakespeare's Prince Hal, and in Thomas More's Utopia. As readers are prompted to emulate the poet's fashioning in their daily lives, the distinction between life and art is blurred, and a greater degree of perfection is transported to the realm of mundane experience.

Within the fifteenth-century poems, attention shifts from the quest for Truth to the attainment of wisdom, harmony, and order in the state, manifested, for example, in the "governance" of the *Kingis Quair,* the "prudence" of Henryson's *Fables,* the piety of Douglas's Aeneas. By means of his heightened language, the poet becomes the instrument of this order, like the noble King Amphion, prompting humans to turn from willfulness and chaos to a civilized state. The poet's words and the wisdom and order they inspire, finally, have the potential to strengthen us against Fortune and help us live prudently. In the sixteenth century, the poet's language acquires a greater power. The poet's words become a form of service to the state, a potent source of political illusion making, rewarded and, as the censoring of the ending of Shakespeare's *Richard II* suggests, feared by monarchs. But more significantly, the poet's language now acquires creative force. More than a source of order, the poet's words, like the creative Word of God, have the power to form a "second nature." As Sidney suggests, the poet,

> lifted up with the vigor of his own invention, doth grow in effect into another nature, in making things either better than nature bringeth forth, or, quite anew . . . so as he goeth hand in hand with nature, not enclosed within the narrow warrant of her gifts but freely ranging within the zodiac of his own wit. Nature never set forth the earth in so rich tapestry as divers poets have done, neither with so pleasant rivers, fruitful trees, sweet-smelling flowers, nor whatsoever else may make the too much loved earth more lovely. Her world is brazen, the poets only deliver a golden.[2]

More simply, Ben Jonson concludes, the poet draws "forth out of his best and choicest flowers, with the Bee, and turn[s] all into Honey."[3] Thus, unlike the philosopher, who is limited to precepts, and the historian, bound by the examples of the past, the poet is free by his words to create whatever forms may serve Protean man. Yet the extreme power of the Renaissance poet's language is double-edged. Unlike the imperfect language of the fallen mortal and the human artist in the Middle Ages, the Renaissance poet's language, when detached from God's higher purpose, is not simply incomplete and erroneous, but, as the examples of Volpone, Iago, and Milton's Satan indicate, it is anticreative, and, rather than ennobling people, it leads them to a bestial state.

Linked to the changing attitudes toward the poet's language is a redefinition of the poet's self-image. In contrast to the Ricardian poets, who present themselves as ordinary men, naive both in their lives and in their craft—for example, Chaucer's simple pilgrim of the *Canterbury Tales* or the awkward outsider from love of the *Troilus, Hous of Fame,* and *Parliament,* Langland's Will, and Gower's Amans—the fifteenth-century poets begin to characterize themselves as professionals in search of recognition for their craft. Commissioned by Henry IV, Queen Katharine, and powerful nobles like Humphrey of Gloucester, Lydgate, though not an official member of the court, in many of his poems represents himself as a public poet, conscious of his service to the realm. Similarly, Dunbar draws attention to his role as self-appointed laureate or official poet, who commemorates people and events, serving as both scourge and celebrator. Hawes and Skelton take the stance of responsible poets who write to offset the corruption in the realm. Significantly, in the fifteenth century, the familiar humility topos of the Middle Ages with the poets' elaborate protests of their lack of skill, disappears. Although this topos is evident in Lydgate's work, the poets at the end of the period characteristically avoid it. Dunbar, for example, presents himself as a poet competent in his craft who is aware of his place in a larger tradition of poets. Moving from the line of great English writers, Chaucer, Lydgate, and Gower, to the native Scots poets past and present, in the "Lament for the Makaris," he assigns himself a place among his "brether" poets. Likewise, Skelton, in the "Garlande of Laurell," his final long poem, in a bold self-advertisement, comically defends his right to the garland of laurel.

Linked to the changes in the poets' stances is a shifting perception of the relation of poetry and fame and the desirability of worldly fame. Although most thirteenth- and fourteenth-century poets link Fama and Fortuna and represent worldly fame as a questionable pursuit, and in poetry at best the uncertain form of reward epitomized by Chaucer's treatment in the *Hous of Fame,* the fifteenth-century poets not only reiterate this view, for example, in Douglas's *Palice of Honour* and Hawes's *Pastime of Pleasure,* but they also begin to articulate the changing notion that worldly fame is a respectable pursuit and that poetry is an effective means of conferring fame. In his prologue to the *Troy Book,* Lydgate first introduces this note, arguing that poets protect people's fame from oblivion. Without the poet:

. . . certeyn the grete worthynesse
Of her dedis hadde ben in veyn;
For-dirked age elles wolde haue slayn
By lenthe of ȝeris þe noble worthi fame
Of conquerours, and pleynly of her name
For-dymmed eke the lettris aureat,
And diffaced the palme laureat,
Whiche þat þei wan by kniȝthood in her dayes,
Whos fretying rust newe and newe assayes
For to eclipse the honour and the glorie
Of hiȝe prowes. . . .[4]

By means of his enameling, Dunbar, likewise, creates artifacts that endure beyond the immediate occasion of the poem. Hedging his position in the "Garlande of Laurell," Skelton both reveals his ability to confer fame and preserve his own reputation in his eleven lyrics in praise of the Countess of Surrey and her ladies, and, by his comic intrusions, hints of the limits of Fame's dictates. In the Elizabethans' "monuments of eternity," much of the ambivalence of the medieval poets' vision of worldly fame is gone. The poem for Spenser in the *Shepheard's Calendar,* Jonson in his epitaphs, Sidney and Shakespeare in their sonnet cycles, can confer immortal fame and hold back the ravages of time.

The change in the position of poetry in the fifteenth century is underscored by the shift in the meaning of the terms used to describe the poet. A good example is provided by the term "makar," which, in the hands of the Renaissance poets, draws together the fifteenth-century conceptions of craftsman, "rethor," "enluminer," "vates," and "true poet." The fourteenth-century poets use the term "makar" almost exclusively to refer to God, but in the fifteenth century, "makar" is applied to the poet in the role of craftsman or fashioner of matter.[5] Thus, Dunbar praises Chaucer in the "Golden Targe" as a "makar" skilled in poetic language: "Thou beris of makaris the tryumph riall; / Thy fresch anamalit termes celicall / This mater coud illumynit have full brycht."[6] Similarly, in the "Lament for the Makaris," he celebrates Chaucer as "The Noble Chaucer of makaris flour."[7] In their effort to distinguish themselves from the vulgar poets or poetasters, the Renaissance poets return to the older English term "makar," considerably expanding its connotations. Tracing the word back to its Greek root, they suggest that "makar" signifies one who makes or feigns, one who both crafts and creates. Sidney, for example, observes:

> Indeed that name of *making* is fit for him, considering that whereas other arts retain themselves within their subject and receive, as it were, their being from it, the poet only bringeth his own stuff and doth not learn a conceit out of a matter but maketh matter for a conceit.[8]

Likewise, Jonson indicates that a poet is a "Maker, or a fainer," "From the word ποιεῖν, which signifies to make or fayne. Hence hee is call'd a *Poet,* not hee which writeth in measure only but that fayneth and formeth a fable, and writes things like the Truth."[9] The connotation of the "makar" as a feigner or creator in the positive sense rather than in the ambiguous sense of the term in Henryson's and Douglas's work, is expanded further by the association of the "makar" with the "vates," the priest or prophet, from the Latin term for poet. As Sidney notes, both the Romans and the Greeks gave "divine names" to poetry, "the one of prophesying, the other of making."[10] The two functions complement each other as aspects of the divine power the poet imitates. Finally, the definition of "makar" takes on the implications of the poet as a good man, the craftsman or feigner who uses his fables to lead others to virtue. Jonson sums up this version in his "Dedicatory Epistle of Volpone":

> For if man will impartially, and not a-squint, looke toward the offices and function of a *Poet,* they will easily conclude to themselues the impossibility of any mans being the good *Poet,* without first being a good Man. He that is sayd to be able to informe *yong-men* to all good disciplines, inflame *growne-men* to all great verties, keepe *old men* in their best and supreme state . . . that comes forth the Interpreter and Arbiter of *Nature,* a Teacher of things diuine no less than humane, a Master in manners: and can alone, or with a few, effect the business of Man-kind.[11]

This true poet is indeed rare. "As that Laurell *Maia* dreamed of," Henry Peacham suggests, he "is made by miracle from his mother's wombe, and like the Diamond onely polished and pointed of him-selfe."[12]

In the Laureate, the "true poet, self-fashioned and perfected like the diamond," the transformations of the fifteenth century come to fruition. The term "laureate" is used only once by Chaucer to refer to the extraordinary laureation of Petrarch in 1341, an event that inflamed the imagination of the poets who succeeded him.[13] In the fifteenth century, the term appears frequently to describe the highest rank of poets, in James I's words, those "Superlatiue as poetis laure-ate / In moralitee and eloquence ornate."[14] Shirley equates the laure-ate's skill and renown, praising Chaucer as "þe laureal and moste famous poets þat euer was to-fore him." Henryson uses the term as an extreme form of praise for his master, Aesop, "Esope, that noble clerk, ane poet worthie to be lauriate."[15] In the early Renaissance, laureation acquires a broader spectrum of meanings as several ideals coalesce. While the old sense of supreme status survives, laureate now also embodies the fifteenth-century ideal of the poet who is effective in ennobling human beings, in moving them to virtue and order by the power of language. Lydgate's Amphion used this power to civilize humanity and to forestall the destructive force of Fortune. The sixteenth-century laureate as courtier and advisor to the prince offers his skills as a form of public service, a means of contributing to the stability and improvement of the realm. Jonson explains, "The study of [poetry] . . . offers to mankinde a Certaine rule and Patterne of living well and happily, disposing us to all Civill offices of Society."[16] In his public role, the poet presents himself at once as an example of the good man devoted to a worthy purpose and as the perpetuator of human fame. Ideally, as poet, he relies upon the primacy of his mind and his power to "make" or "create"; but practically as courtier, he depends upon the system.

The dilemma of the poet who aspires to the ideal of "makar" or laureate reveals the broad implications of the changes in attitudes and assumptions about poetry that occurred in the fifteenth century. With the shift to a literature oriented to the world, to the order of the realm, and to the ability of individuals, inspired by the poet's words, to ennoble and refashion themselves, the poet is compelled to recreate the context and purpose of art as well as its poetic forms. Detached from God's higher purpose, the poets' art may serve the imperfect ambitions of their patrons or rulers or their own aspirations to fame. For this reason, the "true poets" continually must redefine the values and ideals that give meaning to their poetry. The perpetual re-creation of the context of poetry in terms of a purpose larger than immediate human vision is one of the legacies of the end of the Middle Ages that we as moderns still address. With the loss of the medieval Christian framework, poets for the past five centuries have searched for a significant shared context for their art, a search that has led them to the state, to reason and science, to nature, inward to experience, to private myth, to self-consciously recreated tradition, and to a variety of new styles and forms for signifying meaning.

NOTES AND INDEX

Altf. Wb.	*Altfranzosisches Würterbuch,* ed. by A. Tobler and E. Lommatzsch (Wiesbaden: Steiner, 1925–76), Vols. 1–10
E & S	*Essays and Studies*
EIC	*Essays in Criticism*
ELH	*Journal of English Literary History*
ELR	*English Literary Renaissance*
ES	*English Studies*
JEGP	*Journal of English and German Philology*
Littre	*Dictionnaire de la Langue, Française* 7 vols., ed. Émile Littré (Paris: J. Pauvert, 1956–58)
MAE	*Medium Aevum*
MED	*Middle English Dictionary,* ed. Hans Kurath and Sherman M. Kuhn (Ann Arbor: University of Michigan Press, 1952–85) Pts. A–R
Mit. Wb.	*Mittellateinisches Worterbuch* (Munich: C. H. Beck, 1959–76) Vols. 1–2
MLN	*Modern Language Notes*
MLR	*Modern Language Review*
NM	*Neuphilologische Mitteilungen*
OED	*Oxford English Dictionary,* 12 vols. and suppl., ed. J. A. H. Murray et al. (Oxford: Clarendon Press, 1933)
PLL	*Papers on Language and Literature*
PMLA	*Publications of the Modern Language Association of America*
PQ	*Philological Quarterly*
RES	*Review of English Studies*
SAC	*Studies in the Age of Chaucer*
SN	*Studia Neophilologia*
SP	*Studies in Philology*
SSL	*Studies in Scottish Literature*
TSLL	*Texas Studies in Literature and Language*

otes

PREFACE

1 H. S. Bennett, "The Author and His Public in the Fourteenth and Fifteenth Centuries," *E & S* 23 (1937): 7–24; H. S. Bennett, *Chaucer and the Fifteenth Century* (Oxford: Clarendon Press, 1947), chap. 5; A. I. Doyle, "More Light on John Shirley," *MAE* 30 (1961): 93–101; K. L. Scott, "A Mid-Fifteenth-Century English Illuminating Shop and its Customers," *Journal of the Warburg and Courtauld Institutes* 31 (1968): 170–96; A. S. G. Edwards, "The Influence of Lydgate's *Fall of Princes, c.* 1440–1555: A Survey," *Medieval Studies* 39 (1977): 428–30; A. I. Doyle and M. B. Parkes, "The Production of Copies of the *Canterbury Tales* and the *Confession Amantis* in the early Fifteenth Century," in *Medieval Scribes, Manuscripts and Libraries: Essays Presented to N. R. Ker,* ed. M. P. Parkes and A. G. Watson (London: Scholar Press, 1978), pp. 163–210; Richard Firth Green, *Poets and Princepleasers: Literature and the English Court in the Late Middle Ages* (Toronto: University of Toronto Press, 1980); Derek Pearsall, ed., *Manuscripts and Readers in Fifteenth Century England: The Literary Implications of Manuscript Study* (Cambridge: D. S. Brewer, 1983).

2 See, for example, C. S. Lewis, *English Literature in the Sixteenth*

Century (Oxford: Clarendon Press, 1961), p. 120; Thomas Percy, "On the Ancient Metrical Romances," in *Reliques of Ancient English Poetry,* 3 vols. (1886, repr.: New York: Dover, 1966), 3:354; George Ellis, *Specimens of the Early English Poets,* 3 vols. (London: G. and W. Nicol, 1801), 1:273–94; Joseph Ritson, *Bibliographia Poetica* (London: G. and W. Nicol, 1802), pp. 66–90; George Saintsbury, *Historical Manual of English Prosody* (London: Macmillan, 1910), p. 287.

3 This issue is emphasized in some of the studies of fifteenth-century literature that have appeared in the 1980s, including A. C. Spearing, *Medieval to Renaissance in English Poetry* (Cambridge: Cambridge University Press, 1985); Robert F. Yeager, *Fifteenth-Century Studies: Recent Essays* (Hamden, Conn.: Archon Books, 1984); and Lois Ebin, ed., *Vernacular Poetics in the Middle Ages* (Kalamazoo, Mich.: Medieval Institute Publications, 1984), pp. 227–93.

4 Walter F. Schirmer, "The Importance of the Fifteenth Century to the Study of the English Renaissance," *English Studies Today* (series 1), ed. C. L. Wrenn and G. Bullough (London: Oxford University Press, 1951), pp. 104–10; Alain Renoir, *The Poetry of John Lydgate* (London: Routledge & Kegan Paul, 1967), pp. 75–143; 161–73.

5 Bennett, *Chaucer and the Fifteenth Century;* Eleanor P. Hammond, *English Verse Between Chaucer and Surrey* (1927, repr.; New York: Octagon Books, 1965), pp. 3–37; Rossell Hope Robbins, *Historical Poems of the XIVth and XVth Centuries* (New York: Columbia University Press, 1959), pp. xvii–xlvii; Derek Pearsall, *John Lydgate* (London: Routledge & Kegan Paul, 1970); Derek Pearsall, *Old English and Middle English Poetry* (London: Routledge & Kegan Paul, 1977), pp. 212–83; A. S. G. Edwards, *Stephen Hawes* (Boston: Twayne, 1983), chaps. 1 and 4; Green, *Poets and Princepleasers;* N. F. Blake, "The Fifteenth Century Reconsidered," *NM* 71 (1970): 146–57. For other useful considerations of the historical and social contexts of fifteenth-century poetry, see Ethel Seaton, *Sir Richard Roos: Lancastrian Poet* (London: R. Hart-Davis, 1961); John MacQueen, "The Literature of Fifteenth-Century Scotland," in Jennifer M. Brown, ed., *Scottish Society in the Fifteenth Century* (New York: St. Martin's Press, 1977), pp. 184–208; V. J. Scattergood and J. W. Sherborne, eds., *English Court Culture in the Later Middle Ages* (New York: St. Martin's Press, 1983).

6 Bennett, *Chaucer and the Fifteenth Century,* pp. 97–103; Hammond, *English Verse Between Chaucer and Surrey,* p. 7.

7 Pearsall, *John Lydgate,* p. 67; Derek Pearsall, "The English Chaucerians," in *Chaucer and Chaucerians,* ed. D. S. Brewer (University: University of Alabama Press, 1966), p. 68; Rossell Hope Robbins, "Court Literature of the Fifteenth Century," lecture presented to the

Medieval Club of New York, New York City, October 18, 1974. See also
John Stevens, *Music and Poetry in the Early Tudor Court* (Lincoln:
University of Nebraska Press, 1961), p. 212; Green, *Poets and Prince-
pleasers*, pp. 3–12; Glending Olson, *Literature as Recreation in the
Later Middle Ages* (Ithaca, N.Y.: Cornell University Press, 1982).

8 Spearing, *Medieval to Renaissance in English Poetry*, chaps. 3–6.

9 A. J. Minnis, *Medieval Theory of Authorship: Scholastic Literary Attitudes in the Later Middle Ages* (London: Scolar Press, 1984).

CHAPTER I

1 Caroline F. Spurgeon, ed., *Five Hundred Years of Chaucer Criticism and
Allusion*, 3 vols. (1925, repr.; New York: Russell & Russell, 1961), 1:4–
77.

2 For the traditional views of the relation of the fifteenth-century poets to
Chaucer, see H. S. Bennett, *Chaucer and the Fifteenth Century* (Oxford:
Clarendon Press, 1947); G. Gregory Smith, *The Transition Period* (Edin-
burgh: Blackwood & Sons, 1900).

3 Among the many studies of Chaucer's views of poetry and the relation
between the poet's moral and artistic visions, the following are par-
ticularly useful: Robert O. Payne, *The Key of Remembrance: A Study of
Chaucer's Poetics* (New Haven, Conn.: Yale University Press, 1963);
Robert O. Payne, "Chaucer's Realization of Himself as Rethor," in
Medieval Eloquence, ed. James J. Murphy (Berkeley and Los Angeles:
University of California Press, 1978), pp. 270–87; Patricia M. Kean,
Chaucer and the Making of English Poetry (London: Routledge & Kegan
Paul, 1972); John A. Burrow, *Ricardian Poetry* (New Haven, Conn.:
Yale University Press, 1971); Charles Muscatine, *Poetry and Crisis in the
Age of Chaucer* (Notre Dame, Ind.: University of Notre Dame Press,
1972): Donald R. Howard, *The Idea of the Canterbury Tales* (Berkeley
and Los Angeles: University of California Press, 1976); Alfred David,
The Strumpet Muse: Art and Morals in Chaucer's Poetry (Bloomington:
University of Indiana Press, 1976); Donald L. Rose, ed., *New Perspec-
tives in Chaucer Criticism* (Norman, Okla.: Pilgrim, 1981); A. J. Minnis,
*Medieval Theory of Authorship: Scholastic Literary Attitudes in the Later
Middle Ages* (London: Scolar Press, 1984), chap. 5; Winthrop Wether-
bee, *Chaucer and the Poets: An Essay on Troilus and Criseyde* (Ithaca,
N.Y.: Cornell University Press, 1981).

4 For a consideration of the relation of Chaucer's views on poetry to the
philosophical developments of the time, see Sheila Delany, *Chaucer's
House of Fame: The Poetics of Skeptical Fideism* (Chicago: University of
Chicago Press, 1972).

5 For an example of this view, see George Saintsbury, "The English Chaucerians," in *The Cambridge History of English Literature*, 15 vols. (Cambridge: Cambridge University Press, 1963), 2:197–22.

6 Kean, *Chaucer and the Making of English Poetry*, 2:210–40. For a useful examination of the fifteenth-century poets' praise of Chaucer, see A. C. Spearing, *Medieval to Renaissance in English Poetry* (Cambridge: Cambridge University Press, 1985), chap. 2.

7 Spurgeon, *Five Hundred Years of Chaucer Criticism and Allusion*, 1:70.

8 Ibid., 1:14, 20, 21, 27, 36, 42, 47, 57, 58, 68, 70.

9 John Lydgate, *A Critical Edition of John Lydgate's Life of Our Lady*, ed. Joseph A. Lauritis (Pittsburgh: Duquesne University Press, 1961), 2: 1629–37.

10 Spurgeon, *Five Hundred Years of Chaucer Criticism and Allusion*, 1:21.

11 Ibid., 1:19.

12 Lydgate, *Siege of Thebes*, Prol., 46–47.

13 John Lydgate, *The Pilgrimage of the Life of Man*, ed. F. J. Furnivall (London: Kegan Paul, Trench, Trubner, 1899–1904), lines 19775–76.

14 John Lydgate, *Fall of Princes*, ed. Henry Bergen (1924, repr.; London: Oxford University Press, 1967), I, 275–79.

15 Spurgeon, *Five Hundred Years of Chaucer Criticism and Allusion*, 1:22.

16 Ibid., 1:49; see also p. 54.

17 Ibid., 1:58.

18 Ibid., 1:68–69, 73–74.

19 Lydgate, *Troy Book*, III, 4240.

20 Ibid., 4250 ff.

21 Lydgate, *Fall of Princes*, III, 3858–59.

22 Spurgeon, 1:54.

23 The author of *The Floure of Curteyse* first sounds this note in about 1401:

> Chaucer is deed, that had suche a name
> Of fayre makyng, that, without[en] wene,
> Fayrest in our tonge, as the laurer grene.
>
> We may assay for to countrefete
> His gay[e] style, but it wyl not be;
> The welle is drie, with the lycoure swete,
> Bothe of Clyo and of Caliope, . . .
> (Lydgate, *Minor Poems*, II, no. 4)

A few years later, Henry Scogan offers a similar tribute (Spurgeon, 1:18), whereas in 1409–11, Lydgate inserts an elaborate passage in the *Life of Our Lady* which contains many of the elements of future tributes:

. . . in our tunge, was neuere noon hym like
For as the sonne, doth in hevyn shyne
In mydday spere, dovne to vs by lyne
In whose presence, no ster may apere
Right so his dyteʒ withoutyn eny pere

Euery makyng withe his light disteyne
In sothfastnesse, who so takethe hede
Wherfore no wondre, thof my hert pleyne
Vpon his dethe, and for sorwe blede
For want of hym, nowe is my grete nede
That shulde alas, conveye and directe
And with his supporte, amende eke and correcte

The wronge traceʒ, of my rude penne
(*Life of Our Lady,* II, 1637–49)

24 Spurgeon, 1:45.
25 Ibid., 1:53.
26 Ibid., 1:71.
27 John Skelton, *John Skelton: The Complete English Poems,* ed. John Scattergood (New Haven, Conn.: Yale University Press, 1983), "Phyllyp Sparowe," 797–803.
28 Eleanor Prescott Hammond, *Chaucer: A Bibliographical Manual* (1908, repr.; New York: Peter Smith, 1933), section IV, pp. 325–405; *The Works of Geoffrey Chaucer,* ed. F. N. Robinson, 2d ed. (Boston: Houghton Mifflin, 1957), pp. 898–928; B. A. Windeatt, *Geoffrey Chaucer: Troilus and Criseyde, a New Edition of 'The Book of Troilus'* (London: Longman, 1984).
29 The works of Doyle and Parkes ("Paleographical Introduction," in *The Canterbury Tales: A Facsimile and Transcription of the Hengwrt Manuscript, with Variants from the Ellesmere Manuscript,* ed. Paul G. Ruggiers [Norman: University of Oklahoma Press, 1979], pp. xix–xliii) have prompted a significant revaluation of the production of Chaucer manuscripts and the relation of the manuscripts. John M. Manly and Edith Rickert (*The Text of the Canterbury Tales, Vol. 2, Classification of the Manuscripts* [1940, repr.; Chicago: University of Chicago Press, 1967], pp. 78–473) argued that parts of the *Canterbury Tales* circulated separately and were gathered together only after Chaucer's death, but Doyle and Parkes suggest that in the first quarter of the fifteenth century an individual or committee had access to Chaucer's uncirculated text of the *Canterbury Tales* as it existed at his death. Manly and Rickert believed that there were two distinct types of manuscript production of the *Canter-*

bury Tales, commercial and private; Doyle and Parkes have demonstrated that in the early fifteenth century there were no organized scriptoria for vernacular manuscripts and only one type of vernacular manuscript production existed. Doyle and Parkes argue that an individual or committee with access to the exemplars of the text hired scribes to copy the exemplars as necessary and produced the manuscript either to order or as speculation. In the case of the *Canterbury Tales,* the exemplar owned by the committee consisted of unrelated fragments that needed ordering. N. F. Blake ("The Relationships Between the Hengwrt and Ellesmere Manuscripts of the *Canterbury Tales,*" *E & S* n.s. 32 [1979]: 1–18; "The Editorial Assumptions in the Manly-Rickert Edition of the *Canterbury Tales, E & S* 64 [1983]: 385–400; *Pretextual Tradition of the Canterbury Tales* [London: Arnold, 1985]) argues that the committee added missing links, corrected the language, and spruced up the presentation of the text. Thus the order and composition of the tales might change in subsequent manuscripts.

These studies also have changed certain of our assumptions about the order of the tales. Although several early scholars concluded that none of the manuscript sequences of the *Canterbury Tales* had any final authority in determining the order of the groups of tales, a majority of later critics have viewed the Ellesmere order as the poet's own final ordering of the *Canterbury Tales.* See Sheridan Cox, "A Question of Order in the *Canterbury Tales, Chaucer Review* 1 (1967): 228–52; James H. Wilson, "The Pardoner and the Second Nun: A Defense of the Bradshaw Order," *NM* 74 (1973): 292–96; Edward S. Cohen, "The Sequence of the *Canterbury Tales,*" *Chaucer Review* 9 (1974): 190–95; George R. Keiser, "In Defense of the Bradshaw Shift," *Chaucer Review* 12 (1977): 191–201; and Larry D. Benson, "The Order of the *Canterbury Tales" SAC* 3 (1981): 77–120. Doyle and Parkes, Blake, and Roy Vance Ramsey ("The Hengwrt and Ellesmere Manuscripts of the *Canterbury Tales:* Different Scribes," *Studies in Biography* 35 [1982]: 113–54) have raised questions about the supremacy of the Ellesmere manuscript, arguing that Hengwrt represents an earlier and more accurate text. We are thus left with the paradox of an earlier more accurate text with a poorer order of tales. Blake ("Chaucer Manuscripts and Texts," *Review* 3 (1981): 219–32) proposes one solution to this paradox. The committee had "only one exemplar consisting of separate fragments which [it] was continually reordering and revising. If the additions and omissions were noted in the exemplar, it would be changing so much that it would be impossible to consider that exemplar an established text which could be divided into different sections for different scribes to copy simultaneously. A theory along these lines enables us to understand why an improving order is associated with a deteriorating text" (p. 226). Finally, Charles A. Owen, Jr., "The Alternative Reading of the *Canterbury Tales:* Chaucer's Text and the Early Manuscripts," *PMLA* 97 (1982): 237–50, and John M. Bowers, "The Tale of Beryn and *The Siege of Thebes,*" *SAC* 7 (1985): 23–50, challenge the notion that a one-way journey was Chaucer's final design.

30 Charles A. Owen, Jr., "*The Canterbury Tales:* Early Manuscripts and Relative Popularity," *JEGP* 54 (1955): 106–10; see also John M. Manly and Edith Rickert, *The Text of the Canterbury Tales,* vol. 1, *Descriptions of the Manuscripts* (1940, repr.; Chicago: University of Chicago Press, 1967), pp. 52–54; 82–84; 126–29; 189–97; 238–48; 289–94; 302–3; 343–48; 376–80; 472–75; 501–3; 519–21. As M. Deansley has demonstrated in her study of medieval books ("Vernacular Books in England in the Fourteenth and Fifteenth Centuries," *MLR* 15 [1920]: 349–58), religious and moral literature had a better chance of surviving in the Middle Ages than secular literature. In his interesting study, "Chaucer's Fifteenth-Century Audience and the Narrowing of the 'Chaucer Tradition,'" *SAC* 4 (1982): 3–33, Paul Strohm argues that the tales most frequently circulated in the fourteenth century, including the *Franklin's Tale,* the *Canon's Yeoman's Tale,* and the *Miller's Tale,* were among Chaucer's most independent tales. The tales most anthologized in the fifteenth century, including the *Second Nun's Tale,* the *Melibee,* and the *Parson's Tale,* were more conventional and familiar.

31 Spurgeon, 1:4–77.

32 See, for example, *The Bannatyne Manuscript Written in Tyme of Pest, 1568, by George Bannatyne,* 4 vols., ed. W. Tod Ritchie (Edinburgh: Blackwood & Sons, 1928–34), 3:304, no. 283. Another popular passage was the epilogue, particularly lines 1849–55. For fifteenth-century imitations of this passage, see, for example, Lydgate's *Complaint of the Black Knight,* lines 400–406 (John Norton-Smith, ed., *John Lydgate Poems* [Oxford: Clarendon Press, 1966], p. 58); "A Balade in Commendation of Our Lady," lines 5–7 (Norton-Smith, *John Lydgate Poems,* p. 25); *Siege of Thebes,* 4628–30; *Troy Book,* IV, 3210–16.

33 Lee Patterson, "Ambiguity and Interpretation: A Fifteenth-Century Reading of *Troilus and Criseyde,*" *Speculum* 54 (1979): 297–330.

34 Spurgeon, 1:44, 67; John Lydgate, *The Temple of Glas,* in Norton-Smith, *John Lydgate Poems,* pp. 67–112; Gavin Douglas, *The Shorter Poems of Gavin Douglas,* ed. Priscilla J. Bawcutt (Edinburgh: Blackwood & Sons, 1967), pp. 1–134; Gavin Douglas, *Virgil's Aeneid,* ed. David F. C. Coldwell (Edinburgh: Blackwood & Sons, 1957), II, 3–17; *The Poetical Works of John Skelton,* 2 vols., ed. Alexander Dyce (London: T. Rodd, 1843), 1:361–427.

210

35 For a description of some of the anthology manuscripts in which this poem is found, see Manly and Rickert, *The Text of the Canterbury Tales*, 1:170; Hammond, *Chaucer: A Bibliographical Manual*, pp. 378–83; Aage Brusendorff, *The Chaucer Tradition* (1925, repr.; Gloucester, Mass.: Peter Smith, 1965), pp. 137–48. For the allusions to the *Legend of Good Women* in fifteenth-century poetry, see Spurgeon, 1:18, 39, 40, 67, 72. For a description of the fifteenth-century poems that this work has influenced, see Rossell Hope Robbins, "The Chaucerian Apocrypha," in *A Manual of the Writings in Middle English 1050–1500*, 4 vols. (New Haven: Connecticut Academy of Arts and Sciences, 1973), section xi, 4:1095, 1087, 1097, 1074.

36 Robbins, "The Chaucerian Apocrypha," 4:963, 1062, 1084, 1086, 1087.

37 William Dunbar, *The Poems of William Dunbar*, ed. James Kinsley (Oxford: Clarendon Press, 1979), no. 14; John Lydgate, *The Minor Poems of John Lydgate*, ed. Henry Noble MacCracken (London: Oxford University Press, 1934), Part II, nos. 17, 42.

38 See, for example, Donald McDonald, "Henryson and Chaucer: Cock and Fox," *TSLL* 8 (1967): 451–61; Lydgate, *Fall of Princes*, VIII, 673–79; Beverly Boyd, "The Literary Background of Lydgate's 'The Legend of Dan Joos,'" *MLN* 72 (1957): 81–87; Elizabeth Roth Eddy, "Sir Thopas and Sir Thomas Norny: Romance Parody in Chaucer and Dunbar," *RES*, ns 22 (1971): 401–9.

39 Spurgeon, 1:4–77. See, for example, Lydgate, *Siege of Thebes*, 1–17; "The Mumming at Bishopswood," in *The Minor Poems of John Lydgate*, Part II, no. 40, stanza 2.

40 For useful discussions of these interests, see Derek Pearsall, *Old English and Middle English Literature* (London: Routledge & Kegan Paul, 1977), pp. 218–83; Rossell Hope Robbins, "Court Literature of the Fifteenth Century," lecture presented at the Medieval Club of New York, New York City, October 18, 1974; John Stevens, *Music and Poetry in the Early Tudor Court* (Lincoln: University of Nebraska Press, 1961); Glending Olson, *Literature as Recreation in the Later Middle Ages* (Ithaca, N.Y.: Cornell University Press, 1982).

41 Robbins, "The Chaucerian Apocrypha," pp. 1062–1101; Francis W. Bonner, "The Genesis of Chaucer Apocrypha," *SP* 48 (1951): 461–81; Brusendorff, *The Chaucer Tradition*, pp. 433–45. For the text of many of these poems, see W. W. Skeat, *Chaucerian and Other Pieces, Supplement to the Complete Works of Geoffrey Chaucer* (1897, repr.; London: Oxford University Press, 1959). For an analysis of the impact of the fifteenth-century audience on the relative popularity of "Chaucer" texts, see Strohm, "Chaucer's Fifteenth-Century Audience," pp. 25–29.

42 Bonner, "The Genesis of Chaucerian Apocrypha," pp. 461–81. See also

John Gower, *The English Works of John Gower,* 2 vols., ed. G. C. Macaulay (1901, repr.; London: Oxford University Press, 1957), vol. II, Book VIII, lines 2941*–57*; Lydgate, *Fall of Princes,* I, Prol., 316–19, 352–53; Hammond, *Chaucer: A Bibliographical Manual,* pp. 52–53; Brusendorff, *The Chaucer Tradition,* pp. 178–79. "It appears to have been a common publishers' custom during the latter half of the fifteenth century to make one or more scribes copy a number of short poems in separate quires and to unite these very much at random, merely with a view to get up collections as would command a good price and a quick sale" (Brusendorff, p. 179). As the title pages of the early editions reveal, it was a common practice among many fifteenth- and sixteenth-century editors of Chaucer to swell their editions with as many newly discovered "Chaucerian texts" as possible to make their volumes more saleable. Thynne, for example, advertises his 1532 edition as "The Workes of / Geffray Chau / cer newly printed with / dyvers workes whi / che were never in / print before: / as in the table more playnly / dothe appere" (Hammond, p. 116). Likewise, Stow emphasizes that his edition of 1561 contains "divers addicions, which / were neuer in print before" (Hammond, p. 119), and, in the *Annals of England* (1600), he explains that he not only corrected the poems which appeared in Thynne's edition, but he added many pieces which Thynne and the early editors had not discovered (Bonner, p. 472). Thus, Pynson prints five spurious works in his edition of 1526; Thynne includes twenty-one such pieces in 1532 and twenty-two in his edition of 1542. By 1561, Stow has increased the number of apocryphal works to thirty-eight. For a provocative analysis of the literary views of Chaucer's early editors, see R. F. Yeager, "Literary Theory at the Close of the Middle Ages: William Caxton and William Thynne," *SAC* 6 (1984): 135–64. For suggestions about the importance of the activity of Chaucer's scribes and fifteenth-century editors, see Derek Pearsall, "Texts, Textual Criticism, and Fifteenth Century Manuscript Production," in *Fifteenth-Century Studies: Recent Essays,* ed. Robert F. Yeager (Hamden, Conn.: Archon Books, 1984), pp. 121–36; Jeremy J. Smith, "Linguistic Features of Some Fifteenth-Century English Manuscripts," in *Manuscripts and Readers in Fifteenth-Century England: The Literary Implications of Manuscript Study,* ed. Derek Pearsall (Cambridge: D. S. Brewer, 1983), pp. 104–12; for suggestions about the roles of scribes and editors of Gower and Lydgate texts in this period, see A. S. G. Edwards, "Lydgate Manuscripts: Some Directions for Future Research," in *Manuscripts and Readers,* pp. 15–26; Kate Harris, "John Gower's 'Confessio Amantis': The Virtues of Bad Texts," in *Manuscripts and Readers,* pp. 27–40. Finally, Pamela Robinson, "The 'Booklet': A Self-Contained Unit in Composite Manuscripts," *Codicologica* 3

(1980): 46–49, points out that some texts circulated in independent "booklets." Medieval readers often put together a number of these separate "booklets" to form composite volumes, in many cases, revealing an eclectic attitude toward the texts assembled.

43 Robbins, "The Chaucerian Apocrypha," pp. 1075–76. Note Julia Boffey's caveat in "The MS of English Courtly Love Lyrics in the Fifteenth Century," in *Manuscripts and Readers*, pp. 3–14, that courtly lyrics often had the role of fillers in fifteenth-century manuscripts. For a fuller discussion of the role of courtly love lyrics in medieval manuscripts, see Julia Boffey, *Manuscripts of English Courtly Love Lyrics in the Later Middle Ages* (Cambridge: D. S. Brewer, 1985).

44 Robbins, "The Chaucerian Apocrypha," pp. 1087, 1090, 1091, 1096, 1094. As Bonner points out ("The Genesis of Chaucer Apocrypha," p. 481), these conventional pieces were influential in forming faulty conceptions of Chaucer which endured for centuries.

45 Robbins, "The Chaucerian Apocrypha," pp. 1077, 1078, 1082, 1083.

46 Montague Rhodes James, *The Western Manuscripts in the Library of Trinity College Cambridge: A Descriptive Catalogue*, 4 vols. (Cambridge: Cambridge University Press, 1901), 2:71; Hammond, *Chaucer: A Bibliographical Manual*, p. 342.

47 Thomas Raynesford Lounsbury, *Studies in Chaucer: His Life and Writings* (1892, repr.; New York: Russell & Russell, 1962), p. 469. Richard Pynson set the precedent for adding spurious works to the Chaucer canon by including five non-Chaucerian pieces in the second part of his 1526 edition of Chaucer. Thynne reprints only two of these pieces: *La Belle Dame Sans Merci* and *The Lamentation of Mary Magdalene*. Thynne's additions show him to be susceptible to love poetry for he prints for the first time Robert Henryson's *Testament of Cresseid, The Flower of Courtesy, The Assembly of Ladies, A Praise of Women, The Remedy of Love;* Hoccleve's *Letter of Cupid, The Book of Cupide;* and a few ballads. But he also prints for the first time many nonamatory pieces, including the prefactory poems "Eight Godly Questions" and Hoccleve's "To the King's Most Noble Grace," Thomas Usk's *Testament of Love,* and Gower's *In Praise of Peace.* For detailed assessments of Thynne's activities as editor, see James E. Blodgett, "William Thynne," in *Editing Chaucer: The Great Tradition,* ed. Paul G. Ruggiers (Norman, Okla.: Pilgrim, 1984), pp. 35–52; Yeager, "Literary Theory at the Close of the Middle Ages"; Derek S. Brewer, ed., *The Works, 1532, with Supplementary Material from the Editions of 1542, 1561, 1598 and 1602 by Geoffrey Chaucer* (Menston, Yorks.: Scolar Press, 1969); Charles Muscatine, *The Book of Geoffrey Chaucer* (San Francisco: Book Club of California, 1963).

48 Skeat, *Chaucerian and Other Pieces,* p. 191.

49 Derek Pearsall ("Thomas Speght," in *Editing Chaucer: The Great Tradition*, ed. Ruggiers, p. 88) suggests that "*Jack Upland* answers to a different conception of Chaucer, this time as the earnest critic of the old abuses of the Church, and Protestant by premonition." For a review of the textual tradition of *Jack Upland*, see P. L. Heyworth, ed., *Jack Upland, Friar Daw's Reply and Upland's Rejoinder* (Oxford: Oxford University Press, 1968).

50 Robbins, "The Chaucerian Apocrypha," pp. 1082–83. For descriptions of the prints of these poems, see W. W. Skeat, *The Complete Works of Geoffrey Chaucer*, 7 vols. (Oxford: Oxford University Press, 1984), 1:27–46; Hammond, *A Bibliographical Manual;* Muscatine, *The Book of Chaucer;* Brewer, ed., *Geoffrey Chaucer, The Works*, 1532; *Editing Chaucer: The Great Tradition*, ed. Ruggiers, pp. 35–92.

51 See, for example, Lydgate, *Fall of Princes*, I, 461; "Ballade at the Reverence of Our Lady," in *The Minor Poems of John Lydgate*, ed. Henry Noble MacCracken (London: Kegan Paul, Trench, Trubner, 1911), Part I, no. 49, lines 12–14; "Invocation to Seynte Anne," in *Minor Poems of John Lydgate*, Part I, no. 23, line 14; *Life of St. Edmund*, line 221; *Legend of St. Margaret*, line 56; *Troy Book*, Prol., 31.

52 Spurgeon, *Five Hundred Years of Chaucer Criticism and Allusion*, 1:57.

53 Georg Reismuller, *Romanische Lehnwerter bei Lydgate* (Leipzig: A Deichert, 1911), pp. 1–132; Pierrepont Henrick Nichols, "Lydgate's Influence on the Aureate Terms of the Scottish Chaucerians," PMLA 47 (1932): 516–22; and Nichols, "William Dunbar as a Scottish Lydgatian," PMLA 46 (1931): 222–24; Eleanor Prescott Hammond, *English Verse Between Chaucer and Surrey* (1927, repr.; New York: Octagon Books, 1965), p. 87.

54 Andre Courmont, *Studies on Lydgate's Syntax in the Temple of Glas* (Paris: Libraire Felix Alcan, 1912).

55 Derek Pearsall, *John Lydgate* (London: Routledge & Kegan Paul, 1970), pp. 54–55.

56 Ibid., p. 54.

57 Gavin Douglas, *The Palice of Honour*, in *The Shorter Poems of Gavin Douglas*, ed. Bawcutt, Part I, lines 451–62.

58 Dunbar, *The Poems of William Dunbar*, no. 50, lines 50–56.

59 Lydgate, *The Minor Poems of John Lydgate*, Part II, no. 17.

60 Ronald D. S. Jack, "Dunbar and Lydgate," SSL 8 (1971): 220–22.

61 Pearsall, *John Lydgate*, pp. 51–58.

62 For a good example of this view, see Henry Bergen, ed., *Lydgate's Troy Book* (London: Kegan Paul, Trench, Trubner, 1906), intro.

63 Guido della Colonna, *Historia destructionis Troiae*, trans. Mary Elizabeth Meek (Bloomington: Indiana University Press, 1974), p. 199.

64 James I of Scotland, *The Kingis Quair*, ed. John Norton-Smith (Oxford:

214

Clarendon Press, 1971); see, for example, Walter Scheps, "Chaucerian Synthesis: The Art of *The Kingis Quair,*" *SSL* 8 (1971): 143–65; John Preston, " 'Fortunys Exiltree': A Study of *The Kingis Quair,*" *RES,* ns 7 (1956): 339–47; M. F. Markland, "The Structure of *The Kingis Quair,*" *Research Studies of the State College of Washington* 25 (1957): 273–86; Mary Rohrberger, "*The Kingis Quair:* An Evaluation," *TSLL* 2 (1960): 292–302; John MacQueen, "Tradition and the Interpretation of *The Kingis Quair,*" *RES,* ns 12 (1961): 117–31; A. Von Hendy, "The Free Thrall: A Study of *The Kingis Quair,*" *SSL* 2 (1965): 141–51; Ian Brown, "The Mental Traveller, a Study of *The Kingis Quair,*" *SSL* 5 (1968): 246–52; Alice Miskimin, "Patterns in *The Kingis Quair* and the *Temple of Glas,*" *PLL* 13 (1976): 339–61; William Quinn, "Memory and the Matrix of Unity in the *Kingis Quair,*" *Chaucer Review* 15 (1980): 332–55; Vincent Carretta, "The *Kingis Quair* and the *Consolation of Philosophy,*" *SSL* 16 (1981): 14–28.

CHAPTER 2

1 David Diringer, *The Illuminated Book: Its History and Production* (New York: Praeger, 1967), p. 21.

2 Ibid., p. 23.

3 David M. Robb, *The Art of the Illuminated Manuscript* (Philadelphia: Philadelphia Art Alliance, 1973), p. 15.

4 Plato's *Republic,* in *Great Dialogues of Plato,* trans. W. H. D. Rouse (New York: Mentor Books, 1956), 517c. For an excellent study of the rich medieval tradition of thought about the relation between light and creation, see Edgar de Bruyne, *Études d'esthétique médiévale,* Rijksuniversiteit to Gent: Werken uitgegeven door de Faculteit van de Wijsbegeerte en Letteren, vols. 97–99 (Bruges: De Tempel, 1946), 3.3–30.

5 Augustine, *De Trinitate,* in *Patrologiae Latinae cursus completus, series latina,* vols. 32–47, ed. J. P. Migne (Paris, 1865), 42:9, 6, 9, 12, 15, 24; *Enarrationes in Psalmos,* 119 (*Patrologiae Latina* 37); *Sermones* 23 (*Patrologiae Latina* 38).

6 Augustine, *In Psalmos* 118; *Sermones* 18, 4.

7 Bonaventura, *Opera omnia* (Quaracchi: Collegii s. Bonaventurae, 1882–1902), *De Mysterio Trinitatis,* 3, 2 ff.

8 Bonaventura, *Collationes in Hexaemeron,* ed. R. P. Ferdinand Delorme (Florence: Collegii s. Bonaventurae, 1934), Visio II, Collatio V.

9 Thomas Aquinas, *Summa Theologica* in *Opera Omnia* (Parma, 1852–73; repr., New York, 1948). Ia, 5.2; 84,7; 85,2; 86,1; John Duns Scotus, *Commentaria Oxoniensia* (Quaracchi, 1912–14), 1, 3, 4, nos. 2–5.

10 *MED,* s.v. enluminen, v.

11 Geoffrey Chaucer, *The Works of Geoffrey Chaucer,* 2d ed., ed. F. N. Robinson (Boston: Houghton Mifflin, 1957), X (I), 244. All subsequent references to Chaucer's poetry will be to this edition.

12 John S. P. Tatlock, *A Concordance to the Complete Works of Geoffrey Chaucer,* 2d ed. (Gloucester, Mass.: Peter Smith, 1963), pp. 268–69, cites only six uses of the term "enlumyne" in all of Chaucer's writing and the reference in the *Clerk's Tale* is the only usage of the word which applies to poetry. In contrast, Lydgate introduces the word more than fifty times, and, in more than half of these instances, he applies the term specifically to poetry. See, for example, *Life of Our Lady,* I, 58; II, 1635– 36; III, 196, 583, 1029; V, 5; *Siege of Thebes,* 56–57; *Temple of Glas,* I, 283; *Troy Book,* Prol., 59; 218; 362; II, 1029, 4700, 6782; envoy, 100, *Fall of Princes,* III, 3570; IV, 31, 371; VI, 3080; VIII, 70; IX, 2525; *Life of St. Edmund,* 221–22; "Exposition of the Pater Noster," 318; "To Mary, the Queen of Heaven," 41–42. There is no dictionary evidence for an earlier English usage of the term "enlumyne" to refer to poetry other than the one example in Chaucer's work (*MED,* s.v. enluminen, v.; *OED,* s.v. enlumine, v.). As Lowes suggests, Chaucer may have gotten the idea for his one poetic use of the term from Eustache Deschamps who, in the *Marguerite* poems refers to Ovid, "saiges en rethorique, / Aigles tres- haultz, qui par sa theorique / Enlumines la regne d'Eneas." See John Livingston Lowes, "The Prologue to the *Legend of Good Women* as Related to the French *Marguerite* Poems and the *Filostrato,*" *PMLA* 19 (1904): p. 641, note 3). Neither Littre nor the *Altf. Wb.* cite any similar uses of the term (s.v. enluminer, v.a.).

13 John Lydgate, *Fall of Princes* (London: Oxford University Press, 1924), IX, 2525–26. All subsequent references to this poem will be to this text. Note also Dante's related usage in *De Vulgari eloqentia,* I, 17.

14 John Lydgate, *Troy Book* (London: Kegan Paul, Trench, Trubner, 1910), V, 100–101. All subsequent references to this poem will be to this edition. This meaning appears to be a skillful extension of the meaning found frequently both in the English and in French "to give color or light to something." In the *Romance of the Rose,* for example, the rosebud is described as "enlumyned With colour reed. . . . As nature couthe it make faire" (*Romance of the Rose,* 1965 [*MED,* s.v. enluminen, v.]; Littre, s.v. enluminen, v.a.).

15 Caroline F. Spurgeon, ed., *Five Hundred Years of Chaucer Criticism and Allusion,* 3 vols. (1925, repr.; New York: Russell & Russell, 1961), 1:14. Although he neither dates this usage nor does he cite any examples to illustrate it, Littre cites a related figurative meaning of "enluminer" in French; "Enluminer son style, y repandre des ornements qui ont plus d'eclat que de naturel" (Littre, II, 1404).

16 John Lydgate, *A Critical Edition of John Lydgate's Life of Our Lady,* ed. Joseph A. Lauritis (Pittsburgh: Duquesne University Press, 1961), II, 1635–36. All subsequent references to this text will be to this edition.

17 John Lydgate, *Siege of Thebes,* ed. Axel Erdmann and Eibert Ekwall (London: Kegan Paul, Trench, Trubner, 1911), 53–57. For a reading of Lydgate's "Temple of Glas" as a poem in which the poet sheds light on the significance of his content, see Judith M. Davidoff, "The Audience Illuminated, or New Light Shed on the Dream Frame of Lydgate's *Temple of Glas,*" SAC 5 (1983): 105–25.

18 Note that Lydgate's usage of these terms in this sense is earlier than the examples cited in the MED. In developing "adourne" and "enbelissche" as critical terms for poetry, Lydgate appears to have extended some of the earlier senses of these words as well as added new connotations. He obviously draws upon the most common meaning of "adourne," "to beautify," which one finds in the works of Chaucer and other poets, though not with reference to poetry, for example, in the proem to Book III of the *Troilus,* "O blisfull light, of which the bemes clere Adournith al the thyrd hevyn faire." Likewise, Lydgate has in mind the sense "to add lustre to, as a quality does" found in Thomas Usk's lines (*Testament of Love,* 18.135, in *Chaucerian and Other Pieces,* ed. Walter W. Skeat [1897, repr.; London: Oxford University Press, 1959]), "This jewel, for vertue, wold adorne and make fayre al a realme." But when applied to poetry, Lydgate's term "adourne" also carries the significance of "to order" or "to arrange," a usage found in French to refer to the creation of God, for example, in the following lines from the *Chronique des Ducs de Normandie:* "Apres vout Deus le munt former E les elemenz deviser; E quant il out tuit (l. tut) aorné. E us en (l. Eu sen) de sa parfundité" (*Altf. Wb.,* I, 414). Finally, although Lydgate first introduces the term "enbelissche" into English as a critical term for poetry, his usage in part is an extension of a nonpoetic sense of the word "to increase the beauty of an object or person," as in Chaucer's lines from the *Legend of Good Women* (1737), "Hire teres ful of honeste Embelished hire wifly chastite." Significantly, however, we do not find the terms "adourne" and "enbelissche" used with references to poetry before Lydgate in the examples cited in the MED, the OED, or in the French and Latin usages noted by Littre, the *Altf. Wb.,* and the *Mit. Wb.* (MED, s.v. adournen, v.; embelishen, v.; OED, s.v. adorn, v.; embesslish, v.; Littre, II, 1336; *Altf. Wb.,* I, 414–15; III, 42–43; *Mit. Wb.,* I, 242.

19 MED, s.v. embelishen, v.

20 MED, s.v., adournen, v.

21 John Norton-Smith, ed., *John Lydgate Poems* (Oxford: Clarendon Press, 1966), p. 192. See, for example, *Fall of Princes,* I, 461; VIII, 81; VII,

1157; *Troy Book,* Prol., 31, 211; IV, 5202–4; V, 3400; "Exposition of the
Pater Noster," 315; "An Invocation to Seynte Anne," 14; "A Mumming
for the Mercers of London," 34; "Ballade at the Reverence of Our
Lady," 12–14; "Ave Regina Celorum," 7; "As a Mydsomer Rose," 43,
83. Note that in addition to the late Latin uses cited by Norton-Smith, the
Mit. Wb. records the use of the stem *aureus* to refer to the eloquence of an
orator, cf. *Hugeburc, Vita Willibaldi,* 4, p. 101, 20, "Iohannes ille Os
a—us;" *Otto Frisingensis, Chronica,* 4, 19, p. 208, 8. "Chrisostomus
tanquam—i oris propter eloquentiam vocatus" (*Mit. Wb.,* I, 1247).
There is no dictionary evidence of any application of the French term
"dore" to poetic language before Lydgate's time (Littre, II, 1222, *Altf.
Wb.,* II, 2030–31) nor is there evidence of the appearance of the word
"aureat" in English before MED, s.v. aureat, adj.; OED, s.v. aureate, adj.

22 See, for example, Lydgate, *Fall of Princes,* Prol., 449–66; IX, 3441–47.

23 John Lydgate, *The Minor Poems of John Lydgate,* ed. Henry Noble
MacCracken (London: Oxford University Press, 1934), Part II, no. 45,
lines 34–35.

24 See, for example, *Life of St. Edmund,* 221; "The Legend of Seynt
Margarete," 56; "Exposition of the Pater Noster," 315; "An Invocation
to Seynte Anne," 14; "Ballade at the Reverence of Our Lady," 12–14;
Troy Book, Prol., 31.

25 John Lydgate, *The Minor Poems of John Lydgate,* ed. Henry Noble
MacCracken (London: Kegan Paul, Trench, Trubner, 1911), Part I, no.
49, lines 12–14.

26 Ibid., Part I, no. 23, lines 1–14.

27 Ibid., Part II, no. 63, line 82. This usage of the word "goldyn" (from
Anglo Saxon "gold") as a critical term in English for eloquent language
or heightened style, it is important to note, is original with Lydgate.
Chaucer introduces "goldyn" ten or eleven times, but he exploits the
adjective only to describe something made of gold or gold in color
without providing any hint for Lydgate's usage (Tatlock, *A Concordance
to the Complete Works of Geoffrey Chaucer,* p. 380). Although neither the
OED nor the MED record this meaning (OED, s.v. golden, adj.; MED, s.v.
golden, adj.), Lydgate uses "golden" more than six times to refer to good
poetic style. See, for example, *Life of Our Lady,* II, 1633; "An Invocation to Seynte Anne," 12; *Serpent of Division,* Spurgeon, I:14; *Troy
Book,* II, 4699.

28 Lydgate, *Siege of Thebes,* Prol., 52; Lydgate, *The Minor Poems of John
Lydgate,* Part II, no. 63, line 82. Lydgate may have gotten some hint for
his uses of "sugrid" to refer to the sound of poetry from the occasional
application of this term in Middle English to the pleasing sound of
speech. Usk, for example, in the *Testament of Love* (1387–88), uses the

word in this sense to refer to the comforting words of his guide: "she gan deliciously me comforte with sugred wordes" (I, iv, 34). Littre records a similar usage in fifteenth-century French, "Tu m'as cy donne de mos emmielles, de paroles farcis de sucre" (IV, 2068). Lydgate, however, appears to have been the first to introduce the term into English with specific reference to poetry (*OED*, s.v. sugared, ppl. a).

29 Tatlock, *A Concordance to the Complete Works of Geoffrey Chaucer*, p. 262.

30 See, for example, Lydgate, *Troy Book*, Prol., 219, 364; I, 1402; II, 171, 868, 2500, 4699, 4726, 5606; IV, 2792, 3541; *Fall of Princes*, VI, 3084, 3166; 3123–29, 4915, 5606; III, 2305, 3242, 4243; IV, 146, 1698, 2792; 6577; V, 2143; VI, 2956, 3084, 3126, 3152; *Siege of Thebes*, 42, 215, 287. For a useful discussion of the changes in connotations of the words "rethoric" and "elloquence" in the fifteenth century, see Patricia Kean, *Chaucer and the Making of English Poetry*, 2 vols. (London: Routledge & Kegan Paul, 1972), 2:218–26.

31 John Gower, *The English Works of John Gower*, 2 vols., ed G. C. Macaulay (1901, repr.; London: Oxford University Press, 1957), vol. II, Book VIII, lines 2942*–47*.

32 Thomas Usk, *The Testament of Love*, in *Chaucerian and Other Pieces*, ed. Skeat, III, iv, 255–58.

33 Spurgeon, *Five Hundred Years of Chaucer Criticism and Allusion*, 1:21.

34 Ibid., 1:49.

35 Ibid., 1:53.

36 Chaucer's anxiety about the truthfulness of poetry has a long tradition in medieval poetics. This view, for example, is implicit in Augustine's discussion of the ambiguity of words in *De Doctrina Christiana* and is prominent in Philosophy's criticism of poetry in Boethius's *De Consolatione philosophiae*, in Alain de Lille's discussion of man's speech in *Planctus Naturae*, and in Langland's use of language in *Piers Plowman*. For an interesting survey of this tradition, see Alice S. Miskimin, *The Renaissance Chaucer* (New Haven, Conn.: Yale University Press, 1975), pp. 54–80. Among the many studies of Chaucer's view on this subject, the following are particularly useful: Robert O. Payne, *The Key of Remembrance: A Study of Chaucer's Poetics* (New Haven, Conn.: Yale University Press, 1963); Robert O. Payne, "Chaucer's Realization of Himself as Rhethor," in *Medieval Eloquence*, ed. James J. Murphy (Berkeley and Los Angeles: University of California Press, 1978), pp. 270–87; Kean, *Chaucer and the Making of English Poetry;* John A. Burrow, *Ricardian Poetry* (New Haven, Conn.: Yale University Press, 1971); Charles Muscatine, *Poetry and Crisis in the Age of Chaucer* (Notre Dame, Ind.: University of Notre Dame Press, 1972); Donald R.

Howard, *The Idea of the Canterbury Tales* (Berkeley and Los Angeles: University of California Press, 1976); Alfred David, *The Strumpet Muse: Art and Morals in Chaucer's Poetry* (Bloomington: Indiana University Press, 1976); Dorothy Everett, "Some Reflections on Chaucer's 'Art Poetical,'" in *Essays on Middle English Literature*, ed. Patricia Kean (1955, repr.; Oxford: Clarendon Press, 1964), pp. 149–74; Robert J. Allen, "A Recurring Motif in Chaucer's *House of Fame*," JEGP 55 (1956): 393–405; Sheila Delany, *Chaucer's House of Fame: The Poetics of Skeptical Fideism* (Chicago: University of Chicago Press, 1972); Alistair J. Minnis, *Medieval Theory of Authorship: Scholastic Literary Attitudes in the Later Middle Ages* (London: Scolar Press, 1984), chap. 5. Lydgate, in contrast, appears to be influenced by the opposite tradition, most eloquently articulated by John of Salisbury, Dante, and Boccaccio, of poetry as ennobling, a certain source of truth. Although recent critics, including Derek Pearsall and A. C. Spearing, find Lydgate "little interested in poetic theory" (Pearsall, *John Lydgate* [London: Routledge & Kegan Paul, 1970], p. 233) and a "misreader" of Chaucer in Harold Bloom's sense (Spearing, *Medieval to Renaissance in English Poetry* [Cambridge: Cambridge University Press, 1985], p. 84), an investigation of his numerous digressions on poetry reveals that Lydgate not only was familiar with the important medieval views of poetry, but that he repeatedly selected from among these views those which presented poetry as ennobling, a source of truth. Moreover, the terms he coins to define the qualities of good poetry suggest a view of poetry more coherent than the loosely formulated poetic that Pearsall assumes. Although few critics have studied Lydgate's poetics, the following provide a useful discussion of the traditions that underlie his high style: Elfriede Tilgner, *Die Aureate Terms als Stilement bei Lydgate* (Berlin: E. Ebering, 1936); John Allan Conley, "Four Studies in Aureate Terms" (Ph.D. diss., Stanford University, 1956); Walter Schirmer, "Der Stil in Lydgate's religiose Dichtung," *Kleine Schriften* (Tubingen: Max Niemeyer, 1950), pp. 40–56; Isabel Hyde, "Lydgate's 'halff chongyd latyne': An illustration," MLN 70 (1955): 252–54; J. A. Lauritus, "Second Thoughts on Style in Lydgate's *Life of Our Lady*," in *Essays and Studies in Language and Literature*, ed. H. E. Petit (Pittsburgh: Duquesne University Press, 1964), pp. 12–23.

37 Burrow, *Ricardian Poetry*, pp. 44–45.

38 For a description of Humphrey of Gloucester's activities and influence, see, for example, K. H. Vickers, *Humphrey Duke of Gloucester* (London: Constable, 1907), chaps. 9–10; Eleanor P. Hammond, "Lydgate and Coluccio Salutati," *Modern Philology* 25 (1927): 49–57. For a discussion of the activities of other important fifteenth-century patrons, see S. Moore, "Patrons of Letters in Norfolk and Suffolk, c. 1450,"

220

PMLA 27 (1912): 188–207; 28 (1913): 79–106; Derek Pearsall, *Old English and Middle English Poetry* (London: Routledge & Kegan Paul, 1977), pp. 225–26, 230–34, 238–41, 251–52.

39 Pearsall, *Old English and Middle English Poetry*, p. 283. For a more general discussion of the demands of the new reading public, see H. S. Bennett, *Chaucer and the Fifteenth Century* (Oxford: Clarendon Press, 1947); H. S. Bennett, "The Author and his Public in the Fourteenth and Fifteenth Centuries," *E & S* 23 (1937): 7–24; H. S. Bennett, "Caxton and his Public," *RES* 19 (1943): 113–19.

40 Lydgate, *The Minor Poems of John Lydgate*, Part I, no. 49.

41 Compare, for example, Lydgate's treatment with *Anticlaudianus*, V, 487 ff. For a detailed comparison of the relation of the two worlds, see Norton-Smith, *John Lydgate Poems*, pp. 145–50.

42 Laurent de Premierfait, "Le Prologue de Translateur," in Lydgate's *Fall of Princes*, ed. Henry Bergen (1924, repr.; London: Oxford University Press, 1967), Part I, p. liv.

43 Lydgate, *Fall of Princes*, I, 85–91.

44 Geoffrey of Vinsauf, *The New Poetics*, in *Three Medieval Rhetorical Arts*, ed. James J. Murphy (Berkeley and Los Angeles: University of California Press, 1971), p. 41. For a useful discussion of the attitudes toward amplification in medieval literature, see Jane Baltzell, "Rhetorical 'Amplification' and 'Abbreviation' and the Structure of Medieval Narrative," *Pacific Coast Philology* 2 (1967): 32–39.

45 Geoffrey of Vinsauf, *The New Poetics*, pp. 43–44.

46 Evrard l'Allemand, *Laborintus*, in *Les Arts Poetiques du XIIe du XIIIe Siecle*, ed. Edmond Faral (Paris: Libraire Honore Champion, 1958), p. 347.

47 *The Parisiana Poetria of John of Garland*, ed. Traugott Lawlor (New Haven, Conn.: Yale University Press, 1974), pp. 72–73.

48 Giovanni Boccaccio, *De Genealogia deorum gentilium libri* (Bari: Guis. Laterza & Figli, 1951), Liber XIV, chap. 7, p. 699 (trans. Charles G. Osgood, *Boccaccio on Poetry* [New York: Bobbs-Merrill, 1956], p. 39).

49 Ibid., p. 100.

50 Ibid., chap. 11, p. 713.

51 Ibid., chap. 7, pp. 699–700.

52 Ibid., chap. 7, p. 699.

53 It is only in the *Fables* and on one occasion in the *Fall of Princes* that Lydgate explicitly articulates the theory of poetry as a veil (prologue to *Isopes Fabules*, in *The Minor Poems of John Lydgate*, Part II, no. 24, lines 22–28; *Fall of Princes*, III, 3830–31).

54 Marcia L. Colish, *The Mirror of Language: A Study in the Medieval*

Theory of Knowledge (New Haven, Conn.: Yale University Press, 1968), p. 225.

55 Compare Lydgate, *Siege of Thebes,* 4690–4703, with the following lines from the Treaty of Troyes: "& obviertur Occasionibus et Principiis, ex quibus inter eadem Regna, quod absit, Debata, Dissensiones seu Discordiae futuris possent temporibus exoriri" (Erdmann and Ekwall, *Siege of Thebes,* 2:8).

56 Lydgate, *Siege of Thebes,* 183–327; *Fall of Princes,* VI, 337–43; *Temple of Glas,* 1310.

57 Lydgate, *Siege of Thebes,* 183–327. For a consideration of this tale as Lydgate's additional Canterbury Tale, see John M. Powers, "The Tale of Beryn and *The Siege of Thebes,*" SAC 7 (1985): 23–50. For a fuller discussion of the theme of poetry in the *Siege of Thebes* and the *Fall of Princes,* see Lois Ebin, *John Lydgate* (Boston: Twayne, 1985), pp. 52–59, 62–75.

58 Boccaccio, *Genealogia,* Liber V, chap. 30, p. 274. Lydgate, *Siege of Thebes,* 202–3.

59 Boccaccio, *Genealogia,* Liber V, chap. 30, p. 274. "Quod autem a Mercurio cythatam susceperit, est quod eloquentiam ab influentia Mercurii habuerit." (The fact that he received the harp from Mercury, however, suggests that it is from the influence of Mercury that he had eloquence.) Lydgate, *Siege of Thebes,* 219.

60 Boccaccio, *Genealogia,* Liber V, chap. 30, p. 274.

CHAPTER 3

1 For a consideration of the philosophical themes of *The Kingis Quair,* see John Preston, " 'Fortunys Exiltree': A Study of the *Kingis Quair,*" RES, ns 7 (1956): 339–47; John MacQueen, "Tradition and the Interpretation of *The Kingis Quair,*" RES, ns 12 (1961): 117–31; A. Von Hendy, "The Free Thrall: A Study of *The Kingis Quair,*" SSL 2 (1965): 141–51; Ian Brown, "The Mental Traveller, a Study of *The Kingis Quair,*" SSL 5 (1968): 246–52; Vincent Carretta, "*The Kingis Quair* and the *Consolation of Philosophy,*" SSL 16 (1981): 14–28; William Quinn, "Memory and the Matrix of Unity in *The Kingis Quair,*" *Chaucer Review* 15 (1981): 332–55.

2 Lois Ebin, "Boethius, Chaucer, and *The Kingis Quair,*" PQ 53 (1974): 327–29.

3 In the *Consolation,* Philosophy devotes the fifth book to proving the possibility of human free will in a world governed by divine Providence. She first establishes that rational natures must have free will. Boethius

raises the objection that divine foreknowledge and human will are incompatible. Philosophy counters his objection by showing the difference between divine and human knowledge. Unlike human reason, divine intelligence is not hampered by time; rather it sees all things as eternally present. Thus God does not have foreknowledge, that is, knowledge of future events, but knowledge of an unchanging present. What He sees as happening does happen, but Philosophy demonstrates, the necessity is found only in God's knowledge of the event, not in the nature of the event itself. Thus one does have free choice and must use one's will virtuously. Chaucer's Troilus completely reverses the conclusions of the *Consolation* by repeating only Boethius's arguments in the fifth book without Philosophy's response. Like Boethius, Troilus reasons that if God sees everything in advance and cannot be deceived, whatever His providence foresees will happen. If things could happen in any other way, then God's foreknowledge would not be certain. On the other hand, some argue that Providence foresees what is to come because it will happen and that necessity is thus in the things and not in Providence. Troilus attempts to test this assumption with Boethius's example of a man sitting on a chair, but without Philosophy's aid, he is unable to distinguish between simple and conditional necessity and concludes "That thilke thynges that in erthe falle, / That by necessity they comen alle" (IV, 1049–50).

4 For an example of the view that these stanzas are merely a coda, see Von Hendy, "The Free Thrall," pp. 141–51.

5 For a description of this effect in Chaucer's *Troilus,* see E. Talbot Donaldson, *Chaucer's Poetry: An Anthology for the Modern Reader,* 2d ed. (New York: Ronald Press, 1975), pp. 1129–44.

6 *The Poems of Robert Henryson,* ed. Denton Fox (Oxford: Clarendon Press, 1981), pp. 3–110, 132–53. All references to Henryson's poems will be to the Fox edition.

7 Boethius, *The Consolation of Philosophy,* trans. Richard Green (Indianapolis: Bobbs-Merrill, 1962), Book III, poema 12.

8 Fabius Planciades Fulgentius, *Mitologiae,* ed. R. Helm (Leipzig, 1979), III, x, p. 77.

9 Boethius, *Consolation of Philosophy,* trans. Jean de Meun, comm. Nicholas Trivet, B. N. Lat. 18424, folio 101 v.

10 Ibid., "Iste autem per suavitatem citharea id est eloquentiae impies brutales et silvestres reduxit ad mormam rationis." For a useful account of the myth of Orpheus in medieval texts, see John Block Friedman, *Orpheus in the Middle Ages* (Cambridge, Mass.: Harvard University Press, 1970).

11 Boethius, *The Consolation of Philosophy,* Book III, poema 12.

12 *Orpheus and Eurydice,* lines 226–39. For a consideration of Henryson's

conception of the poet Orpheus, see Friedman, *Orpheus in the Middle Ages*, pp. 195–211; Kenneth Gros Louis, "Robert Henryson's *Orpheus and Eurydice* and the Orpheus Traditions of the Middle Ages," *Speculum* 41 (1966): 643–55; Dorena Wright, "Henryson's *Orpheus and Eurydice* and the Tradition of the Muses," *MAE* 40 (1970): 41–47; John Mac-Queen, *Robert Henryson: A Study of the Major Narrative Poems* (Oxford: Clarendon Press, 1967), pp. 24–44.

13 *Orpheus and Eurydice*, lines 507–13; 585–87. For an analysis of Henryson's attitude toward Orpheus's failure and the lesson provided for his contemporaries, see Douglas Gray, *Robert Henryson* (Leiden: Brill, 1979), pp. 228–31.

14 Compare Henryson's "Prologue" in *The Poems of Robert Henryson*, ed. Fox, 1–63, with *Gualteri Anglici Fabulae*, in *Les Fabulistes Latins depuis le siecle d'Auguste jusqu'a la fin du moyen age*, ed. Leopold Hervieux (Paris: Didot, 1894), pp. 316 ff; *Caxton's Aesop*, ed. R. T. Lenaghan (Cambridge, Mass.: Harvard University Press, 1967); *The History of Reynard the Fox by William Caxton*, ed. N. F. Blake (London, New York, Toronto: Oxford University Press, 1970); John Lydgate, *Isopes Fabules*, in *The Minor Poems of John Lydgate*, ed. Henry Noble MacCracken (London: Oxford University Press, 1934), Part II, no. 24. For detailed discussions of the relation of the *Fables* to their sources, see A. R. Diebler, *Henrisone's Fabeldichtungen* (Halle, 1885); G. Gregory Smith, *The Poems of Robert Henryson* (Edinburgh: Blackwood & Sons, 1906–14); MacQueen, *Robert Henryson*, pp. 200–221; Gavin Bone, "The Source of Henryson's 'Fox, Wolf, and Cadger,' " *RES* 10 (1934): 319–20; Marshall Stearns, "A Note on Henryson and Lydgate," *MLN* 60 (1945): 101–3; Richard Bauman, "The Folktale and Oral Tradition in the Fables of Robert Henryson," *Fabula* 6 (1963): 108–24; Ian Jamieson, "The Poetry of Robert Henryson: A Study of the Use of Source Material" (Ph.D. diss., University of Edinburgh, 1964); Ian Jamieson, "A Further Source of Henryson's 'Fabillis,' " *Notes & Queries*, ns 14 (1967): 403–5; A. W. Jenkins, "Henryson's 'The Fox, the Wolf, and the Cadger' Again," *SSL* 4 (1966): 107–12; John B. Friedman, "Henryson, the Friars, and the Congession Reynardi," *JEGP* 66 (1967): 550–61; Denton Fox, "Henryson and Caxton," *JEGP* 67 (1968): 586–93; Robert L. Kindrick, *Robert Henryson* (Boston: Twayne, 1979), pp. 57–117; Marianne Powell, *Fabula Docet: Studies in the Background and Interpretation of Henryson's Morall Fabillis* (Odense: Odense University Press, 1983), chaps. 4–8. For a word of caution about Henryson's use of Italian sources, see R. J. Lyall, "Henryson and Boccaccio: A Problem in the Study of Sources," *Anglia* 99 (1981): 38–59.

15 For a detailed examination of the distinction in the Middle Ages between

fable as a short moral tale and fable as fictitious writing, see R. T. Lenaghan, "The Nun's Priest's Fable," *PMLA* 78 (1963): 310–17. For a useful context of this issue, see Wesley Trimpi, "The Ancient Hypothesis of Fiction: An Essay on the Origins of Literary Theory," *Traditio* 27 (1971): 1–78; Wesley Trimpi, "The Quality of Fiction: The Rhetorical Transmission of Literary Theory," *Traditio* 30 (1974): 1–11. Peter Dronke, *Fabula: Explorations into the Uses of Myth in Medieval Platonism* (London: Brill, 1974).

16 For a comparison of Chaucer's and Henryson's techniques, see Donald MacDonald, "Henryson and Chaucer: Cock and Fox," *TSLL* 8 (1967): 451–61. For further discussion about Chaucer's use of the fable form see Lenaghan, "The Nun's Priest's Fable," pp. 301–7; John M. Steadman, "Flattery and the Moralitas of the *Nonne Preestes Tale*," *MAE* 28 (1959): 172–79; Stephen Manning, "The Nun's Priest's Morality and the Medieval Attitude Towards Fables," *JEGP* 50 (1960): 403–16; Constance B. Hieatt, "The Moral of *The Nun's Priest's Tale*," *SN* 42 (1970): 3–8; Walter Scheps, "Chaucer's Anti-Fable: *Reductio ad Absurdum* in the *Nun's Priest's Tale*," *Leeds Studies in English* 4 (1970): 1–10; D. E. Myers, "Focus and 'Moralite' in the *Nun's Priest's Tale*," *Chaucer Review* 7 (1973): 210–20; Paul A. Shallers, "The 'Nun's Priest's Tale': An Ironic Exemplum," *ELH* 42 (1975): 319–37; Jill Mann, "The *Speculum Stultorum* and the *Nun's Priest's Tale*," *Chaucer Review* 9 (1975): 262–82; Karl P. Wentersdorf, "Symbol and Meaning in Chaucer's *Nun's Priest's Tale*," *Nottingham Medieval Studies* 26 (1982): 29–46. For a useful review of the criticism of Chaucer's poem, see Derek Pearsall, ed., *A Variorum Edition of the Works of Geoffrey Chaucer*, vol. II, *The Canterbury Tales, Part 9, The Nun's Priest's Tale* (Norman: University of Oklahoma Press, 1984).

17 John MacQueen has argued ("The Text of Henryson's *Morall Fabillis*," *Innes Review* 14 [1963]: 3–9; "The Text of the Morall Fabillis," Appendix I in *Robert Henryson*, pp. 189–99) that the text of the Bannatyne manuscript, which antedates the Bassandyne manuscript and differs markedly in the ordering of the ten of the thirteen extant *Fables* it preserves, provides in many cases readings that are superior to Bassandyne's. Although his notes about individual readings are convincing, his suggestion about the Bannatyne order is not conclusive. Henryson may have begun with the Bannatyne order and then revised as he added more tales as Chaucer did in the *Canterbury Tales*. Ramson, in his thoughtful study of Bannatyne's editing, indicates that Bannatyne exerted a considerable degree of editorial control over the selection and ordering of his manuscripts, often organizing texts around a particular theme. In considering the *Fables*, William Ramson makes a convincing case for Ban-

natyne's thematic ordering of Henryson's work, in "On Bannatyne's Editing," in *Bards and Makaris*, ed. A. Aitken, M. McDiarmid, D. Thomson (Glasgow: University of Glasgow Press, 1977). In his edition of Henryson's poems (pp. lxxv–lxxxi), Fox defends the Bassandyne order on the basis of internal thematic development. More recently, Powell (*Fabula Docet*, pp. 41 ff) concludes that, despite the frequent verbal superiority of the Bannatyne manuscript, it would be unwise to draw any conclusion as to the order and overall intention of the *Morall Fabillis* on the basis of this manuscript.

18 See, for example, *Gualteri Anglici Fabulae*, no. 1; *Caxton's Aesop*, Book I, no. 1. For a useful comparison of this tale with its sources, see Ian Jamieson, "The Beast Tale in Middle Scots: Some Thoughts on the History of a Genre," *Parergon* 2 (1972): 27–30.

19 Jamieson ("The Beast Tale in Middle Scots," p. 29) suggests that, in this tale, "we are left with these two totally contradictory ways of existence; a relativism, which surely leads to tolerance, because it demands of those professing it knowledge and self-awareness." I agree that Henryson changes his sources to make us support the Cock's views at the outset, but his exploitation of the narrator and the tale's contrasting styles make us uneasy about the Cock's judgment before we reach the *moralitas*. For further discussion about the relation between the tale and *moralitas* in this fable, see Kurt Wittig, *The Scottish Tradition in Literature* (Edinburgh: Oliver & Boyd, 1958), p. 40; Denton Fox, "Henryson's *Fables*," *ELH* 29 (1962): 341–48; MacQueen, *Robert Henryson*, pp. 100–110; Stephen Khinoy, "Tale-Moral Relationships in Henryson's *Moral Fables*," *SSL* 17 (1982): 99–115. In an interesting analysis of the first *moralitas*, Khinoy effectively demonstrates that the "Iasp" refers to the jacinth not the jasper as most critics have assumed.

20 For references to the recurrent theme of human blindness in the *Fables*, see lines 1020–21; 1304–6; 1622–49; 1902–8.

21 MacDonald, "Henryson and Chaucer," pp. 451–61. For a discussion of this fable in relation to its sources, see also Jamieson, "The Beast Fable in Middle Scots," pp. 30–31.

22 Henryson, "The Cock and the Fox," lines 495–543. Compare Henryson's version with Chaucer, *The Nun's Priest's Tale*, in *The Works of Geoffrey Chaucer*, 2d ed., ed. F. N. Robinson (Boston: Houghton Mifflin, 1957), VII, 2821–3446, and Caxton's version (*Caxton's Aesop*, Book V, no. 3).

23 Compare the emphasis of Henryson's *moralitas* with Caxton's *Aesop*, Book I, no. V: *Gaulteri Anglici Fabulae*, no. IV; Lydgate, *Isopes Fabules*, no. IV. For informative discussions about the social context of the *Fables*, see Ian Jamieson, "Some Attitudes to Poetry in Late 15th Cen-

tury Scotland," *SSL* 15 (1980): 28–40; Craig McDonald, "The Perversion of Law in Robert Henryson's Fable of the *Fox, the Wolf, and the Husbandman*," *MAE* 49 (1980): 244–53; Robert L. Kindrick, "Politics and Poetry at the Court of James III," *SSL* 19 (1984): 40–55.

24 Compare Henryson's version with *Caxton's Aesop*, Book I, no. 4; *Gualteri Anglici Fabulae*, no. IV, Lydgate, *Isopes Fabules*, no. IV.

25 Henryson, *Fables*, lines 1292–99. For a consideration of this *moralitas*, see MacQueen, *Robert Henryson*, pp. 130–31.

26 See note 17 of this chapter. In his article, "Central and Displaced Sovereignty in Three Medieval Poems," *RES*, ns 33 (1982): 247–61, A. C. Spearing demonstrates the centrality of this fable numerologically in the collection of thirteen fables and the centrality of the theme of mercy emphasized in stanzas 21–23 of the fable, the center point of the 43-stanza tale. Spearing argues that in this fable, sovereignty is qualified and diminished in favor of mercy.

27 For a similar view of the relation of tales nos. 6, 7, 8 to the rest of the *Fables*, see Howard Henry Roereche, "The Integrity and Symmetry of Robert Henryson's *Moral Fables*" (Ph.D. diss., Pennsylvania State University, 1970).

28 For a consideration of this tale in terms of the political events of the time, see MacQueen, *Robert Henryson*, pp. 170–73; Nicolai von Kreisler, "Henryson's Visionary Fable: Tradition and Craftsmanship in *The Lyon and the Mous*," *TSLL* 15 (1972): 391–403. For a more general consideration of the political allusions in the *Fables*, see Marshall W. Stearns, "Henryson and the Political Scene," *SP* 40 (1943): 380–89.

29 See line 1754; "Whatever we foresee does less hurt"; for a consideration of this tale in terms of the theme of prudence, see John Burrow, "Henryson: The Preaching of the Swallow," *EIC* 25 (1975): 25–37.

30 Compare Henryson's version of this tale with *Gualteri Anglici Fabulae*, no. II; *Caxton's Aesop*, Book I, no. 2; Lydgate *Isopes Fabules*, no. II.

31 Compare Henryson's tale with *Gualteri Anglici Fabulae*, no. III, *Caxton's Aesop*, Book I, no. 3.

32 Jamieson, in contrast, argues (" 'To preue thare preching be a poesye,' " pp. 24–36) that we are left with contradictory views of the nature of poetry in the *Fables*, citing the discrepancies in perspectives in many of the tales between poetry as an effective moral instrument and poetry as an alluring or witty tour de force and the frequent lack of resolution between tale and *moralitas*. He suggests that, like Chaucer, Henryson in the *Fables* is an experimentor, examining his themes from different points of view. I agree that Henryson provides a much more problematical view of poetry in the *Fables* than he had earlier in the *Orpheus and Eurydice*, but in contrast to Chaucer, Henryson finally affirms the value of poetry in the

Fables. The contradictions within the tales are part of his strategy and introduce an analogy between the "fenʒeit" surface of the poem and the world which the narrator challenges us to come to terms with (see discussion later in this chapter).

33 For examples of this device, see *Fables,* lines 495–515; Fox, *Testament of Cresseid,* in *The Poems of Robert Henryson* (Oxford: Clarendon Press, 1981), lines 126–365; 407–80; 546–74; 610–16. For useful critical considerations of the style and structure of *The Testament of Cresseid,* see A. C. Spearing, "*The Testament of Cresseid* and the High Concise Style," *Speculum* 37 (1962): 208–25; Fox, *Testament of Cresseid,* pp. 20–58; MacQueen, *Robert Henryson,* pp. 45–93; Duncan Douglas, "Henryson's *Testament of Cresseid,*" *EIC* 11 (1961): 128–35; Sydney Harth, "Henryson Reinterpreted," *EIC* 11 (1961): 471–80; E. Duncan Aswell, "The Role of Fortune in *The Testament of Cresseid,*" *PQ* 46 (1967): 471–87; Del Chessel, "In the Dark Time: Henryson's *Testament of Cresseid,*" *Critical Review* 12 (1969): 61–72; Dolores L. Noll, "*The Testament of Cresseid:* Are Christian Interpretations Valid?" *SSL* 9 (1971): 16–25; John McNamara, "Divine Justice in Henryson's *Testament of Cresseid,*" *SSL* 11 (1973): 99–107; John McNamara, "Language as Action in Henryson's *Testament of Cresseid,*" in *Bards and Makaris,* pp. 41–52; Walter Scheps, "A Climatological Reading of Henryson's *Testament of Cresseid,*" *SSL* 15 (1980): 80–87.

34 *The Poems of Robert Henryson,* ed. Fox, pp. 154–56; 167–69. For a critical consideration of these poems, see Ian Jamieson, "The Minor Poems of Robert Henryson," *SSL* 9 (1971–72): 125–47; John Stephens, "Devotion and Wit in Henryson's Annunciation," *ES* 51 (1970): 323–31; A. M. Kinghorn, "The Minor Poems of Robert Henryson," *SSL* 3 (1965): 30–40.

35 Giovanni Boccaccio, *De Genealogia deorum gentilium libri* (Bari: Guis. Laterza & Figli, 1951), Liber XIV, chap. 9 (trans. Charles G. Osgood, *Boccaccio on Poetry* [New York: Bobbs-Merrill, 1956], p. 48).

36 Henryson, *Fables,* lines 1–18; 586–89; *Orpheus and Eurydice,* lines 415–20.

37 *MED,* s.v. feinen, v. For Henryson's use of the term in the *Fables,* see, for example, lines 1, 18, 402, 460, 523, 589, 589, 600, 1960. See also Fox, *Testament of Cresseid,* line 66; *Orpheus and Eurydice,* lines 416, 464, 586.

38 See, for example, Ian Jamieson, "Henryson's 'Taill of the Wolf and the Wedder,' " *SSL* 6 (1969): 248–57; Ian Jamieson, "The Beast Tale in Middle Scots," p. 29.

39 William Dunbar, *The Poems of William Dunbar,* ed. James Kinsley (Oxford: Clarendon Press, 1979). Unless otherwise indicated, all further

references to Dunbar's poetry will be to this text. For incisive observations about the Dunbar text and canon, see Priscilla Bawcutt, "The Text
and Interpretation of Dunbar," MAE 50 (1981): 88–100.

40 Of the eighty-three poems edited by Kinsley, more than half celebrate a
particular person or event. For useful considerations of the "Golden
Targe," see Denton Fox, "Dunbar's *The Golden Targe*," ELH 26 (1959):
311–34; John Leyerle, "The Two Voices of William Dunbar," *University of Toronto Quarterly* 31 (1962): 316–38; Isabel Hyde, "Poetic Imagery: A Point of Comparison between Henryson and Dunbar," SSL 2
(1965): 183–97; Isabel Hyde, "Primary Sources and Associations of
Dunbar's Aureate Imagery," MLR 51 (1956): 481–92; Tom Scott, *Dunbar: A Critical Exposition of the Poems* (Edinburgh: Oliver & Boyd,
1966), pp. 40–46; Roderick J. Lyall, "Moral Allegory in Dunbar's
'Golden Targe,'" SSL 11 (1973): 47–66; Walter Scheps, "*The Golden
Targe:* Dunbar's Comic Psychomachia," PLL 11 (1975): 339–56; Pamela M. King, "Dunbar's *Golden Targe:* A Chaucerian Masque," SSL 19
(1984): 115–31.

41 For a similar view, see Fox, "Dunbar's *The Golden Targe*," pp. 317–18,
and Scheps, "*The Golden Targe:* Dunbar's Comic Psychomachia," pp.
354–56.

42 For useful descriptions of the process of enameling in the Middle Ages,
see Mary Chamot, *English Medieval Enamels* (London: Benn, 1930);
Philippe Burty, *Les emaux cloisonnés anciens et modernes* (Paris: Martz,
1868); Lewis Foremann Day, *Enameling: A Comparative Account of the
Development and Practice of the Art* (London: B. T. Batsford, 1907);
Marie Madeline S. Gautier, *Emaux limousins champleyes des XIIe, XIIIe
& XIVe siecles* (Paris: G. le Prat, 1950); Louis Elie Millenet, *Enameling
on Metal: A Practical Manual on Enameling and Painting on Enamel,*
trans. H. de Koningh (London: Technical Press, 1947); Victoria and
Albert Museum, *A Picture Book of Medieval Enamels* (London: Board of
Education, 1927); Walters Art Gallery, *Catalogue of the Painted Enamels
of the Renaissance,* ed. Philippe Verdier (Baltimore: Walters Art Gallery,
1967); Isa Barsali Belli, *European Enamels,* trans. R. Rudorff (London,
N.Y.: Hamlyn, 1969).

43 For illustrations of this technique, see Henry H. Cunnynghame, *European Enamels* (London: Methuen, 1906), pp. 105 ff.

44 MED, s.v. enamelen, v.

45 I have not been able to find earlier usages in Middle Scots or in Middle
English texts. For an examination of the relation of Dunbar's poetry to the
tradition of aureate diction, see John Cooper Mendenhall, *Aureate Terms:
A Study in the Literary Diction of the Fifteenth Century* (Lancaster, Penn.:
Wickersham, 1919); Pierrepont Henrick Nichols, "William Dunbar as a

Scottish Lydgatian," *PMLA* 46 (1931): 214–24; and Nichols, "Lydgate's Influences on the Aureate Forms of the Scottish Chaucerians," *PMLA* 47 (1932): 516–22; Hyde, "Primary Sources and Associations of Dunbar's Aureate Imagery," 418–92; John A. Conley, "Four Studies in Aureate Terms" (Ph.D. diss., Stanford University, 1956).

46 For an analysis of this poem, see Scott, *Dunbar: A Critical Exposition of the Poems,* pp. 179–211; James Kinsley, "The Tretis of the Tua Mariit Wemen and the Wedo," *MAE* 23 (1954): 31–35; Arthur K. Moore, "The Setting of 'The Tua Mariit Wemen and the Wedo,' " *English Studies* 32 (1951): 56–62; Priscilla Bawcutt, "Dunbar's 'Tretis of the Tua Mariit Wemen and the Wedo' 185–87 and Chaucer's 'Parson's Tale,' " *Notes and Queries,* ns 11, 209 (September 1964): 332–33; Ian Rose, *William Dunbar* (Leiden: Brill, 1981), pp. 217–37; A. C. Spearing, *Medieval to Renaissance in English Poetry* (Cambridge: Cambridge University Press, 1985), p. 218.

47 For a consideration of Dunbar's display of his craft, see Florence Ridley, "The Prosodiae Irony of William Dunbar," paper presented to Modern Language Association, New York City, December 27, 1976. For other examinations of Dunbar's technical virtuousity, see Hyde, "Poetic Imagery: A Point of Comparison between Henryson and Dunbar," pp. 183–97; Hyde, "Primary Sources and Associations of Dunbar's Aureate Imagery," pp. 481–92; Edwin Morgan, "Dunbar and the Language of Poetry," *EIC* 2 (1952): 138–58; Priscilla Bawcutt, "Aspects of Dunbar's Imagery," in *Chaucer and Middle English Studies,* ed. Beryl Rowland (Kent, Ohio: Kent State University Press, 1974), pp. 190–200; Wilhelm F. H. Nicholaisen, "Line and Sentence in Dunbar's Poetry," in *Bards and Makaris,* pp. 61–71; Florence H. Ridley, "Scottish Transformations of Courtly Literature: William Dunbar and the Court of James IV," in *The Expansion and Transformation of Courtly Literature,* ed. Nathaniel B. Smith and Joseph T. Snow (Athens: University of Georgia Press, 1980), pp. 171–84; Fox, "Dunbar's *The Golden Targe,*" pp. 331–32.

48 Ronald D. S. Jack, "Dunbar and Lydgate," *SSL* 8 (1971): 220.

49 Compare the ending of the "Thrissil and the Rois" with Chaucer, *Parliament of Fowls,* 680–99.

50 *The Minor Poems of John Lydgate,* ed. Henry Noble MacCracken (London: Kegan Paul, Trench, Trubner, 1911), Part I, pp. 254–311. Note that Dunbar's no. 36, "The Ballade of Lord Bernard Stewart, Lord of Aubigny," shows some similarity in technique to these two poems.

51 For an interesting consideration of Dunbar's images of the poet, see Gerard Kinneavy, "Metaphors of the Poet and his Craft in William Dunbar," in *Aeolian Harps,* ed. Donna G. Fricke and Douglas C. Fricke (Bowling Green, Ohio: Bowling Green University Press, 1976), pp. 57–

64. For a comparison of Dunbar's and Villon's poet-narrators, see A. M. Kinghorn, "Dunbar and Villon: A Comparison and a Contrast," *MLR* 62 (1967): 195–208; Jean-Jacques Blancot, "William Dunbar and Francois Villon: The Literary Personae," in *Bards and Makaris,* pp. 72–87.

CHAPTER 4

1 Gavin Douglas, *The Shorter Poems of Gavin Douglas,* ed. Priscilla J. Bawcutt (Edinburgh: Blackwood & Sons, 1967). All subsequent references to the *Palice of Honour* will be to the Edinburgh text printed in this edition.

2 For a treatment of the *Palice of Honour* as a poem about poetry, see Gerald B. Kinneavy, "The Poet in *The Palice of Honour,*" *Chaucer Review* 3 (1969): 280–303; Mark E. Amsler, "The Quest for the Present Tense: The Poet and the Dreamer in Douglas's *The Palice of Honour,*" *SSL* 17 (1982): 186–208. For a comparison of Chaucer's and Douglas's journeys as poets in the *Hous of Fame* and the *Palice of Honour,* see Gregory Kratzmann, *Anglo-Scottish Literary Relations, 1430–1550* (Cambridge: Cambridge University Press, 1980), pp. 104–28.

3 Alice Miskimin, "The Design of Douglas's *Palice of Honour,*" in *Acts du 2ᵉ Colloque de Langue et de Litterature Ecossaises (Moyen Age et Renaissance)* (Strasbourg: Université de Strasbourg, 1978), pp. 396–421.

4 *The Palice of Honour,* 1921. For a consideration of this pun, see C. S. Lewis, *The Allegory of Love* (New York: Oxford University Press, 1958), p. 290. For a more extended discussion of this scene in the context of the poem's development, see A. C. Spearing, *Medieval Dream Poetry* (Cambridge: Cambridge University Press, 1976), pp. 210–11.

5 Gavin Douglas, *Virgil's Aeneid,* ed. David F. C. Coldwell (Edinburgh: Blackwood & Sons, 1964). All references to the *Eneados* will be to this text. For the view of the prologues as disparate poems, see W. Geddie, *A Bibliography of Middle Scots Poets* (Edinburgh: Blackwood & Sons, 1912), pp. 226–30; G. Gregory Smith, "The Scottish Chaucerians," in *The Cambridge History of English Literature,* 15 vols., ed. A. W. Ward and A. R. Waller (Cambridge: Cambridge University Press, 1963), 2:262; and, more recently, Denton Fox, "The Scottish Chaucerians," in *Chaucer and Chaucerians,* ed. D. S. Brewer (University: University of Alabama Press, 1967), p. 191. For a more extended consideration of the nature prologue, see Charles R. Blyth, "Gavin Douglas' Prologues of Natural Description," *PQ* 49 (1970): 164–77; Penelope Schott Starkey, "Gavin Douglas's *Eneados:* Dilemmas in the Nature Prologues," *SSL* 11 (1973): 82–98; Priscilla Bawcutt, *Gavin Douglas: A Critical Study* (Edinburgh: Edinburgh University Press, 1976), pp. 164–91.

6   Charles R. Blyth, "The 'Knychtlyke Style': A Study of Gavin Douglas's *Aeneid*" (Ph.D. diss., Harvard, 1963), pp. 65–130.

7   For a useful analysis of the relation of Douglas to these commentators, see Bawcutt, *Gavin Douglas*, pp. 69–78. For a more general survey of the views of these commentators, see Don Cameron Allen, *Mysteriously Meant: The Rediscovery of Pagan Symbolism and Allegorical Interpretation in the Renaissance* (Baltimore: Johns Hopkins University Press, 1970), pp. 135–64.

8   Compare Douglas, *Eneados*, VI, xvi, with Virgil, *Aeneid*, VII, 1–24.

9   Starkey, "Gavin Douglas's *Eneados*," pp. 86–88.

10 Compare Douglas's prologue with Robert Henryson's prologue to "The Lion and the Mouse," in *The Poems of Robert Henryson*, ed. Denton Fox (Oxford: Clarendon Press, 1981), pp. 54–64.

11 Virgil, *Georgics*, Book III; Horace, *Ars Poetica*, 19 ff and 156 ff; Geoffrey of Vinsauf, *The New Poetics*, in *Three Medieval Rhetorical Arts*, ed. James J. Murphy (Berkeley and Los Angeles: University of California Press, 1971), pp. 60–89; Alexander Barclay, *Eclogues* (London, 1928), I, 83–88; *The Arte of English Poesie, by George Puttenham*, ed. G. D. Willcock and A. Walker (Folcroft, Penn.: Folcroft Press, 1969).

12 Bawcutt, *Gavin Douglas*, pp. 173–74.

13 William Dunbar, *The Poems of William Dunbar*, ed. William Mackay Mackenzie (London: Faber & Faber, 1960), no. 56.

14 Bawcutt, *Gavin Douglas*, p. 177.

15 Starkey, "Gavin Douglas's *Eneados*," pp. 92–93; Bawcutt, *Gavin Douglas*, pp. 189–90.

16 Henryson, *Fables*, prologue to "The Lion and the Mouse"; John Lydgate, *Fall of Princes* (London: Oxford University Press, 1924); Giovanni Boccaccio, *De Casibus illustrium virorum* (Gainesville, Fla.: Scholars Facsimiles & Reprints, 1962).

17 For earlier uses of these terms in this sense, see *MED*, s.v. crafti, adj; curious, adj.; derk, n.; *OED*, s.v. sly, adj., adv.; quaint, adj.; misty, adj.

18 Geoffrey Chaucer, *The Works of Geoffrey Chaucer*, 2d ed., ed. F. N. Robinson (Boston: Houghton Mifflin, 1957), *Troilus and Criseyde*, V, 898–99; Henryson, "Tale of the Paddock and the Mouse," line 2913.

19 See, for example, *MED*, s.v. crafti, adj.; curious, adj.; derk, n.; *OED*, s.v. sly, adj.

20 *MED*, s.v. curious, adj.

21 *MED*, s.v. derk, n.

22 *MED*, s.v. derk, n.

23 Augustine, *On Christian Doctrine*, trans. by D. W. Robertson, Jr. (Indianapolis: Bobbs-Merrill, 1958), p. 37.

232

24 For a consideration of the techniques of these poets, see Frederick Goldin, *Lyrics of the Troubadours and Trouveres: An Anthology and a History* (Garden City, N.Y.: Anchor Books, 1973).

25 Dante Alighieri, *De Vulgari eloquentia*, in *Literary Criticism of Dante Alighieri*, ed. and trans. Robert S. Haller (Lincoln: University of Nebraska Press, 1973), Book II, chap. 6.

26 Erich Auerbach, *Literary Language and Its Public in Late Latin Antiquity and in the Middle Ages*, trans. Ralph Manheim (New York: Pantheon Books, 1965), pp. 223–24.

27 Ibid., p. 224.

28 "Similitudes et exempla"; see Macrobius, *Saturnalia*, ed. J. Willis (Leipzig: B. G. Teubner, 1963), I, ii. 6–25.

29 *Servii Grammitici qui feruntur in Vergilii carmina commentarii*, ed. George Theio and Herman Hagen (Hildesheim: Georg Olms, 1961), Book I, 20.

30 *Fulgentius the Mythographer*, trans. Leslie George Whitbread (Columbus: Ohio State University Press, 1971), p. 119.

31 Bernard Silvestris, *Commentum super sex libros Eneidos Virgilii*, ed. W. Riedel (Leipzig, 1784), Preface.

32 Petrarch, *Petrarch's Secret or the Soul's Conflict with Passion*, trans. William H. Draper (London: Chatto & Windus, 1911), p. 83.

33 Christoforo Landino, *Virgil, Opera* (Basel, 1577), pp. 3051, 3001–2.

34 Bawcutt, *Gavin Douglas*, pp. 95–102; Priscilla Bawcutt, "Gavin Douglas and the Text of Virgil," *Edinburgh Bibliographical Society Transactions* 4 (1973): 213–31.

35 See, for example, *Eneados*, III, x, 63 ff; V, xiii, 71; VIII, iii, 167; VIII, iv, 149. For examples of Douglas's skillful use of language in translating, see Florence Ridley, "The Distinctive Character of Douglas's *Eneados*," *SSL* 18 (1983): 110–22.

36 See, for example, *Eneados*, X, ii, 12; VII, iii, 90–92; VIII, x, 95–96; XII, viii, 57–58.

37 For a more detailed account of Douglas's changes in Book IV, see Quentin George Johnson, "Gavin Douglas as Poet-Translator: *Eneados* and *Aeneid* IV" (Ph.D. diss., University of Oregon, 1967), and Penelope Schott Starkey, "Douglas's *Eneados:* Virgil in 'Scots' " (Ph.D. diss., City University of New York, 1971), pp. 33–36.

38 Compare Douglas, *Eneados*, I, xii, 1–24, with Virgil, *Aeneid*, II, 1–13. For a detailed consideration of Douglas's changes in Book II, see Blyth, "The 'Knychtlyke Style,' " pp. 182–209.

39 Virgil, *Aeneid*, ed. H. Rushton Fairclough (Cambridge, Mass.: Harvard University Press, 1940), II, 65–66. Unless otherwise noted, all subsequent references to the *Aeneid* will be to this text.

40 Boethius, *The Consolation of Philosophy*, trans. Richard Green (Indianapolis: Bobbs-Merrill, 1962), Book I, metrum 1; Chaucer, *Troilus and Criseyde*, V, 197–245; *The Canterbury Tales*, II (B¹) 421–27; VII, 2407–62; B², 3597–3652.

41 For a consideration of the way in which the Man of Law's style undermines the sentence of his tale, see Walter Scheps, "Chaucer's Man of Law and the Tale of Constance," *PMLA* 89 (1974): 292; Hope Weisman, "The Chaucer Performance," lecture presented to the Medieval Club of New York, New York City, February 1, 1974.

42 Compare Douglas, *Eneados*, II, x, 167, with Virgil, *Aeneid*, II, 655.

43 Compare Douglas, *Eneados*, II, xi, 95–110, with Virgil, *Aeneid*, II, 739–46.

44 Compare Douglas, *Eneados*, Prologue XI, with John Barbour, *The Bruce*, ed. Walter W. Skeat (Edinburgh: Blackwood & Sons, 1894), Book VI, 325–72.

45 Barbour, *The Bruce*, Book XIV, 273–82; XVIII, 49–56.

46 Compare with Virgil, *Aeneid*, IX, 132–34: "terra autem in nostris manibus; tot milia gentes / arma ferunt Italae, nil me fatalia terrent, / si qua Phryges prae se iactant, responsa deorum" (But the earth is in our hands: in such thousands are the nations of Italy under arms. Naught do I dread all the fateful oracles of heaven whereof these Phrygians boast).

47 For an analysis of the meaning of the term "style," see Blyth, "The 'Knychtlyke Style,'" pp. 229–31.

48 Douglas, *Eneados*, I, iv, 41 n.

49 Compare with Virgil, *Aeneid*, VI, 687–88.

50 Virgil, *Aeneid*, I, 220, 305, 378; X, 545.

51 Blyth, "The 'Knychtlyke Style,'" p. 261.

CHAPTER 5

1 Stephen Hawes, *The Conforte of Louers*, in *Stephen Hawes: The Minor Poems*, ed. Florence Gluck and Alice Morgan (London: Oxford University Press, 1974), line 135. All subsequent references to the *Conforte* will be to this text.

2 John Lydgate, *The Pilgrimage of the Life of Man*, ed. F. J. Furnivall (London: Kegan Paul, Trench, Trubner, 1899–1904); John Lydgate, *The Temple of Glas*, in *John Lydgate Poems*, ed. John Norton-Smith (Oxford: Clarendon Press, 1966); Gregor Reisch, *Margarita Philosophica* (Strasbourg: Schott, 1504); *Assembly of Ladies*, ed. Derek Pearsall (London: Nelson, 1962); *Courte of Sapyence*, ed. Robert Spindler (Leipzig: Bernard Tauchmitz, 1927). For a useful consideration of the sources of the *Pastime*, see A. S. G. Edwards, *Stephen Hawes* (Boston: Twayne, 1983),

p. 30, who argues that it is doubtful whether a specific model exists for the *Pastime*. For an interesting discussion of the relation between text and picture in Hawes's work, see A. S. G. Edwards, "Poet and Printer in Sixteenth Century England: Stephen Hawes and Wynkyn de Worde," *Gutenberg Jahrbuch* (1980): 82–88. For an analysis of the different kinds of allegory in the poem, see John N. King, "Allegorical Pattern in Stephen Hawes's the *Pastime of Pleasure*," *Studies in Literary Imagination* 11 (1978): 57–67.

3 Stephen Hawes, *The Example of Virtue*, in *Stephen Hawes: The Minor Poems*, pp. 1–71. All subsequent references to this *Example* will be to this text.

4 Stephen Hawes, *The Pastime of Pleasure*, ed. William Edward Mead (London: Oxford University Press, 1928). All subsequent references to the *Pastime* will be to this edition.

5 See, for example, *The Example of Virtue*, 260–66; *The Pastime of Pleasure*, 5523–85; *Example*, 204–25; *Pastime*, 358–65; *Example*, 463–90; *Pastime*, 4050–76.

6 *Pastime*, 174. Note that similar greyhounds, part of the livery of Henry VII, also appear prominently in the *Conforte of Louers*, 263–64. In the opening lines of the *Pastime*, Hawes praises Henry VII for the "gouernaunce" and "grace" which have guided him so well, and, in this passage, he transfers those qualities to the questing narrator in the form of the emblematic greyhounds who accompany him.

7 Compare, for example, the narrator of the *Pastime* with the figure in the *Courte of Sapyence*. For a useful consideration of the relation of this poem to *The Example of Virtue* and *The Pastime of Pleasure*, see Whitney Wells, "Stephen Hawes and the Court of Sapience," RES 6 (1930): 284–94.

8 See, for example, the similar conceptions in Giovanni Boccaccio, *De Genealogia deorum gentilum libri* (Bari: Guis. Laterza and Figli, 1951), Liber XIV, chap. 9; Gavin Douglas, *Virgil's Aeneid*, ed. David F. C. Coldwell (Edinburgh: Blackwood & Sons, 1964), Prol. I.

9 Dante, *Letter to Can Grande Della Scala* in *Literary Criticism: Plato to Dryden*, ed. Allan H. Gilbert (Detroit: Wayne State University Press, 1962), pp. 202–6; Boccaccio, *Genealogia*, Liber XIV, chap. 9.

10 For a survey of other treatments of this theme in late medieval literature see Priscilla Bawcutt, *The Shorter Poems of Gavin Douglas* (Edinburgh: Blackwood & Sons, 1967), pp. xxxv–xxxvi.

11 Zeak Monroe Buckner, "An Allegorical Analysis of Stephen Hawes's *Pastime of Pleasure*" (Ph.D. diss., University of Texas, Austin, 1972), pp. 47–49. Similarly, Edwards (*Stephen Hawes*, p. 47) emphasizes how little space is given to Grand Amour's actions, for Hawes was more

interested in what Grand Amour confronts than in the way he confronts it. Hawes's emphasis is on how Grand Amour's confrontations demonstrate the efficacy of his education as poet.

12 Sam Freeman, "The Poems of Stephen Hawes" (Ph.D. diss., University of Oklahoma, 1962).

13 Hawes, *The Conforte of Louers*, in *Stephen Hawes: The Minor Poems*.

14 See, for example, *The Pastime of Pleasure*, 24–28, 1130–34, 1164–65, 1317–20, 1373–75.

15 See, for example, ibid., 25, 34–42, 720–820, 870–72, 932, 943, 981–82, 1353.

16 For additional examples of Hawes's treatment, see ibid., 32, 34, 44, 49, 945, 953, 988, 996, 1357, 1389; *The Conforte of Louers*, 4. See chapter 5 for a comparison with Henryson's and Douglas's use of the word and *MED*, s.v. feinen, v., for contemporary treatment.

17 *MED*, s.v. fatal, adj.

18 *OED*, s.v. scripture, sb. For additional examples of Hawes's usage of the two terms, see *The Example of Virtue*, 901, 903; *The Pastime of Pleasure*, 33, 35, 721, 727, 807, 869, 934, 987, 1028; *The Conforte of Louers*, 3.

19 "Joyful Meditatioun," in *Stephen Hawes: The Minor Poems*, 176–82; for a fuller consideration of this allusion, see Gluck and Morgan's comments, p. 152, note, lines 176–82; p. 154, note, lines 167–78.

20 *The Conforte of Louers*, 139–40. For an attempt to elucidate the mysterious allusions in this stanza, see Gluck and Morgan's comments in *Stephen Hawes: The Minor Poems*, p. 154, note, lines 139–40. For a reading of the poem as a personal allegory for Hawes, see Edwards, *Stephen Hawes*, pp. 77–87.

21 For a fuller discussion of these images, see Gluck and Morgan's comments in *Stephen Hawes: The Minor Poems*, p. 155, note, lines 233–34; and Buckner, "An Allegorical Analysis of Stephen Hawes's *Pastime*," pp. 78–79.

22 For an attempt to elucidate these lines, see Gluck and Morgan's comments in *Stephen Hawes: The Minor Poems*, pp. 160–62, note, lines 890–96. For the view that Hawes had come to believe his poems were "fatyll fyccyons" foretelling a future of which he knew nothing, see A. C. Spearing, *Medieval to Renaissance in English Poetry* (Cambridge: Cambridge University Press, 1985), p. 259.

23 For the image of the preeminence of the right hand, see Psalms 15.18, 16.18, 20.9, 59.7, 109.1.

24 Compare with Psalms 7.16; 9a.16, 17; 10.7; 56.7, 123.7, 141.4.

25 Compare with Psalms 7.17, 139.11.

26 For a discussion of the figure of David in the Middle Ages and early

Renaissance, see Edward Alberic Gosselin, *The King's Progress to Jerusalem: Some Interpretations of David During the Reformation Period and their Patristic and Medieval Background* (Malibu, Calif.: Undena Publications, 1976); for a consideration of David as *auctor,* see Alastair J. Minnis, *Medieval Theory of Authorship: Scholastic Literary Attitudes in the Later Middle Ages* (London: Scolar Press, 1984), pp. 103–9.

27 Augustine, *Enarrationes in Psalmos,* in J. P. Migne, ed., *Patrologiae Latinae cursus completus* (Paris: Garnier, 1844–80), vols. 36–37.

28 Augustine, *Patrologiae Latina,* XXXVI, *Psalms* 54–56, col. 628–73. For the medieval versions, I will cite the old numbers of the Psalms.

29 Augustine, *Patriologiae Latina,* XXXVI, *Psalm* 55, col. 648. "Therefore 'the foreigners [*allophyli,* i.e., Philistines or nonbelievers] have held in Geth' David our lord Jesus Christ, born of the seed of that David; and they hold him there still. The Geth I refer to is a city. But if the interpretation of its name is examined, it means 'press-room.' According to this chapter, Christ—the saviour of the flesh, he who was born of a virgin and crucified, who through the resurrection of his flesh now shows us the model for our own resurrection, who sits at the right hand of the father and intercedes for us—he is here as well, but in his body which is the church" (trans. Bruce W. Frier).

30 Augustine, *Patriologiae Latina,* XXXVI, *Psalm* 55, col. 648. "His body, i.e., his church, is held in the press-room. What does this mean, 'in the press-room'? Under pressure. But in a press-room the pressure is fruitful. On the vine a grape feels no pressure, it seems whole, but nothing flows from it. It is sent into a press-room, it is trodden and pressed. Injury seems to be done to the grape, but this injury is not fruitless; indeed, were no injury to occur, it would remain fruitless" (trans. Bruce W. Frier).

31 Gosselin, *The King's Progress to Jerusalem,* chap. II. For the text of this commentary, see Nicolaus of Lyra, *Postilla super totam bibliam* (Rome: Conradus Sweynheym and Arnoldus Pannartz, 1471–72).

32 Nicolaus of Lyra, *Psalm* 5, fol. p. 8, recto and verso.

33 Gosselin, *The King's Progress to Jerusalem,* p. 30.

34 Nicolaus of Lyra, *Psalm* 85, fol. t 4, recto.

35 Nicolaus of Lyra, *Psalm* 26, fol. q 8 recto. "I have explained this psalm as literally concerning David's position when, after Saul's death in Ebron, he rose and began to rule over the tribe of Judah, although his enemies were still present in great number. But it can be explained as morally concerning any believer who reaches adulthood, for then the passion of his soul should begin its rule by ruling well. And since it encounters difficulty in this, it should call upon the lord for his governance" (trans. Bruce W. Frier).

36 James S. Preus, *From Shadow to Promise: Old Testament Interpretations from Augustine to the Young Luther* (Cambridge, Mass.: Harvard University Press, 1969). For an analysis of Luther's development in his early commentaries on the Psalms, see also E. Gordon Rupp, *The Righteousness of God: Luther Studies* (London: Hodder and Stoughton, 1963), pp. 130–57.

37 John Calvin, *Commentary on the Book of the Psalms,* 5 vols., trans. Rev. James Anderson (Edinburgh: Calvin Society, 1845–49), 1:xliv.

38 Ibid., "The Author's Preface," 1:xxxviii–xxxix.

39 For a useful consideration of the link between Orpheus and David in the Middle Ages, see John Block Friedman, *Orpheus in the Middle Ages* (Cambridge, Mass.: Harvard University Press, 1970), pp. 147–56.

40 John Lydgate, *The Minor Poems of John Lydgate,* ed. Henry Noble MacCracken (London: Kegan Paul, Trench, Trubner, 1911), Part I, no. 15.

41 Bartholomaeus Anglicus, *De Proprietatibus rerum,* trans. John Trevisa (Westminster, 1495), mii, cols. a, b. For similar treatments, see also P. Studer and J. Evans, *Anglo-Norman Lapidaries* (Paris: Champion, 1924); *Courte of Sapyence,* lines 1072–73: "The grene Smaragd that ys right medicinable / Ayenst tempest, sekenes and fantasy."

42 Augustine, *Patrologia latina cursus completus,* XXXVIII, Psalm 128, col. 1689.

43 Ibid., col. 1689–96.

44 Ibid., col. 1695.

45 Richard Rolle of Hampole, *The Psalter or Psalms of David,* ed. Rev. H. R. Bramleu (Oxford: Clarendon Press, 1884), pp. 446–48.

46 Ibid., p. 447.

47 Calvin, *Commentary on the Psalms,* Psalm 129, 5:119.

48 For an attempt to elucidate these lines, see Gluck and Morgan's comments in *Stephen Hawes: The Minor Poems,* pp. 160–62.

49 This use of style has disturbed some of Hawes's critics, including Derek Pearsall, *Old English and Middle English Poetry* (London: Routledge & Kegan Paul, 1977), pp. 267–68, who remarks that the contrast between the aureate manner and the "threadbare diction of [Hawes's] unmannered style" in the *Pastime* is sufficient "to make the former appear tawdry and the latter drab."

CHAPTER 6

1 John Skelton, *The Complete English Poems,* ed. John Scattergood (New Haven, Conn.: Yale University Press, 1983), pp. 29–35. All further references to Skelton's poems will be to this edition.

2 See, for example, Skelton, "The Bowge of Courte," 16 ff.

3 Geoffrey of Vinsauf, *The New Poetics*, in *Three Medieval Rhetorical Arts*, ed. James J. Murphy (Berkeley and Los Angeles: University of California Press, 1971), p. 47.

4 The world of the poem is presided over by "Luna, full of mutabylyte, / As emperes the dyademe hath worne / Of our pole artyke, smylynge halfe in score / At our foly and our unstedfastnesse; / The tyme whan Mars to werre hym dyde dres" (3–7). For useful criticism of this poem, see Paul D. Psilos, "Dulle, Drede and the Limits of Prudential Knowledge in Skelton's Bowge of Court," *Journal of Medieval and Renaissance Studies* 61 (1976): 297–317; Judith Larsen, "What is the Bouge of Courte?" *JEGP* 61 (1962): 288–95; Leigh Winser, "*The Bowge of Courte:* Drama Doubling as Dream," *ELR* 6 (1976): 3–39; A. R. Heiserman, *Skelton and Satire* (Chicago: University of Chicago Press, 1961), pp. 14–65; Stanley Eugene Fish, *John Skelton's Poetry* (New Haven, Conn.: Yale University Press, 1965), pp. 54–81; Stanley K. Kozikowski, "Allegorical Meanings in Skelton's *The Bowge of Court*," *PQ* 61 (1982): 305–15; A. C. Spearing, *Medieval to Renaissance in English Poetry* (Cambridge: Cambridge University Press, 1985), pp. 264–65.

5 For important studies of these concerns, Stanley Eugene Fish, "Aspects of Rhetorical Analysis: Skelton's 'Philip Sparrow,' " *SN* 24 (1962): 218–38; Fish, *John Skelton's Poetry*, pp. 98–125; J. Swart, "John Skelton's Philip Sparrow," *ES* 45 (1964): 161–64; Nan Cooke Carpenter, *John Skelton* (Boston: Twayne, 1967), pp. 60–65.

6 William Caxton, *The Prologues and Epilogues of William Caxton*, ed. W. J. B. Crotch (London: Oxford University Press, 1928), pp. 108–9.

7 Fish, *John Skelton's Poetry*, p. 23.

8 For a consideration of Skelton's relation with the Howard family, see William Nelson, *John Skelton, Laureate* (1939, repr.; New York: Russell & Russell, 1964), pp. 210 ff; H. L. R. Edwards, *Skelton: The Life and Times of an Early Tudor Poet* (London: British Book Center, 1949), pp. 200–208; Carpenter, *John Skelton*, pp. 102–4.

9 For a consideration of the political allusions in these works, see R. L. Ramsay, ed., *Magnyfycence* (London: Kegan Paul, Trench, Trubner, 1908); Nelson, *John Skelton, Laureate*, pp. 185–88; Maurice Pollet, *John Skelton, Poet of Tudor England* (1962, repr.; London: J. M. Dent & Sons, 1971), pp. 80–103; Carpenter, *John Skelton*, pp. 82–83; William O. Harris, "Wolsey and Skelton's 'Magnygycence': A Re-evaluation," *SP* 57 (1960): 99–122; William O. Harris, *Skelton's "Magnyfycence" and the Cardinal Virtue Tradition* (Chapel Hill: University of North Carolina Press, 1965), pp. 3–45. For examples of Skelton's manipulation of proverbial wisdom in *Magnyfycence*, see Paula Neuss, "Proverbial Skelton," *SN* 54 (1982): 237–46.

10 Edwards, *Skelton*, pp. 193–99.

11 Nelson, *John Skelton, Laureate*, pp. 167–68.

12 Ibid., pp. 148–57.

13 Nancy S. Struever, *The Language of History in the Renaissance: Rhetoric and Historical Consciousness in Florentine Humanism* (Princeton, N.J.: Princeton University Press, 1970), pp. 38–82.

14 Desiderius Erasmus of Rotterdam, *Opera Omnia*, ed. J. Clericus (Leiden, 1703–6); Erasmus, *Opera omnia* (Amsterdam: North-Holland, 1969–85); Erasmus, *Erasmi Opuscila: A Supplement to the Opera omnia*, ed. Wallace K. Ferguson (The Hague: Martinus Nijhoff, 1953); Erasmus, *Erasmi Epistolae*, ed. P. S. Allen et al. (Oxford: Clarendon Press, 1906–58).

15 Marjorie O'Rourke Boyle, *Erasmus on Language and Method in Theology* (Toronto: University of Toronto Press, 1977), p. 41.

16 *Apologia Erasmi Roterodami palam refellens quorundam seditiosos clamores apud Populum ac Magnates, quibus ut impie factum iactitant, quod in evangelio Ioannis verterit, in principio erat sermo* (Nuremberg: Friedrich Peypus, c. 1520).

17 For a consideration of the traditions that Parrot inherits, see Nelson, *John Skelton, Laureate*, pp. 182–83. Note also F. W. Brownlow's interesting suggestion ("The Boke Compiled by Maister Skelton, Poet Laureate, Called Speake Parrot," *ELR* 1 [1971]: 3–26) that the figure of Parrot is influenced by Lydgate's *The Churl and the Bird* and the later alchemical interpretations of this poem.

18 Acts of the Apostles 2.1–14.

19 For useful studies of the poem's allegory, see F. W. Brownlow, "Speke, Parrot': Skelton's Allegorical Denunciation of Cardinal Wolsey," *SP* 65 (1968): 124–39; John Chalker, "The Literary Seriousness of John Skelton's 'Speke, Parrot,'" *Neophilologus* 44 (1960): 39–47; Fish, *John Skelton's Poems*, pp. 135–76.

20 For a consideration of the issues in the Grammarians' War that Parrot sums up in lines 145–87, see Nelson, *John Skelton's Poems*, pp. 148–57.

21 Brownlow, "The Boke Compiled by Maister Skelton, Poet Laureate, Called Speake Parrot," pp. 15–16.

22 "Candidi lectores, callide callete vestrum fovete Psittacum" (Fair readers, shrewdly cherish your parrot).

23 Edwards, *Skelton*, pp. 192–92.

24 Nelson, *John Skelton, Laureate*, pp. 165–74.

25 Kenneth J. Atchity, "Skelton's Colin Clout: Visions of Perfectibility," *PQ* 52 (1973): 722.

26 Fish, *John Skelton's Poems*, p. 197. For a consideration of the possible link between this poem and the patronage of the Howard family, see

Edwards, *Skelton*, pp. 204–17. For a useful critical study of Skelton's strategy in this poem, see Robert S. Kinsman, "Voices of Dissonance: Patterns in Skelton's *Colyn Cloute*," *Huntington Library Quarterly* 26 (1963): 291–313.

27 Edwards, *Skelton*, pp. 26–29. For interesting studies of the background of the "Garlande," see Leigh Winser, "The Garland of Laurell" Masque Spectacular," *Criticism* 19 (1976): 51–69; M. J. Tucker, "The Ladies in Skelton's 'Garland of Laurel,' " *Renaissance Quarterly* 22 (1969): 333–45; David A. Lowenstein, "Skelton's Triumph: *The Garland of Laurel* and Literary Fame," *NM* 68 (1984): 611–22.

28 Nelson, *John Skelton, Laureate*, p. 198; Edwards, *Skelton*, p. 231. Spearing (*Medieval to Renaissance*, p. 243) suggests that in the *Garlande*, the anxiety of Chaucer's influence for Skelton is over. Skelton's poem celebrates itself. "The tradition of poetry exists in order that Skelton may be its latest and most glorious representative."

29 For the critical debate about Skelton's motive in shifting from criticism to praise of Wolsey, see John Bale, *Scriptorum Catalogus* (Basel, 1559), pp. 651–52; Nelson, *John Skelton, Laureate*, pp. 185–220; Edwards, *Skelton*, pp. 229–33; Carpenter, *John Skelton*, pp. 105–10; Fish, *John Skelton's Poems*, p. 238.

30 Skelton, "A Replycacion," 72 ff.

31 See, for example, Fish, *John Skelton's Poems*, pp. 256–61.

32 David Lawton ("Skelton's Use of Persona," *EIC* 30 [1980]: 9–28) suggests that Skelton's juxtaposed styles are linked to his use of open and closed personae. "Most of Skelton's major poetry is essentially a rhetoric of moral values, and his clear preference is for the open type of *persona* that finally draws attention to these values rather than to itself" (p. 19).

33 T. S. Eliot, *The Waste Land*, in *T. S. Eliot: The Complete Poems and Plays, 1909–1950* (New York: Harcourt, Brace & World, 1952), lines 426, 431.

CONCLUSION

1 Geoffrey Chaucer, *The Works of Geoffrey Chaucer*, 2d ed., ed. F. N. Robinson (Boston: Houghton Mifflin, 1957), *Troilus and Criseyde*, V, 1840–41.

2 Sir Philip Sidney, "The Defense of Poesie," in *Literary Criticism: Plato to Dryden*, ed. Allan H. Gilbert (Detroit: Wayne State University Press, 1962), pp. 412–13.

3 Ben Jonson, *Timber, or Discoveries*, in *Critical Essays of the Seventeenth Century*, ed. J. E. Spingarn (Bloomington: Indiana University Press, 1963), p. 54.

4 John Lydgate, *Troy Book,* ed. Henry Bergen (London: Kegan Paul, Trench, Trubner, 1906), Prol., 206–16.

5 See, for example, Chaucer, *Canterbury Tales,* VII (B) 2270–75; VII (B) 2815–20; III (D) 150: VIII (G) 41; *Troilus,* III, 1437; John Gower, *Confessio Amantis,* in *The English Works of John Gower,* ed. G. C. Macaulay (1900 repr.; London: Oxford University Press, 1957), II, 916; VII, 1508.

6 William Dunbar, "The Golden Targe," in *The Poems of William Dunbar,* ed. James Kinsley (Oxford: Clarendon Press, 1979), lines 256–58.

7 Dunbar, "Lament for the Makaris," line 50.

8 Sidney, "The Defense of Poesie," p. 435.

9 Jonson, *Timber, or Discoveries,* p. 50.

10 Sidney, "The Defense of Poesie," p. 435.

11 Ben Jonson, "Dedicatory Epistle of Volpone," in *Critical Essays of the Seventeenth Century,* p. 116.

12 Henry Peacham, from *The Compleat Gentleman* in *Critical Essays of the Seventeenth Century,* 3 vols. (Bloomington: Indiana University Press, 1963), 1:116.

13 Chaucer, *The Canterbury Tales,* IV (E) 31.

14 James I of Scotland, *The Kingis Quair,* ed. John Norton-Smith (Oxford: Clarendon Press, 1971), lines 1376–77.

15 John Shirley, "The Prologue of the Knyghtes Tale," M.S. Harl. 7333, fol. 37, col. 1, reprinted in Caroline Spurgeon, *Five Hundred Years of Chaucer Criticism and Allusion* (1925, repr.; New York: Russell & Russell, 1961), 1:54; Robert Henryson, *Fables,* in *The Poems of Robert Henryson,* ed. Denton Fox (Oxford: Clarendon Press, 1981), lines 1888–89.

16 Ben Jonson, *Timber, or Discoveries,* p. 51. For a consideration of the poet as laureate in the Renaissance, see Louis A. Montrose, "Celebration and Insinuation: Sir Philip Sidney and the Motives of Elizabethan Courtship," *Renaissance Drama* 8 (1977): 3–35; Louis A. Montrose, " 'The Perfect Paterne of a Poete': The Poetics of Courtship in *The Shepheardes Calendar,*" *TSLL* 21 (1979): 34–67; Richard Helgerson, "The Elizabethan Laureate: Self-Presentation and the Literary System," *ELH* 46 (1979): 193–220; Richard Helgerson, *Self-Crowned Laureates* (Berkeley and Los Angeles: University of California Press, 1983); Stephen Greenblatt, *Renaissance Self-Fashioning: From More to Shakespeare* (Chicago: University of Chicago Press, 1980).

ndex